T0115291

WEEDOPEDIA

An A to Z Guide to All Things Marijuana

ADAMS MEDIA

NEW YORK LONDON TORONTO SYDNEY NEW DELHI

Adams Media
An Imprint of Simon & Schuster, Inc.
57 Littlefield Street
Avon, Massachusetts 02322

Copyright © 2020 by Simon & Schuster, Inc.

All rights reserved, including the right to reproduce this book or portions thereof in any form whatsoever. For information address Adams Media Subsidiary Rights Department, 1230 Avenue of the Americas, New York, NY 10020.

First Adams Media hardcover edition January 2020

ADAMS MEDIA and colophon are trademarks of Simon & Schuster.

For information about special discounts for bulk purchases, please contact Simon & Schuster Special Sales at 1-866-506-1949 or business@simonandschuster.com.

The Simon & Schuster Speakers Bureau can bring authors to your live event. For more information or to book an event contact the Simon & Schuster Speakers Bureau at 1-866-248-3049 or visit our website at www.simonspeakers.com.

Interior design by Colleen Cunningham
Image credits listed at the end of this book

Manufactured in the United States of America

10 9 8 7 6 5 4 3 2 1

Library of Congress Cataloging-in-Publication Data has been applied for.

ISBN 978-1-5072-1288-2
ISBN 978-1-5072-1289-9 (ebook)

Many of the designations used by manufacturers and sellers to distinguish their products are claimed as trademarks. Where those designations appear in this book and Simon & Schuster, Inc., was aware of a trademark claim, the designations have been printed with initial capital letters.

Certain sections of this book deal with activities that would be in violation of various federal, state, and local laws if actually carried out. We do not advocate the breaking of any law. The authors, Adams Media, and Simon & Schuster, Inc., do not accept liability for any injury, loss, legal consequence, or incidental or consequential damage incurred by reliance on the information or advice provided in this book. The information in this book is for entertainment purposes only.

Contains material adapted from the following title published by Adams Media, an Imprint of Simon & Schuster, Inc.: *Weedopedia* by Will B. High, copyright © 2010, ISBN 978-1-4405-0645-1.

INTRODUCTION

MARIJUANA *Biological genus category* Cannabis sativa, Cannabis indica, *and* Cannabis ruderalis, *marijuana is a medically relevant, recreationally useful, naturally grown intoxicant of the safest and most benign kind. A historically misunderstood, yet massively popular drug, marijuana is sometimes incorrectly considered the "gateway drug" into other deviant behavior. It's also a great way to spend a Friday night (or any night, really; we won't judge).*

Time to set aside those boring, incorrect, and downright annoying misconceptions—here are the *real* answers to all your cannabis-related questions. Whether you're looking to expand your own knowledge, learn some fun trivia, or share some essential basics with nonbelievers and newbies, you'll find what you're looking for here. We're covering all the important stuff, like:

- Is weed actually legal in **AMSTERDAM**? (Surprisingly not. It's only decriminalized. Not to worry: Cannabis cafés are still legal, and the weed is just as strong as you'd hoped.)
- How do you make an **APPLE PIPE**? (It's quick and simple—and makes an easy snack when the munchies hit!)
- What year did **D.A.R.E.** start teaching kids to say no to drugs? (That would be 1983—also the year a group of University of Vermont kids started a little jam band called **PHISH**.)
- Does the **G-13** strain actually exist? (Let's just say if you've ever claimed to smoke it, you're probably lying...or really, really gullible.)
- And so much more.

3

Just like a regular encyclopedia, these entries cover the entire spectrum of cannabis culture: different strains, influential smokers, munchie options, slang, paraphernalia, pot etiquette, even a few on how to quit smoking (not that one would ever want to). But unlike a regular encyclopedia, this one doesn't suck. A bit like pot smokers themselves, *Weedopedia* is lighthearted, nonthreatening, self-deprecating, and genuinely fun to have around.

So sit back, break out the snacks, and learn everything one could possibly want to know about marijuana. Best if served with an open mind and, of course, a burning joint.

1, 2, 3

2001: A SPACE ODYSSEY A trippy 1968 Stanley Kubrick film whose legend has taken on epic proportions as time and marijuana-influenced viewings have boosted its status to among the greatest films ever made. The movie begins with about five minutes of black, and then shows pre-Homo erectus creatures as they fight and hunt, before a monolith is inexplicably dropped in their small community. The film then follows future man (when the movie was released, the year was 2001) and a space mission to Jupiter featuring the supercomputer HAL, who attempts to ambush the mission after the human astronauts discuss possibly disconnecting him. This culminates in a man-versus-machine showdown that is likely a prelude of the coming war. The movie can really only be appreciated after smoking a joint—shocking, we know.

4 WAY A strand of marijuana that is a crossbreed of four potent strains. 4 Way is frequently advertised on marijuana seed–selling websites as a supergroup of marijuana product, taking only the best from four different strands and putting them all together in a new strand. Not surprisingly, 4 Way weed is typically about as enjoyable as a supergroup—good, but not as good as the originals. ▼

40-YEAR-OLD VIRGIN, THE A comedy film directed by Judd Apatow. The film stars Steve Carell as the titular character and includes many familiar faces from Apatow films, including Seth Rogen. Unsurprisingly, the plot tells the story of Andy's (Carell) quest to finally lose his virginity. It's also a great opportunity to see an apple pipe in action. **See also Apatow, Judd; apple pipe; Rogen, Seth**

42 The answer to life, the universe, everything, as defined in *The Hitchhiker's Guide to the Galaxy*. While the answer is known, unfortunately the question remains a mystery, especially for weed aficionados. Their possible theories include: "How many stoners does it take to screw in a light bulb?" "What is 420 divided by ten?" "How many hits are too many?" ▼

420 A term used to declare oneself a part of the pot-smoking culture by saying one is "420 friendly" or, more bluntly, "Let's smoke some 420." It is perhaps one of the most misunderstood marijuana terms, as several urban legends exist to explain its origin. Some claim it derives from the penal code section in California for marijuana use. It doesn't. Others claim it is the number of chemical compounds in marijuana. It's not. Some mistakenly believe it's the date Jim Morrison died or the room the Grateful Dead always stayed in on tour. Nope. In fact, the term derives from a group of pothead high schoolers at San Rafael High School in California who used it as a reminder for the time they planned to toke up. Really. Yeah, kind of disappointing. **See also 420 celebrations; toke**

420 CELEBRATIONS An annual weed-friendly holiday falling on April 20 meant to celebrate the rich culture of marijuana smoking. In actuality, it's just another excuse to get high. Some 420 events have political overtones in supporting decriminalization efforts, but the rest of the world never takes it seriously. **See also 420; decriminalization; joint**

420 MAGAZINE A marijuana-focused magazine whose stated mission is "to repeal cannabis prohibition by promoting international cannabis awareness to the masses." Founded in 1993, the magazine serves its ends by posting decriminalization-related news, promoting the benefits of smoking reefer, reviewing cannabis strains, providing instructions on how to grow marijuana, and listing doctors who will prescribe medical marijuana. **See also** *High Times*

50-YARD LINE A long white strip that separates one half of a football field from the other. In one of the final scenes of the film *Dazed and Confused*, several of the main characters share a joint on this portion of the field, which has resulted in millions of smokers replicating this experience at high schools around the world. In theory it is a terrible place to smoke: It's out in the open, there's usually only one exit, and it's near a school so the penalty if one is caught is often more severe. However, there is a certain sense of satisfaction to giving a metaphorical middle finger to one's local high school and sparking up a fatty right in plain sight. **See also** *Dazed and Confused* ▼

99 CENT STORE The greatest store ever to someone who's high. If it is a true dollar store, everything is only ninety-nine cents. Invisible ink, plastic handcuffs, sassy bumper stickers, toy soldiers, fake mustaches, goggly-eye glasses, paper plates, sudoku books, whoopee cushions, tennis balls, and every off-brand candy and snack one could dream of. It's easy to spend an entire evening walking up and down the aisles, leave with bags full of munchies and novelty items, and still have enough money to buy an eighth. And they often do just that. **See also eighth**

Aa

ABDUL-JABBAR, KAREEM (BORN APRIL 16, 1947) The all-time NBA leader in points scored (38,387) and goggles-wearing, skyhook-shooting, *Airplane!*-starring Lakers center who retired as a nineteen-time All-Star and one of the most accomplished players in NBA history. In addition to being inducted into the Hall of Fame and earning his place as a member of the NBA's 50th Anniversary All-Time Team, Abdul-Jabbar's retirement has been punctuated by the news that the six-time MVP might also be a pot smoker. After surrendering a small amount of marijuana to authorities at a Toronto airport in 1998, Abdul-Jabbar was arrested for a DUI in 2000 after an officer smelled marijuana emanating from his car. To this day, Abdul-Jabbar maintains that he smokes pot to alleviate migraines—and that he has a proper prescription. Sure, Kareem. **See also sports**

ACTIVE SMOKER A contradiction of sorts, this variety of marijuana user likes nothing more than to get high and seize the day. For most smokers, post-toking activities like hiking, bike riding, marathon running, and cross-country skiing sound like buzz-kills, but the active smoker actually seeks out these sorts of physical activities as a means to enhance the high. It is best that active smokers keep to their own kind, as their trademark enthusiasm and get-up-and-go attitude are sure to bother anyone who was under the impression that the day would be spent sitting around and watching Netflix. **See also enhancement smoker; handy smoker; intellectual smoker; lazy smoker; social smoker; talkative smoker**

ADULT SWIM A ten-or-so-hour block of mindless, shamelessly lowbrow TV that pot smokers can proudly call their own. Airing in the early evening to sunup hours on Cartoon Network, Adult Swim is the epitome of stupid humor (in the best way) designed and explicitly intended for consumption by pot smokers. The programming block contains such favorites as *Aqua Teen Hunger Force*, *Rick and Morty*, and *Robot Chicken*. Uncontrollable fits of laughter for reasons that even the viewer is unaware of are commonly heard. Contemplating what exactly makes the shows funny is equally frequent and extremely puzzling. Luckily the majority of these programs last only a few minutes, so if one does not understand what's going on, it will be over soon enough.

ADVENTURELAND A 2009 coming-of-age comedy starring Jesse Eisenberg and the girl from the Twilight movies about the two could-be lovers working a summer job at an amusement park. The plot involves some twists and turns, largely based around the use of marijuana that main character James (Eisenberg) got at the beginning of the summer, which every attractive woman in the movie seems to want and that seems somehow to last three months. **See also Stewart, Kristen**

AEROPONICS A form of cultivation that completely defies all previously held universal truths of growing marijuana. Normally, weed is grown in soil and less frequently in water. In aeroponics, it grows while suspended in

the *air*. No dirt, no planter, no water, no magic. Just air. The roots of the plant are simply sprayed with a nutrient-rich liquid from time to time. Many feel this method is superior to all others because the grower can completely isolate the plants from external dangers commonly found in water and soil. Others feel this method is superior to all others because the plants are literally floating—and that's cool as shit. **See also greenhouse; hydroponics ▼**

AFGHAN KUSH A desirable strain of marijuana indigenous to areas of Afghanistan, Turkmenistan, Uzbekistan, and Tajikistan. The first strains hit the US market in the mid-1970s and have remained strongly favored since. Authentic Afghan Kush can run about $600 an ounce and is not intended for novices. The high can be described as heavy and hard-hitting and can pound smokers into a two-hour, couch-sitting, blank-eyed submission of the best kind. **See also kush**

AFROMAN (BORN JULY 28, 1974) A moderately successful, narrowly marketed rapper whose name is synonymous with the song "Because I Got High," probably because the man liked to get high. The song details the narrator's difficulties from smoking weed: failing classes, missing child support payments, masturbating after not having sex with his girlfriend—all of which took place...because he got high. The song became a worldwide hit and was even nominated for a Grammy award...probably because *they* got high.

ALCOTT, LOUISA MAY (NOVEMBER 29, 1832–MARCH 6, 1888) Author of *Little Women* and apparent psychedelic whose prose is peppered with references to mind-bending substances. Sometimes they're expressly marijuana, as in her short story "Perilous Play," in which two potential mates eat pot bonbons, bringing the two together. "Heaven bless hashish, if its dreams end like this!" reads the

story's final line. Alcott expanded on the effects of "hasheesh" in *A Modern Mephistopheles*, as the drug helps improve the innocent Gladys's singing voice and is used by the devious Jasper to "violate the sanctity of the human soul." Theories about whether Alcott had firsthand experience with pot vary. Some claim her hashish references were drawn from the Gunjah Wallah Company's maple sugar hashish candy of the time. Others claim anyone willing to write a 550-page children's book must have been on something. **See also books**

ALMOST FAMOUS A 2000 comedy-drama depicting the behind-the-scenes life of the fictional band Stillwater as they tour with a fifteen-year-old rock journalist for *Rolling Stone* magazine. The story details the rampant drug use, groupies, and all-around fun they have as the once-innocent protagonist is exposed to the rock star's life of vice and indulgence. A close bond is formed, and in the end they all learn a valuable lesson about friendship and love. An important element of the film is the line "I am a golden god!" which is said just before a band member jumps from a house's roof into a pool. It is also a line a pot smoker will genuinely say after smoking some G-13 or Christmas Tree. The movie is a favorite among pot smokers, partly because of the great soundtrack and partly because every teenage pot smoker hopes to someday become a rock star. **See also Christmas Tree; G-13**

AMERICAN BEAUTY A 1999 American drama starring Kevin Spacey as born-again pothead Lester Burnham. Dissatisfied with his marriage, job, and life in general, Lester regresses to his pre-suburban lifestyle and spends the majority of his day smoking G-13 with a neighbor/pot dealer/high school student, working at a local fast-food restaurant, and getting in shape to impress his daughter's superattractive (and superunderage) best friend. Everything goes wonderfully until, due to circumstances only tangentially related to his rediscovered cannabis habit, his newfound euphoria is cut short thanks to a sexually confused retired Marine colonel and a really, really big gun. **See also G-13**

AMSTERDAM The capital of the Netherlands and a wonderland of marijuana consumption. A little-known fact about Amsterdam is that weed is technically only decriminalized there. Due to international antidrug treaties, there remains a formal ban on marijuana in Amsterdam, though cannabis cafés are legally allowed to operate. All this is mere formality, as Amsterdam is and will for the foreseeable future be the go-to destination of college freshmen looking to experience the ultimate spring break. Amsterdam weed is famously strong, on average twice as potent as American weed, and also comes in an assortment of tastes and textures. Welcome to cannabis paradise. **See also decriminalization; hash bar ▶**

ANNIE HALL The 1977 Best Picture–winning comedy from writer-director Woody Allen. Following the on-again/off-again relationship between neurotic Jewish comedian Alvy Singer (Allen) and life-embracing Annie Hall (Diane Keaton), the film pioneered many formal and structural elements of the modern romantic comedy. More important, it contains one of the classic weed-centric film scenes in which Annie, who fancies pot as an incomparable sexual aid, proposes the drug to Alvy as a panacea for all his nervous tics and anxieties. Spoiler alert: If only he had smoked up, perhaps they would have stayed together.

ANSLINGER, HARRY J. (MAY 20, 1892–NOV. 14, 1975) Notable buzzkill who used his position as commissioner of the Federal Bureau of Narcotics (FBN) to launch numerous cultural attacks on marijuana use in America. He's the man responsible for propagating the now-ubiquitous fallacy that pot is a "gateway drug" to heroin use. Throughout the 1930s, Anslinger used a didactic column in *The American Magazine* to recount gruesome and unsubstantiated pot-linked crimes. In the 1940s, he started gunning for Hollywood, using threats of judicial action to force studios to excise drug content from their movie scripts. Then, in the 1950s, Anslinger unveiled his gateway-drug propaganda. A large part of modern conservative anti-weed sentiment is informed by the lingering influence of Anslinger's dishonest fear-mongering. **See also gateway drug**

ANTISOCIAL SMOKER A breed of pot enthusiast who prefers to smoke in seclusion. They are prone to bouts of introspection and contemplation and are significantly less likely to come up with highdeas, which are generally a symptom of groupthink. It's not that they are elitists. They just prefer to get high and ponder the great mysteries of the universe without being interrupted by a group of cackling idiots who just realized God is dog spelled backward. On second thought, perhaps they are elitists. **See also artistic smoker; closet smoker; highdea; hungry smoker; intellectual smoker; lazy smoker; paranoid smoker; quiet smoker; social smoker**

APATOW, JUDD (BORN DECEMBER 6, 1967) Writer, director, and producer extraordinaire whose works include *Freaks and Geeks, The 40-Year-Old Virgin, Knocked Up, Superbad, Pineapple Express, Get Him to the Greek, Bridesmaids, This Is 40,* and

Trainwreck. Despite a resume of work that suggests the contrary, Apatow claims not to smoke pot: "No, I'm not a pot guy....When I smoke pot I just wind up laying in the corner, sucking on my fist, crying, saying 'When's it going to end? When's it going to end?'" **See also** *Knocked Up; Pineapple Express; Superbad*

APPLE PIPE A makeshift but perfectly serviceable novelty contraption that looks completely harmless in someone's hand, but, if necessary, can be disposed of with ease. Apple pipes mimic the chamber system of a typical pipe: one long chamber across the width of the apple and a half-drilled chamber to place a finger on while inhaling. The apple pipe is surprisingly effective, easy to make, and gives its user a sense of joy and accomplishment upon completion. Another benefit: It can be eaten when those munchies suddenly kick in. **See also coconut bong** ▼

APPLES TO APPLES A simplistic card game that is fun only when everyone gets really high and completely ignores the laws of common sense. To play, everyone picks seven red apple cards containing nouns or phrases, and one player known as the judge picks a single green apple card with an adjective. All other players then look through their cards to find the word that best fits the adjective. If the adjective were something like "smelly," a sober player might select "garbage" and assume she will win. If the judge is high, she will be sorely mistaken. The inebriated individual is far more likely to select something crazy like "Batman." After a few bong rips, it will all make perfect sense.

ARMSTRONG, LOUIS (AUGUST 4, 1901–JULY 6, 1971) An American jazz trumpeter, one of the most influential musicians of the twentieth century, and a lifelong marijuana enthusiast. Armstrong, whose influence on pop music is almost immeasurable, was introduced to pot in the mid-1920s, when it was still legal in most states, and he called it an essential part of his life and health. One Armstrong biographer claims the musician smoked "three cigar-sized joints a day, at least."

Pops was as well known for getting high prior to recordings and performances as he was for his unintelligible scat singing, masterful improvisational skills, and cartoonish gravelly voice, though Armstrong's eternal pot legacy will always be the recording "Muggles," a slang term for the drug. It's still unclear how the man was able to remember the thousands of tunes he penned with a head full of smoke though.

ARRESTED DEVELOPMENT A far too short-lived TV series that follows an unimaginably self-centered family of misfit socialites who try to scrape their lives back together after the collapse of their real estate company and coinciding incarceration of the CEO and family patriarch, George Bluth Sr. The show contains sporadic references to drug use, ranging from a frozen banana stand that resembles a marijuana cigarette to a staged drug deal gone wrong orchestrated by a band of "hot cops" (male strippers for hire). In order to fully appreciate the series, a staggering level of canonical knowledge is required that can be gained only through repeated viewings. This makes it an ideal show to watch with a group of friends, a substantial amount of pot, and a buttload of free time.

ARTISTIC SMOKER A variety of pot smoker who will often use the drug as a means of boosting his or her creativity. At first, the incorporation of marijuana is simply an enhancement to the creative process. Before long, however, artistic smokers can become incapable of producing any meaningful painting, sculpture, song, or sonnet without the benefit of marijuana. Often they are also incapable of producing anything meaningful even with the help of cannabis. However, this usually goes unnoticed by them. **See also antisocial smoker; creativity; enhancement smoker; intellectual smoker; quiet smoker; social smoker ▶**

ASH A gray, dusty by-product of combustion produced whenever any organic carbon-based substance like marijuana is burned beyond all recognition. When marijuana reaches this state, it serves no useful purpose and should be discarded quickly before depression sets in due to a sudden lack of weed. **See also ashtray; fire** ▼

ASHTRAY A dedicated receptacle used for the storing of ash, cigarette butts, roaches, and, for some odd reason, chewing gum. While one can purchase these trays cheaply at any number of home goods stores, it is often much easier and more economical to use an empty beer can, unwanted coffee mug, or paper plate instead. While the ashtray is more sanitary and clean than simply allowing ash and roaches to build up on a table, it can also be rather incriminating if not emptied regularly. **See also ash; cigarettes; roach**

Bb

BABYSITTING A slang term used to describe the act of holding onto a joint, bowl, bong, or other marijuana delivery mechanism for an inordinate amount of time without the intention of actually smoking it. Unlike some instances of marijuana hording like bogarting and leeching, babysitting is generally unintentional and entered into without malice. The subject is often caught up in recounting an important story, stuffing his or her face with munchies, or is unable to remember the third portion of the "puff, puff, pass" method of smoking. Similar to a traditional babysitter, the subject will often seem catatonic and take little interest in what's going on around him or her. This is normal and can be easily remedied with a sharp object, loud music, or two fingers rubbed together in a snapping motion. **See also bogart; leech**

BACON The single greatest food known to man. In its most basic form, bacon is a thin strip of pig flesh that has been cured with salt and then dried, smoked, or served fresh. Due to its high salt content and ease of preparation, bacon has earned a welcome place in the list of quality munchies among stoners. Independent of weedophile culture, the food experienced an unprecedented rise in popularity in the 1980s and 1990s thanks in part to a protein-centric way of eating called the Atkins Diet. Currently there are scores of cookbooks, fan clubs, and websites devoted to the food, so much so that the threat of a bacon shortage seemed likely in 2017. The rise in popularity is clear evidence that the rest of the world has started to realize a simple fact that pot smokers have known for centuries—bacon makes everything better. ▼

BAGGIE A plastic sandwich bag of varying size in which weed is frequently distributed. Baggies are usually sold as eighths but smaller bags are used to hold seeds as well. The baggie is practical on all fronts. It's a reliable way to ensure no marijuana is lost during transfer, it's freezer safe for storing purposes, and it's easy to open, allowing each buyer the time-honored tradition of buying the bag, unsealing the flap, taking a quick whiff, and eliciting a satisfying, "Ahhhhhhhh, that smells good." **See also dealers; dime bag; eighth; nickel bag** ▶

BAKED A slang term used to describe somebody who has consumed marijuana in some way, shape, or form and is now high. Really high. Symptoms include bloodshot eyes, inexplicable and insatiable hunger, decreased attention span when performing important tasks, increased attention span when performing unimportant tasks, short-term memory loss, heightened ability to contemplate life's great mysteries, and a general feeling of euphoria. **See also high; stoned; wasted; zonked**

BAKER, JEROME A glassblower and bong maker extraordinaire, Baker's designs are widely considered works of art by weed connoisseurs and are a favorite of celebrity tokers, including Snoop Dogg, George Clooney, the Grateful Dead, and Phish. Although a DEA raid in 2003 shut Baker's operation down, his business has come back stronger than ever. Baker's bongs are stylistically unique and artistically alluring, and they may occupy a stoner's mind for the duration of a smoking experience if not properly hidden after being smoked out of. **See also bong**

BALANCE The ability to firmly stand upright without tipping over. Balance requires some athletic ability, strong muscles, and a low center of gravity. Balance becomes an issue when a person is inebriated and under the influence of alcohol or drugs, as the chemicals somehow interact with the inner ear fluid, causing an inability to walk straight. Cannabis users are most vulnerable after a particularly strong bong hit, as the impact of the smoke sometimes feels almost literally like a punch in the face.

BANANA STAND A purveyor of frozen bananas to legions of overheated pot smokers that exists solely in the *Arrested Development* universe. The location spawned the song "Big Yellow Joint," a ditty recorded by Jimmy Jane in the 1970s to pay homage to the Bluth Frozen Banana Stand and its iconic resemblance to a yellow marijuana cigarette. The banana stand served as a meeting place for pot smokers looking to get high while enjoying a delicious frozen treat. When it isn't being pushed into the harbor or burned to the ground, there is always money in it. **See also Arrested Development**

BANANADINE A fictional drug that many people once believed could be extracted from banana peels. Originally intended as a satirical jab at the American government's overactive legislation of psychoactive chemicals, the Bananadine myth first appeared in the form of an extraction recipe featured in the *Berkeley Barb*, a politically active underground newspaper. Though many readers got the joke, William Powell, author of *The Anarchist Cookbook*, did not. He published the fallacious recipe in the cookbook, which led to a profusion of rumors that Donovan's hit song "Mellow Yellow," released before the *Barb*'s article was even published, was all about the singer's penchant for the smooth, fruity high. The resulting cultural collision resulted in a ridiculous fad in which gullible pot smokers rode out wicked placebo effects while smoking banana peels.

BARR AMENDMENT A part of legislation that was attached to the DC appropriations act of 1999 introduced by then-Georgia congressman Bob Barr effectively eliminating the District of Columbia from implementing medical marijuana. The amendment prevented DC from spending money on a ballot initiative that would legalize or reduce penalties for any substances associated with the Controlled Substances Act, even though 69 percent of DC voters supported legalizing medical marijuana. In an ironic twist fully appreciated only while stoned, Barr reversed positions and became a lobbyist for the Marijuana Policy Project, which seeks to legalize, tax, and regulate marijuana. In 2009, the US Congress overturned the Barr Amendment, freeing DC of the shackles of bullshit political tactics and maneuvering once and for…well, once.

BASEMENTS Subterranean extensions of modern homes used to store boxes of crap, bicycles, power tools, and degenerate twenty-somethings who can't seem to get a job despite possessing a degree from a rather expensive university. When not rifling through the boxes of crap, the degenerate twenty-somethings will often use the space as a secluded place to smoke pot with other degenerate twenty-somethings. While there are numerous products one can purchase to deal with pest problems like cockroaches or mice, there is currently no spray or trap on the market to help a homeowner deal with an infestation of pot smokers.

BEACH, THE A sandy location near a large body of water where individuals go to relax, suntan, swim, play volleyball, surf, dig holes, and look at the scantily clad beach patrons. Surfers, especially, are known to smoke

the ganja, as their wild, long hair and laid-back attitudes are just the sort of things weedophiles are known for. ▾

BEATLES, THE A British rock band of modest success and acclaim. Consisting of four lads from Liverpool named John, Paul, George, and Ringo, The Beatles began smoking marijuana in 1964 at the behest of fellow musician Bob Dylan. Soon after, many Beatles songs began containing actual drug references. Some of the best examples include "A Day in the Life" and "Everybody's Got Something to Hide Except for Me and My Monkey." The Beatles also claim their trippy movie *Help!* was shot "in a haze of marijuana." Within months, pot had given way to LSD. Then they turned to Eastern religion. Then they wrote seven straight historic albums. Then they split up. Then they became one of the most enduring drug bands ever. **See also Dylan, Bob**

BECK, GLENN (BORN FEBRUARY 10, 1964) A conservative TV host who clearly favors marijuana as his drug of choice and has openly supported its legalization. When most smokers explain their pot-addled theories, they enjoy only a small audience of other marijuana users. Beck, however, enjoys an audience of millions with access to a team of "researchers," a world-class studio, and all the Ben & Jerry's he wants.

BEER The beverage of choice for most humans aged twenty-one and older when eating pizza, peanuts, or pretzels; hanging among friends; or trying to get drunk. Beer is a hallmark of American culture, a companion during adolescence, college, and beyond. Beer is also the companion drug to marijuana. Alcohol and marijuana are often compared when pundits are debating legalizing marijuana, but more important, beer is a delicious beverage to accompany the pot-smoking experience. It's important

not to confuse the beer bottle with the bong, though, or else a pot smoker will drink the worst-tasting beer of his or her life. ▼

BEING JOHN MALKOVICH A 1999 comedy film whose premise involves a floor 7½ in an office building, a multilayered love rectangle, and a door behind a file cabinet that serves as a portal into John Malkovich's brain. Written by Charlie Kaufman and directed by Spike Jonze, it's an essential film to watch while high. For the ensuing week after watching the film, viewers are prone to move long-stationed file cabinets, announce their pledge to become a world-famous puppeteer, and insist that all caged orangutans should be immediately released. They are also likely to crawl through the first small heating vent they see, an act that ends with a call to the fire department and a lifetime's worth of humiliating remarks. **See also Jonze, Spike**

BENSON, DOUG (BORN JULY 2, 1964) A pun-loving stand-up comic who has appeared on *Getting Doug with High, Comedy Central Presents,* and *Best Week Ever,* and was a contestant on season five of *Last Comic Standing.* Benson's humor is centered mostly on marijuana, and his most famous works have taken pre-existing ideas and substituted pot themes in their place. He starred in the 2007 documentary film *Super High Me,* when he smoked marijuana all day for thirty consecutive days to see how it affected his physical and mental agility. It was a flop among critics but unanimously embraced by weed aficionados. **See also *Super High Me***

BIG LEBOWSKI, THE A 1998 film written and directed by the Coen brothers starring Jeff Bridges as the perpetually high, White Russian-slurping, bowling enthusiast Jeffrey "The Dude" Lebowski. People who aren't in the proper state of mind (a.k.a., high) will often write it off as childish, disjointed, and, for lack of a better word, stupid. They will ask things like, "Why didn't he just get the rug cleaned after they peed on it?" Improve their viewing experience by introducing them to the "Big Lebowski Game" in which players smoke a joint and/or drink a White Russian whenever a character on-screen indulges. A far simpler solution is to find cooler friends.

BIKE RIDING An activity involving the pedaling of wheels on piping constructed and engineered for speed, balance, and efficiency. Bikes come in different styles—city, mountain, or hybrid—and are a frequent choice of transportation for pot dealers in urban areas, since they can cover a lot of ground quickly, easily, and cheaply. They are the perfect companions to the messenger bag, which many pot dealers use to hold baggies. **See also baggie** ▶

BIONIC An adjective in broad English usage that describes something related to the field of bionics. More specifically, an artificial process that reproduces and enhances normal biological processes, such as a mechanical arm or RoboCop. As such, it has been adapted by the pot-smoking community as a noun to refer to bud, as it enhances the normal biological process of sitting around and doing nothing.

BIRKENSTOCK The official brand of sandal of the pot-smoking community. Produced by a German manufacturer since the 1960s, the sandal's iconic cork insole contours to the wearer's foot, making for a customized fit. When combined with the mind-altering effects of marijuana use, it can give the impression that the subject isn't wearing anything at all and is simply walking on air. Wearing Birkenstocks is a surefire sign that one is 420-friendly. However, if one encounters somebody playing hacky sack while wearing Birkenstocks, a Che Guevara T-shirt, a hemp necklace, and a hat with a pot leaf, one should approach with caution—only narcs dress like that. **See also Che Guevara T-shirts**

BLACK CROWES, THE A hard blues-rock group that released eight studio albums and had a decidedly outspokenly pro-marijuana stance. Like that kid in high school who dreadlocked his hair and wore dirty jeans and tie-dye shirts, The Black Crowes were not shy about letting people know they enjoyed smoking weed. In addition to being featured on the July 1992 *High Times* cover and playing the Great Atlanta Pot Festival, lead singer Chris Robinson wore leaf-patterned pants to the MTV Video Music Awards and the band routinely unraveled marijuana-leaf banners at concerts. Journalists even offered The Crowes pot or bongs in exchange for time, and the band sometimes got high during interviews, which lead to some of the most rambling, incoherent exchanges ever seen in print. Unfortunately, the band broke up in 2015 and all the members moved on to other projects…although it's likely they're still smoking pot in their spare time.

BLACK, JACK (BORN AUGUST 28, 1969) The name of an American comedic actor whose performances are punctuated by attempts at slapstick humor that occasionally elicit a mild chuckle. Black is a prime example of a comedian who is funny only when both his character and audience are under the influence of no fewer than three different drugs. One can actually determine how funny a Jack Black comedy will be based on whether he is playing a straight-laced character like Hal in *Shallow Hal* (unfunny) or staying true to his pot-addled roots as drug guru Devlin in *Bongwater* (hilarious). Many of his movies share a unique characteristic in that they become increasingly funny the more marijuana the viewer smokes, although several independent studies have demonstrated that a plateau is reached after roughly one-eighth of an ounce. Subsequent smoking beyond that point somehow actually makes his films less comical. **See also bong water**

BLACK LIGHT A form of visible light that is also frequently referred to as ultraviolet light. Under the right circumstances, black light has the unique ability to completely transform a mundane, boring object or place into a really cool, awesome sight to behold—especially if the viewer also happens to be high. Human teeth, while normally unassuming, become blinding-white pearls. A room full of lame posters and dirty clothes instantly turns into a mystical den where anything can happen. Unfortunately, a bowling alley continues to be really lame and boring no matter how many black lights one hangs in it. **See also posters**

BLOODSHOT EYES An obvious side effect of smoking marijuana wherein excess blood flows to vessels in the conjunctiva, giving the iris a red-tinged hue. The condition is a telltale sign that someone has been smoking pot, so it is critical that the necessary precautions be taken. Pot smokers should keep a small bottle of eye drops on hand at all times and be prepared to list off any number of possible allergens or other eye irritants that could be causing the symptoms. Ragweed and pollen are good scapegoats in the summer, as are dust and mold in the winter months. Care should be taken not to overdo the act however, as one could easily find him- or herself taking inhaler hits instead of bong hits if the ruse is too believable. **See also sunglasses**

BLOOMBERG, MICHAEL (BORN FEBRUARY 14, 1942) Moneybags McBillionaire, owner of Bloomberg

L.P., and former mayor of New York City. Bloomberg, ranked by *Forbes* as the eighth-richest person in America, shocked the political establishment in 2001 when he admitted that he had in the past both smoked weed and enjoyed it. Yes, this passes as shocking. So the City's mayor is totally hip and enjoys toking up, right? Not really. Bloomberg said he regretted making the comments publicly. He also opposes decriminalizing marijuana and thinks the laws as they're written should be enforced. But that may change if he ever tries the kind of chronic they're growing nowadays. **See also politics**

BLUNT A popular method for smoking pot in large groups. A blunt is rolled using special rolling papers or the more popular method of "gutting" an inexpensive cigar, discarding the tobacco, and rerolling it with marijuana. There is some debate over which direction the blunt moves from person to person, but the "puff, puff, pass" rule is a widely accepted term of etiquette. It is interesting to note that this rule is almost always forgotten by at least one smoker in any given group. Because the remainder of the circle is generally too high

to notice, this is rarely an issue. **See also cigar; Dutch Master; puff, puff, pass; shotgun ▼**

BOGART (For the famous 1940s actor, see another encyclopedia.) A rather negative slang term directed at someone who missed the key developmental stage of childhood where humans learn to share. Somebody who bogarts might take too long with his or her turn on a joint, or might even go so far as to horde a cache of marijuana in secret and claim to be fresh out when it comes time to contribute. In general, pot smokers are passive and congenial. However, an instance of bogarting will inevitably elicit the worst insult a marijuana user is capable of delivering: "Yo, dude. Not cool." **See also buzzkill; leech**

BOMB A term used to describe a grade of pot so high that it will blow a smoker's mind. Not specific to a certain strain or kind, bomb can be used to describe any high-grade weed. Avoid using while watching news coverage of war, as smokers may bug out from realizing its multilayered application.

BONG A decadent piece of paraphernalia used for smoking marijuana. Often, smokers will impart human names and characteristics to their bongs and treat them far better than they do most actual humans. This behavior is considered to be normal and is generally encouraged within the pot-smoking community. **See also gravity bong; paraphernalia; party bong; piece ▼**

BONG WATER A substance found in most bongs consisting of ordinary H_2O mixed with trace amounts of ash, marijuana, THC particles, and an element that is indefinable by modern science called "gross." Bong water acts as a cooling agent that reduces the temperature of marijuana smoke before it reaches the lungs, thus making it possible to hold large quantities of smoke in the lungs for a longer period of time than possible with a regular joint. While it does perform this useful purpose, it is generally understood to be a vile by-product of the smoking experience that will stain anything it comes into contact with. Under no circumstances should one attempt to imbibe bong water unless one is being forced to do so at gunpoint. **See also water**

BONNAROO One of the major annual music festivals and the number one reason to take a road trip to Tennessee. Over the years, Bonnaroo has attracted some of the biggest names in rock, hip-hop, electronica, comedy, and other assorted genres. Some acts who have appeared: Radiohead, Phish, Jay-Z, Wilco, MGMT, *The Daily Show* correspondents, Zach Galifianakis, Dave Matthews Band, Jack Johnson, and tons of others. Bonnaroo is unofficially the opposite of a drug-free zone. People walk through the crowd offering anything a person needs: weed, mushrooms, LSD, ecstasy, etc. Pot smokers love to retell their favorite Bonnaroo stories over a good toke, usually beginning with "First of all, I was so high…" **See also Burning Man; Woodstock**

BOOKS Literary tomes containing combinations of letters, words, and sentences to construct everything from clever works of fiction to historical textbooks and everything in between. Because they often sit untouched on bookshelves for years at a time, they can serve as fairly decent hiding places for pot. One need simply pull out an oft-untouched tome, like *War and Peace*, slip some pot into the hole, and gently slide the book back in. One could also hollow out the book à la *The Shawshank Redemption*, although the additional security really isn't worth the effort. ▼

BOSTON FREEDOM RALLY An annual gathering of pro-marijuana enthusiasts that takes place on the third Saturday of every September on the Boston Common and includes speakers and musical performances. The rally has been a source of discontent between the city and the rally's two organizers, the Massachusetts Cannabis Reform Coalition (MassCann) and NORML, since the groups had to sue the city for a permit to hold the rally in 1997. The two sides have traded lawsuits since, though MassCann and NORML won a fairly decisive victory in 2008 by getting marijuana decriminalized across the state. As of 2019, the length of the event was shortened to one day (instead of the usual three) due to permit violations. However, the event will continue simply because it's the pot smoker's dream come true: protesting for the right to get high while at a music festival. **See also decriminalization; Massachusetts; NORML**

BOWL A relatively small item made of glass, plastic, wood, or ceramic used to smoke marijuana. However, if parents, police officers, or other persons of authority ask, it's actually an intricate sculpture with no practical use whatsoever. In many states, bowls are perfectly legal to own and sell as long as they are purchased for use solely with tobacco products. The feigned ignorance punctuated by exaggerated winking necessary to purchase a bowl is pretty humiliating but still infinitely better than smoking out of a soda can. **See also paraphernalia; piece; pipe ▼**

BRAZIL A South American country whose corrupt police force, strong gang presence, and warm climate make it a hot spot for growing, buying, and selling marijuana. While few smokers will be able to explain why, the general consensus is that pot from this country (and generally any country south of the United States) is infinitely better than American weed. Pot smokers returning from a trip to Brazil are likely to wax poetic about the potent, inexpensive weed being handed out in the streets like candy. However, if one asks specifics they will likely change the subject and insist that one must go and see it for oneself. Like many forward-thinking countries, Brazil is toying around with the idea of legalizing marijuana. Such a move would likely cut down on organized crime, improve the economy, and, in all likelihood, double the population overnight. **See also Amsterdam; Mexico**

BREAKFAST CLUB, THE A 1985 teen comedy directed by the late John Hughes starring members of the infamous "Brat Pack" that follows five high school students during the course of a Saturday detention. The movie is fairly uneventful until marijuana, the greatest equalizer high school has to offer, unites the stereotypical jock, popular girl, tough outcast, nerd, and crazy weirdo. In their heightened state of awareness, the unlikely friends are able to break down social barriers, divulge their deepest secrets, outwit an inexplicably bitter principal determined to squash any semblance of fun, and (with the exception of the nerd) find true love. This is pretty impressive for a bunch of stoned teenagers on a Saturday.

BREAKING BAD A TV drama starring the dad from *Malcolm in the Middle* (Bryan Cranston) as a high school chemistry teacher recently diagnosed with terminal cancer who, knowing his family won't have enough money once he dies, uses his scientific prowess to team up with a former student,

Jesse Pinkman (Aaron Paul), to start selling meth. While the drug of choice in the show is crystal meth, marijuana makes cameo appearances on several occasions, one of which finds the teacher dipping into his student's stash—a welcome role reversal from the traditional "student smokes pot, teacher finds pot, student gets detention" plot device.

BRIBES Offers of money, goods, or sexual acts in exchange for gaining the favor of an authority figure. Bribes are the preferred method of gaining entry into an exclusive club, moving to the front of a long line, or escaping the grips of the law when caught with pot. An attempted bribe usually involves the pot smoker interacting with an officer of the law, uncrumpling a wrinkled $20 bill, flashing a bleary-eyed smile, and moving his eyebrows up and down in a suggestive manner before cracking up uncontrollably. As a result, they will likely spend the night in jail.

BRICK A large compact bar of marijuana that typically weighs either one pound or one kilogram, depending on the country of origin. Pot is bundled in this manner for ease of shipment and subsequent storage, as it is much easier to stack a box full of bricks than it is a box full of glass jars. If one should ever happen to come across a brick, it is best to push all thoughts of running off with it out of one's head. Just leave it alone. While it would certainly be enough pot to last a couple of months, those would likely be the last months of one's life. The owner of said brick might just use a real, far more painful brick as a means for getting it back. ▼

BROAD CITY A popular sitcom created by and starring Ilana Glazer and Abbi Jacobson as two women trying to survive their twenties in New York City. Abbi's character is an aspiring illustrator, while Ilana's is a pretty successful slacker and troublemaker. This is a great show to watch while high, if only because the two main characters are such pot aficionados themselves that the viewer almost starts to feel left out otherwise. **See also New York City**

BROWN, BOBBY (BORN FEBRUARY 5, 1969) A former member of the group New Edition, solo pop star, and legally troubled ex-husband of the late singer Whitney Houston. Brown has claimed that marijuana was his "drug of choice." His ignoble history has turned him into one of the late-night circuit's most reliable punch lines and one of the pot-smoking circuit's most insulting descriptors. Any low-grade, dried-up, headache-inducing schwag can be distinguished as Bobby Brown. If a smoker claims, "This is some Bobby Brown shit," during a smoke-out, immediately apologize and buy some new stuff ASAP.

BUBBLEBERRY A strain of marijuana derived by combining characteristics from bubblegum and blueberry varieties. For the average smoker, pot is pot. For marijuana connoisseurs, the flavors and varieties available in strains like Bubbleberry are as abundant and unique as in fine wines. Similar to wine snobs, it is not uncommon for pot aficionados to develop preferences based on subtle flavor differences undetectable to those who don't possess a particularly sophisticated palate. Among these sommeliers of the pot world, Bubbleberry is highly regarded as both potent and pleasant to smoke. It is also generally more expensive than other varieties of marijuana, so great care should be taken as to when and how it is smoked. There's no sense in cracking open a pricey single-malt scotch for shot number twenty on a friend's twenty-first birthday. The same rules apply to weed. **See also Northern Lights; Purple Haze; White Widow** ▼

BUBBLER A glass smoking device with a pouch under the chamber where cold water can be placed to cool the smoke as it is inhaled. Bubblers fall somewhere between a pipe and a bong on the smoking-device evolutionary chain. While the bubbler adds the cooling effect that a pipe lacks, it fails to incorporate the slide of a bong. Still, some smokers prefer bubblers because they're smaller, easier to transport, lighter weight, and easier to hide. **See also bong; paraphernalia; piece; pipe**

BUD One of the thousands of slang terms for marijuana and among the most common. Bud works on two tracks. Bud is short for a buddy, which marijuana certainly is. Bud is also a botanical term for an undeveloped flower, which marijuana technically is not, but since it's a plant it still kind of works. **See also Buddha; ganja; Mary Jane; pot; reefer** ▶

BUDDHA An enlightened being in the Buddhist religion often depicted as a serene, portly gentleman sitting cross-legged. In some cultures, it is also a euphemism for marijuana. The link between the green leafy substance and achieving ultimate spiritual oneness makes absolute sense to anyone who has ever gotten high and little to no sense to anyone who hasn't. **See also bud; ganja; Mary Jane; pot; reefer**

BUDTENDER An awesome job for a serious pot smoker. Budtenders work at dispensaries or anywhere where medicinal or recreational weed is sold. It's not all fun and games though. Budtenders are expected to be knowledgeable about their products and actually spend a lot of time working face-to-face with customers. If you're not a people person and you're just here for the pot, this probably isn't the right job for you. **See also dispensary** ▼

BUMMER A slang term used by pot smokers and surfers to express disappointment in the outcome of a given situation. The term is especially versatile, as it can be used after any range of unfortunate incidents.

BURNED OUT A state of being after a particularly intense session of smoking pot that can become permanent if one continues to smoke with the same level of reckless abandon. Symptoms include droopy bloodshot eyes, cotton mouth, oversleeping, general contentment with life, and an intense desire to continue getting high. **See also cotton mouth; perma-burned**

BURNING MAN A weeklong excuse to hang out in the desert, experiment with mind-altering drugs, and ignore the fact that there is anything else going on in the world aside from Burning Man. The event attracts people from all walks of life, but the most common attendees are artistic smokers seeking validation for a lifetime of devoted avoidance of the corporate mainstream or anything that could potentially kill their perpetual buzz. **See also artistic smoker; Bonnaroo; Woodstock ▼**

BURROUGHS, WILLIAM S. (FEBRUARY 5, 1914–AUGUST 2, 1997) A heroin, cocaine, pills, meth, and everything else addict who penned *Junky, Queer,* and *Naked Lunch. Naked Lunch* is influential in the weed-smoking culture as the ultimate anti-gateway drug. Pot-smoking readers of *Naked Lunch* will never be tempted to try anything harder once they finish reading this book, which was informed by Burroughs's own heroin habit.

BUSH, GEORGE W. (BORN JULY 6, 1946) A businessman, the forty-sixth governor of Texas, and the forty-third president of the United States whose two presidential wins either saved or ruined the country, depending on the perspective. While most experts credit Bush's two electoral wins to the idea that he was the guy voters would most like to have a beer with, they overlook the fact that he was also the candidate voters would most like to share a joint with. Bush has never admitted to smoking weed directly (although some sources suggest it's definitely been implied), but given his confused use of the English language, questionable decision-making, and penchant for taking long vacations, he was certainly the most pot smoker-like president of the modern era. **See also politics**

BUZZED The initial state of being high achieved after a minimal ingestion of smoke from the *Cannabis sativa* plant. Many argue that this state of being is the most pleasant type of high, as one is still relatively coherent and has not yet achieved a status of baked or stoned. **See also baked; high; stoned ▾**

BUZZKILL Any number of people, places, objects, or events that can completely and utterly ruin the experience of getting high. They should be avoided at all costs while high and can include, but are not limited to, police officers, parental units, bogarting, ex-boyfriends/girlfriends, unexpected encounters with coworkers, running out of pot, running out of munchies, and younger siblings. **See also bogart; cops; narc; volcano**

Bb

Cc

CADDYSHACK A 1980 film that introduced the world to the unfortunate plight of the American golf caddy. Faced with long hours of standing around a golf course holding bags, a group of misfits are forced to turn to drugs, alcohol, and tomfoolery to pass the time. Thanks to its impressive cast list of Bill Murray, Chevy Chase, Ted Knight, and Rodney Dangerfield, the movie has become a cult classic among two polarizing circles: pompous rich golfers and the young, underpaid pot-smoking caddies who serve them. While the camps disagree on the overall message, it is generally understood that the scene where the assistant greenkeeper (Murray) and prominent club member Ty Webb (Chase) share a giant joint, do cannonballs, and discuss the finer points of grass is the greatest four minutes of cinematic history.

CALIFORNIA America's thirty-first state and the United States's own little Amsterdam-style haven for cultivating and purchasing marijuana. Thanks to Proposition 215, passed in 1996, Californians earned the ambiguous legal right to buy marijuana for medical purposes. However, the road for recreational marijuana has been a bit longer. Despite medical research programs, medical marijuana factories, and input from Governor Arnold Schwarzenegger himself, Proposition 19 was defeated in 2010 and recreational marijuana was not legalized. Fortunately, there was a shift in public opinion and, in 2016, Proposition 64 was approved by voters. That means that as of 2018, marijuana has been legalized for recreational use in the state of California. See also medical marijuana

CAMPING A recreational sport that modern-day humans indulge in as a means to escape the fast-paced stop-and-go of city life. The activity usually takes place in secluded wooded areas far away from the prying eyes of law enforcement, so it is not uncommon for campers to use the excursion as an excuse to get high and commune with nature. A word of advice: One should pitch the tent *before* one gets high. Not after.

CAN BONG The minimalist's makeshift bong, since it can be made with an empty beer or soda can and a sharp object. One creates a can bong by denting an empty can, poking small holes through the dent (where the pot will sit), and poking a hole in the bottom of the can to use as a carb. The user then inhales smoke through the can opening. Not the most highbrow smoking contraption, can bongs are a rite of passage for the novice smoker. The practice of can bong–making becomes increasingly pathetic with age. **See also apple pipe; carb**

CANADA America's neighbor to the north, a beacon of clean cities, low crime rates, free health care, a low drinking age, and Ryan Gosling. Canadians are much more tolerant of marijuana smoking generally, although the legal status of the drug was a bit wishy-washy for a while as different courts made contrasting rulings regarding its legality. In the early 2000s, Canada definitively allowed patients to use marijuana for medical purposes, but it wasn't as good as it sounds since they needed a physician's seal of approval. Today, marijuana has been legalized for both medical and recreational use across the nation. **See also Amsterdam; Brazil; Canadian Rockies; Mexico**

CANADIAN ROCKIES The portion of the Rocky Mountains that extends into Canada, inhabiting land in Alberta and British Columbia. The beauty of nature to the recreational smoker in combination with legalized marijuana consumption makes the Canadian Rockies a frequent spot for smokers to get high and look at nature. One of the top activities to do while stoned there: relax in the Banff Upper Hot Springs, a naturally occurring hot spring that allows patrons to sit in the water and look out onto the peaks. **See also Canada** ▶

CANNABIS (PLANT) The wacky tobaccy, sticky icky, devil's lettuce, Mary Jane, green rooster, bud, envy, trees, or any other of the unlimited names that describe the magical plant. In fact, smokers tend to call it *anything* but "cannabis"; it's mostly DEA officers, poorly trained narcs, judges, scientists, and botanists who employ the term. Smokers who use the term are usually engaging in a discussion with one of those officials regarding the drug's legal status or its effects on human health. It's known to cause red eyes, dry mouth, an increased heart rate, and extremely desirable intoxication. **See also every entry in this book** ▼

CANNABIS (TV SHOW) A show available on streaming platform Netflix that's about—you guessed it!—cannabis. After a major shipment of marijuana is stolen, the show introduces all major players in the drug trade, in a way that's almost certain to confuse a pot smoker almost immediately. **See also Netflix**

CANNABIS CULTURE* MAGAZINE** A Canadian pro-marijuana, online-only magazine "dedicated to liberating marijuana, freeing pot-prisoners around the globe, and bringing an end to the vicious worldwide war on drugs." So far its success has been limited. The magazine is a favorite among the politically outraged and indignant, and it doesn't hurt that its publisher is Marc Emery, the famed marijuana seed–seller who has faced legal trouble in the United States. *Cannabis Culture* magazine is the true anti-corporate, anti-capitalist marijuana magazine, which is to say it probably takes itself a little more seriously than, say, *High Times*, for better or worse. **See also *High Times

CANNABUTTER Cannabis-infused butter that's a key ingredient in edibles. It's a two-step process that involves a lot more "big words" than your average pot smoker can handle post-toke. At its most basic, the process is as follows: decarbing + infusion = pot butter. It's best to make cannabutter before getting high since you'll need to spend some time in the kitchen. Or just give up early and smoke your stash instead. See also decarboxylate; edibles; pot butter; pot oil ▼

CANNONBALL A self-induced challenge performed by experienced smokers wherein one inhales a large quantity of marijuana smoke, takes a full shot of hard liquor, and then exhales the hit. When done properly, the stunt is harmless, albeit a little immature. When timed poorly, however, this can result in aspirated liquor being sprayed all over everyone else in the room. It is customary to finish the maneuver by shouting "Cannonball!" at the top of one's lungs before passing both pot and liquor to the next willing participant. While this step is not required, the whole process is just kind of silly without it. See also *Caddyshack*; strikeout

CANOEING Occurs when a novice is sparking a joint and burns one side more than the other. The resultant heat differential produces a canoe-shaped jay, which is not cool. The appropriate course of action is to shout "Bro! It's canoeing!" and apply flame to the opposite side, bringing the joint and the session back to equilibrium.

CARB A hole in a bubbler or a pipe that allows the user to clear the smoke in the chamber by increasing the volume of air that flows into the device. It was first proposed by Dutch-Swiss mathematician/confirmed pot smoker Daniel Bernoulli, whose pioneering work in fluid mechanics was widely read in his 1738 book *Hydrodynamica*. Further evidence that drug technology proceeds at a far faster pace than the clean world: Karl Benz didn't patent the automotive carburetor until 1888. See also bubbler; pipe ▼

CARLIN, GEORGE (MAY 12, 1937– JUNE 22, 2008) A linguistically acute, unapologetically obscene, cross-generationally followed writer and one of the most respected and groundbreaking comedians with the best ponytail of all time. Carlin began his career as a conventional comic who

did cute voices and talked about growing up in New York. This was largely before he was funny. Carlin switched his act on his 1972 comedy album *FM & AM*. Side one, *FM*, featured Carlin's regular, family-oriented bits. Side two, *AM*, saw Carlin tackling issues like sex, drugs, and birth control and marked his transformation into the counterculture. In a *Playboy* interview in 1982, Carlin said, "I was a stonehead for 30 years. I'd wake up in the morning and if I couldn't decide whether I wanted to smoke a joint or not, I'd smoke a joint to figure it out. And I stayed high all day long." It is no wonder that Just before his death at seventy-two, he was more associated with the college crowd than anyone else.

CARMELICIOUS A strain of weed that is green with orange hairs sticking out of it, which can give a distinctly caramel taste when smoked or smelled. Carmelicious is a favorite among beginner growers because it's relatively easy to grow and it produces a happy high.

CASUAL SMOKER A person who participates in an occasional smoking session but does not feel the need to indulge on a regular basis. He or she is unlikely to possess a personal stash of marijuana, although the casual smoker will gladly contribute munchies or money toward the cause—a defining characteristic that separates them from leeches. **See also antisocial smoker; closet smoker; quiet smoker; social smoker; talkative smoker**

CATNIP The common name for the *Nepeta cataria* plant, so dubbed because of the sense of euphoria it creates in felines. Essentially pot for cats. Once a cat smells catnip, it will immediately stop everything it is doing, run over to the catnip, and start purring and rolling around in it. Minus the rolling around, this almost identically mirrors the reaction most pot smokers have when they smell weed. However, cats don't typically check around the room for cops first before indulging in their drug of choice.

CBD A.k.a. cannabidiol. One of the 113 cannabinoids found in cannabis plants. CBD has been suggested as a tool to relieve everything from migraines and insomnia to anxiety and PMS symptoms. Although some people feel there's not enough research to support sustained use of CBD, others are willing to give it a shot and many are liking the results. Unlike THC, however, CBD does not get the user "high," so most real pot smokers will have no need for it. **See also CBD oil** ▼

CBD

THC

CBD OIL A combination of CBD and a carrier oil like coconut oil that's currently all the rage in the wellness world. For best effect, many people simply place the oil under their tongue and hold for a few seconds before swallowing. Others prefer to add it to their favorite food or drink for help with everything from anxiety to other major ailments like multiple sclerosis and cancer. **See also CBD; tincture**

CEPEDA, ORLANDO (BORN SEPTEMBER 17, 1937) A former Major League Baseball player and Hall of Famer who hit .297 career with 379 home runs in seventeen seasons. Cepeda admits in his autobiography, *Baby Bull*, that after injuring his knee in 1964 he turned to marijuana to deal with the external pain of his knee and the internal pain of not playing. Cepeda apparently got only deeper into the marijuana game after retiring, as he was arrested in 1975 at a San Juan airport for trying to pick up 150 pounds of marijuana, about $400,000 worth and enough to fill a car trunk. His troubles continued well into the early 2000s when he was again arrested for possessing marijuana and other drugs, although he claimed that the drugs weren't his. Willie Mays once said of Cepeda, then a rookie, "He's the most relaxed first-year man I ever saw," lending credibility to the idea that Cepeda may have been into the stuff even earlier than he lets on. **See also sports**

CEREAL The most basic, easy, and delicious breakfast food, which can also be eaten, by the sophisticates in society, for lunch or dinner. Cereal is a great choice for binge eating, depending on which cereal is purchased, as it can be extremely delicious while remaining relatively not unhealthy. This all goes down the toilet, however, when sugary cereals are introduced into the mix since anyone with the munchies is capable of going through several entire boxes in one sitting without so much as stopping to play the word search on the back of the box.

CEREAL BOX A common hiding spot for weed. It's inconspicuous and totally ordinary looking. Cereal boxes occasionally end up in odd places when they're storing weed. So if you happen to find a cereal box in the freezer, it is usually best just to pretend as if one sees cereal boxes in the freezer all the time and not ask too many questions. **See also cereal; deodorant**

CHAMBER The hollow area of any pot-smoking apparatus that is used to collect smoke before it is inhaled into the lungs, where it belongs. The larger the chamber, the more smoke can accumulate, and the higher the user will get from each hit. However, it is often speculated that individuals who purchase absurdly large bongs and pipes are merely compensating for other areas in which they are lacking. **See also bong; bowl; pipe**

CHAMPAGNE A strain of weed popularly grown in outdoor gardens due to its relatively mild stench. Champagne is also popular due to its strength, which will cause some smokers to declare it the "best pot I've ever smoked!" though this claim is often made by the sort of people who declare the most recent book they've read their favorite book of all time. Champagne shouldn't be discounted though. One fat joint can make five or six smokers very happy, as the weed gives a clear-headed sort of high.

CHAPPELLE, DAVE (BORN AUGUST 24, 1973) A slacker comedian who has somehow amassed a massive following while smoking weed and bullshitting around. Chappelle's comedic breakthrough came with the 1998 classic *Half Baked*, and he became a national figure with his mega-successful TV series *Chappelle's Show* on Comedy Central. His comedy specials have consistently appeared on Netflix (earning him a Grammy in 2018), and he received an Emmy Award for his appearance on *Saturday Night Live*. Chappelle is a pot smoker's dream comedian: he's unpretentious, can be funny without punch lines, and has stories that somehow get funnier and more bizarre as they go on. Chappelle is so conversational, smokers are prone to think he's literally sitting in their smoking circle while watching him on TV. **See also *Half Baked***

CHE GUEVARA T-SHIRTS A shirt, usually red, worn by hipsters to denote their anti-corporate, anti-institutional, anti-power, anti–The Man stance on whatever issue happens to be in the news that week. When pointing out that Guevara was a communist and that his likeness is being mass-produced in a capitalist country, most Che T-shirt wearers will reply with the merits of socialism and public upheaval. While some Che Ts have marijuana leafs next to his face, the shirt's only real connection to weed culture is that they are worn by the leftist hippie culture, which is heavily populated by pot smokers. Pot smokers who wear one while getting high are at risk of being such a cliché that a black hole spontaneously forms. **See also hipsters** ▶

CHEECH AND CHONG A dude-saying, pot-advocating, Grammy Award–winning comedy duo consisting of Richard "Cheech" Marin and Tommy Chong whose routine revolved around the hippie counter-culture and especially drug culture. One of their most famous bits is about a drug dealer trying to deliver pot and discreetly knocking on the door. "It's Dave, man, open up," he says. The stoner replies, "Who? Dave? Dave's not here." For the 1970s, this passed for groundbreaking comedy. The two have released comedy albums and movies and have gone on tour and amassed a lifetime of work and money dedicated to smoking the herb. The two are so synonymous with smoking weed that Cheech and Chong also serve as a way to describe any eternally pot-smoking duo. **See also** *Up in Smoke*

CHERRY The smoldering ember of delicious THC-laden marijuana that rests at the end of a joint or blunt. Once the end of the joint or blunt is lit, the cherry will continue to ignite the marijuana resting behind it, which will then become the cherry. This process continues until the joint is finished or until someone interrupts it by ashing too hard and knocking the cherry on the ground. **See also blunt; joint**

CHICKEN WINGS A late-night snack of choice for smokers. This may be because they're easily accessible, inexpensive, and just straight-up delicious.

CHOCOLATE MILK Ordinary milk that achieves its full munchie potential thanks to the addition of chocolate syrup. The typical technique used to make the concoction is to fill a glass with milk, squirt syrup into said glass, and stir. If one is lacking a glass, one can simply fill the mouth with milk, squirt syrup into said mouth, and shake one's head around to mix.

CHRISTMAS TREE A variety of marijuana with a pine-like smell, fuzzy texture, and white-sprinkly, snowflake-like exterior that makes it a natural choice for the holiday shopper. Christmas Tree is seasonal, grown in sunny California, and is among the most potent strands of marijuana in the United States. Christmas Tree is a rare and strong breed, up to three times as expensive as regular bud. It makes for the perfect stocking stuffer. **See also Bubbleberry; Northern Lights; Purple Haze**

CHRONIC A widely used and acceptable slang term for high-quality marijuana. Depending on who and where one is, it could refer to weed laced with cocaine or a certain strain of herb so magical and pure that one can count the crystals of THC and reddish fibers perched among its buds. Be very sure which definition the dealer subscribes to before buying chronic: One could have the best high of one's life, or quite possibly the last. **See also Dr. Dre**

CHUBBY BUNNY A wholesome game requiring nothing more than a bag of marshmallows and a group of friends. The game is equally popular among elementary school students and pot smokers of any age. Players sit in a circle and take turns placing marshmallows in their mouths and exclaiming "Chubby bunny!" until all players are laughing too hard to continue or until all the marshmallows are gone, whichever comes first. For an explanation as to why this is so entertaining, one should smoke some pot and try it. **See also highdea**

CIGAR A bundle of dried, fermented tobacco leaves that are either rolled into a cylinder whole or chopped up and then rolled. Whole tobacco leaves or specially designed paper are then used to wrap the contents of the cigar. Flavor variations and differences in quality of tobacco can vary greatly from cigar to cigar depending on where the tobacco was grown, how it was processed, how the cigar was rolled, and a number of other factors. These subtle differences are generally lost on most pot smokers, as their only interest in the product is to harvest the tobacco leaf wrappings for use when rolling blunts. Purchasing an expensive cigar as a present for a weedophile is generally not recommended, as the experience is similar to giving an expensive toy to a toddler only to watch in horror as he ignores the contents and spends the next several hours climbing into and out of the box. **See also blunt; cigar box; Dutch Master**

CIGAR BOX A small wooden receptacle used primarily by children for storing baseball cards, marbles, jacks, and chewing gum, and secondarily for storing marijuana and associated paraphernalia when the owner grows up. **See also cigar**

CIGARETTES Cylindrical paper tubes filled with tobacco, one end of which can be ignited to create smoke that

can then be inhaled through the opposite end. They appear similar to joints in shape and color. When lit, the resulting smoke is far less mind-altering than that of a joint, yet shockingly more addictive. **See also cigarette joint** ▼

CIGARETTE JOINT A form of joint that is crafted by sacrificing a perfectly sociable cigarette in order to fashion a makeshift marijuana receptacle. The smoker gently coaxes the tobacco out of the cigarette by rubbing it between the thumb and forefinger until there is nothing left but a hollow tube, which can then be filled with pot. Filling the resulting tube with weed bit by bit can be a painstaking process; however, it is a useful skill to develop for instances when one lacks more elaborate paraphernalia. Also, the resulting joint can be discreetly slipped into a pack of cigarettes where it can hide in plain sight. A pot smoker just needs to be sure to remember which one is which. **See also cigarettes** ▼

CIRCLE A geometric shape created by connecting several points equidistant from a central location to form a continuous loop. Due to its uniform shape and never-ending chain, it is the ideal configuration for passing any number of objects from person to person, such as hacky sacks, hot potatoes, and, most importantly, marijuana cigarettes. **See also square**

CLEAN The state one attains by refraining from smoking marijuana or ingesting drugs of any kind for an extended period of time. This is occasionally done willingly as an attempt to kick an unwelcome drug habit. However, more often than not it is done begrudgingly in order to pass a drug test and secure employment or to placate nosy parental units. Thankfully, this state is not permanent. **See also cold turkey; drug test; rehab**

CLERKS A low-budget American comedy written and directed by Kevin Smith that follows a single day in the lives of Dante Hicks, a disgruntled convenience store clerk, and his friend Randal Graves, a self-important video rental clerk. While Dante and Randal are busy berating unsuspecting customers, a pair of drug dealers named Jay and Silent Bob (played by Smith) set up a cottage industry outside of the convenience store. The obvious disparity in job satisfaction between the understandably miserable store clerks and the genuinely contented pot purveyors makes one wonder if an alternative title, *Just Sell Weed*, was ever considered. **See also *Jay and Silent Bob Strike Back*; Mewes, Jason; Smith, Kevin**

CLICHÉS A story technique, way of acting, or expression of thought that has been overused to the point of losing any authenticity or originality. Examples include romantic comedies about women and men who hate each other at first before realizing they're meant to be together, hipsters who wear tight jeans and man buns, and pot smokers who get their hair dreadlocked and wear tie-dye shirts. Clichés are cousins of stereotypes but are more devastating on a person's self-image since they have nothing to do with one's race, gender, or religion but with one's actual personality. If someone looks in the mirror and the reflection is wearing a pot leaf T-shirt, smoking a joint, and has dreadlocks, one might be a cliché.

CLINTON, BILL (BORN AUGUST 19, 1946) The forty-second US president and Southern-accented, sweet-talkin' serial womanizer. Slick Willie was a master at tightrope walking through some tough situations, be it his philandering, accidental bombing of a Sudanese pharmaceutical plant, or having to answer the inevitable question all presidential candidates face: "Did you ever smoke pot?" Clinton said he did, but "I didn't inhale," which has become something of a legendary answer, as not only do few believe him, even fewer care. Clinton's tightrope walking continued through his presidency, as he tripled the amount of annual marijuana arrests, but, at the end of 2000, claimed marijuana should be decriminalized. The statement came just in time for him to leave office and do nothing about it. **See also politics**

CLOGGED A worrisome state for a bong or pipe to be in where the chamber becomes blocked with resin, ash, and grime. As a result, smoke cannot escape and the device is transformed into an elaborate sculpture that serves no useful purpose. As hard as one might try, it is impossible to inhale a decent hit once the piece reaches this state. A poker or cleaning solution can be employed to remedy the situation, although it is far more likely that the owner will simply set the piece aside with the intention of cleaning it later and smoke out of something else. While it may appear that smokers with vast collections of bowls and bongs have a greater appreciation for the craft of piece-making than others, it is far more likely they just haven't gotten around to unclogging the first one yet. **See also bong; bowl; Formula 420; pipe; poker (device)**

CLOSET SMOKER A self-loathing breed of pot smoker so ashamed of the smoking lifestyle that he or she will do everything possible to hide the habit from society. They often give no outward signs of being a weedophile, shunning the characteristic long hair, laid-back attitude, and thoughtful manner of speech adopted by other breeds. When they believe no one is paying attention, however, they will quickly bust out a concealed joint, light up, take a few hits, extinguish the roach, swallow it, spray cologne or perfume, and go about their day as if nothing strange has just occurred. It is best to avoid outing closet smokers, as admitting their love of herb is a decision each closet smoker must come to on his or her own terms. See also antisocial smoker; casual smoker; enhancement smoker; intellectual smoker; lazy smoker; paranoid smoker; quiet smoker

CLOWNS Face-painted, ball-nosed, floppy-shoed, children's entertainers who are known to terrify their intended audience as well as play a starring role in the nightmares of adults. Clowns and pot smokers never got along, ever since movies featuring evil clowns started scaring smokers into shaking fits. Clowns and pot smokers have been on terse terms ever since. ▼

COCONUT BONG A bong for the true tropical island experience. Coconut bongs are beneficial in several ways. Not only do they look cool, they come with built-in bong water that helps flavor the smoke. On the downside, it's a lot of work to put into something that's going to rot in a few days. See also apple pipe

COINCIDENCES Happenstances that take place when two uncoordinated but somehow related events meet in time and space in a way that confuses, surprises, and shocks the participants. Coincidences can be devastating to pot smokers, as they usually manifest themselves in a way that places the inebriated, red-eyed, stumbling pot smoker in direct physical proximity with a parent, police officer, or other authority figure. Pot smokers can escape such predicaments in the most efficient and logical way imaginable, as taught by Ferris Bueller: sneaking into the same cab said authority figure is attempting to hail while his back is turned and hoping an identical one pulls up just as the pot smoker's is taking off.

COLBERT REPORT, THE A satirical late-night talk show that was hosted from 2005 to 2014 by faux right-wing political pundit Stephen Colbert. On the show, Colbert is a constructed right-wing news host, allowing him to wear multiple farcical faces (figuratively) and take multiple absurd positions (literally). His segments have always been dangerous for a pot smoker to watch, as the host may convincingly argue that Barack Obama wears an evil moustache, that we should send sick people overseas to spread disease and win wars, or that we should move to a lead-based economy. The pot smoker may come out of his or her stupor believing certain such things are true, but will not be certain why. This can lead to

unnecessary confusion and frustration and a desire to become high again.

COLD TURKEY The process of eliminating a vice from one's lifestyle that one deems undesirable, such as smoking pot. The subject, often on a whim and without warning, ceases to indulge the habit immediately. Subjects will generally delude themselves into believing it was totally their idea, although the decision is usually preceded by an ultimatum dictated by a loved one such as cutting off financial support if the offending subject does not kick the habit. It almost never works for anybody. However, perhaps one should give it a shot anyway. **See also clean ▼**

COLLEGE On the surface, it is a respected institution of higher learning. Upon further inspection, it devolves into summer camp for adults. Students are expected to spend only about fifteen hours of their entire week in the classroom, giving them ample time to experiment with drugs, alcohol, and the finer nuances of microwave cooking. It is in college where many pot smokers are first introduced to the wonders of marijuana, and they often spend the rest of their college careers making up for lost time. ▼

COLORS The visual manifestation of light bouncing off of objects as perceived by the human mind with the eyes. During one's daily life, the concept of color is fairly inconsequential. However, this changes after one has smoked marijuana. Once high, pot smokers will often begin to question the existence of colors and wonder if they are viewed in the same way universally, or if some people see them differently. For example, what if what one sees as red actually appears to others as the color yellow, although both parties still call it red? This line of thought can be dangerous, however, eventually leading to the belief that nothing is real. Best to stick to watching cartoons and playing video games instead.

COMMERCIALS Paid programming on TV or radio during which time advertisers can pitch products that most people don't need and sculpt an image they wish to project for said product. Were commercials taken literally, they would convince humanity that haircuts give people super strength and oil companies care about the environment. However, it is, of course, sometimes difficult to figure these things out after smoking a blunt.

COMPASSIONATE INVESTIGATIONAL NEW DRUG PROGRAM A program started by the US government in 1978 that grew, shipped, and legally allowed certain citizens to smoke marijuana because of medical reasons. The program began after a sufferer of glaucoma brought a lawsuit against the Food and Drug Administration, the Drug Enforcement Agency, and several other government organizations. The court ruled in *United States v. Randall* that "(w)hile blindness was shown by competent medical testimony to be the otherwise inevitable result of the defendant's disease, no adverse effects from the smoking of marijuana have been demonstrated. Medical evidence suggests that the medical prohibition is not well-founded." The outcome was that the FDA sent the defendant government-grown marijuana each month. At its height, the program had thirty patients, but George H.W. Bush closed the program in 1992. The patients were grandfathered in, but several have died and as of 2019 only three remain active. **See also medical marijuana**

CONCENTRATE A multi-functional term that can be used to describe both a skill that some pot smokers lose after a fat joint and a highly potent, concentrated mass of THC that looks a bit like honey. Concentrates can be four times stronger than high-quality marijuana with THC levels up to 40–80 percent. Concentrates have become increasingly popular, with sales data from Washington state showing as much as a 146 percent increase in sales of concentrates between 2014 and 2016. Also known as wax, shatter, and dabs. **See also dabs**

CONCERTS Locations where musicians perform before audiences large and small. Concerts are one of many places pot smokers go to get high and enjoy experiences. Dave Matthews Band, Phish, Radiohead, and the Grateful Dead are just a few bands whose concerts require both a ticket and a joint. However, pot smokers are known for overindulgence, which is why concerts quickly lead to music festivals. This is the music bender for stoners: typically three- to four-day events in which music is played by dozens of bands virtually nonstop on multiple stages and at overlapping times. Music festivals are unofficial free zones for weed, as no one can either endure that much music or live in a tent for that long without having at least a little buzz on. **See also music**

CONNECT The dude who provides one with pot, or the dude who sells pot to the dude who provides one with pot. **See also dealers**

CONTACT HIGH A phenomenon wherein a person not directly involved in a smoking session still exhibits many of the same symptoms and behaviors of those who are active participants. This can usually be attributed to breathing in secondhand smoke that has accumulated in a small, confined, poorly ventilated area. **See also hotbox**

CONTROLLED BREATHING A form of respiration utilized during a smoking session where the number of people present in a smoking circle exceeds the amount of available pot necessary to get everyone high. By inhaling deeply and holding one's breath for several seconds, one can give the THC-laden smoke as much time as possible to percolate in the lungs and increase the likelihood that the desired state of bakedness will be attained. The pot smoker just needs to remember to start breathing again after exhaling.

COOKIE A dessert consisting of varying levels of sugar, butter, flour, eggs, and additional ingredients like nuts and chocolate to produce everything from the humble sugar cookie to the hulking oatmeal raisin. Under normal circumstances, the average human can consume two or three cookies before becoming full. This number, however, does not apply to humans who have recently smoked pot. For such individuals the maximum number of cookies is nearly without limit. **See also cookie dough ▾**

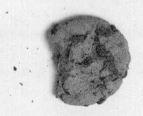

COOKIE DOUGH A combination of raw materials that, when exposed to high temperatures, magically becomes cookies. While cookie dough is by no means complicated to make from scratch, it can be a bit of a challenge for those under the influence. Many popular cookie companies, clearly aware of the plight of the average pot smoker, began selling cookie dough in refrigerated tubes for easy slicing and baking. Later, those same companies made it even easier by creating tear-away, prepackaged blocks. The new packaging makes little difference to the average pot smoker, however, as the vast majority had never considered baking the dough in the first place, preferring to eat it raw. **See also cookie**

COOL A versatile colloquialism whose meaning can shift depending on what circle it is being used in. For example, the general public uses it to imply that something is impressive, neat, or generally good. In pot-smoking circles these meanings still apply, but the word can also mean that somebody has been indoctrinated into the cannabis culture and is most certainly not a cop. It can also mean that somebody has had enough pot to smoke at a given moment and does not need any more. **See also uncool**

COPS Members of the law enforcement community whose admirable primary role is to protect the world's citizens from people with dangerous, harmful intentions, like murderers and thieves. Their secondary and far less productive role is to protect the world's citizens from themselves in the form of traffic tickets, DUI stops, and drug busts. Second only to lighter gnomes, cops are a relentless enemy of pot smokers, often pursuing them through town parks, wooded areas, and dark alleys. If one does find him or herself being pursued by a cop, evasive maneuvers such as running away, apologizing and promising never to do it again, and throwing a concealed cache of doughnuts on the ground have proved effective. **See also DEA; narc; police station** ▶

CORNER STORE A place of business that carries chocolate milk, tortilla chips, doughnuts, other assorted foodstuff, lottery tickets, lighters, and other impulse purchases. The corner store is a friend of the pot smoker as it carries everything he or she needs for the post-smoke binge.

CORNERING An obscure piece of pot etiquette observed by considerate smokers to ensure that all parties involved in a session can experience the first hit of a fresh bowl. Instead of shoving the lighter nearly into the bowl head and scorching the entire cache of pot, the smoker lights only a small portion of the weed and passes it to the next person. It is a surefire way to make new friends. **See also green hit**

CORTÉS, RICARDO Steel-balled author of *It's Just a Plant*, a children's book that promotes legalizing marijuana and paints a picture of pot as a harmless drug. To kids. To be fair, the book states that only adults should consume marijuana. It starts with the main character, a girl named Jackie, walking in on her parents as they smoke weed. The parents then explain to Jackie where marijuana comes from, that it has many medical applications, and that people from all walks of life smoke pot. Spoiler alert: At the end, police arrest someone for smoking the drug, and a confused Jackie vows to vote to overturn marijuana laws when she's old enough.

COSTA RICA One of the world's most progressive countries in terms of environmental policy, use of military, and availability of marijuana. Although the laws continue to be a bit fuzzy, Costa Rica is like a pot dealer who opens his trench coat and has different grades of weed hanging on every hook. Most people can find dealers pitching in most of the tourist spots: San Pedro, San José, Jaco, or Tamarindo.

COTTON MOUTH (If seeking information about the poisonous reptile because of a recent snakebite, stop flipping through an encyclopedia about marijuana and seek immediate medical attention.) An unfortunate side effect of smoking marijuana wherein the mouth transforms from a moist, relatively cooperative environment to a dry, barren wasteland, thus making it nearly impossible to speak, eat, and worse, continue smoking. Effective temporary solutions include drinking large quantities of water, chewing gum, sucking on ice, or playing chubby bunny. Ineffective temporary solutions include spitting, eating saltines, and rubbing the tongue with sandpaper.

COUCH An oblong, cushioned seating device that typically holds up to four people but can accommodate more if individuals squeeze or sit on laps. Couches come in a variety of colors, shapes, and comfort levels, and they're the number one destination location for friends to "crash." The couch is as integral to the smoking experience as pot itself. Couches are the good friends who never let their companions down. Smokers sit, lie, spill, and pass out on them, and the couch keeps doing its job without complaint. The sitting experience is maximized when the couch is combined with a TV, as comfort and entertainment team up with marijuana to form the perfect situation for pot smokers.

COUGHING An unfortunate response resulting from the body's reluctance to breathe marijuana smoke instead of air. The reflex evolved because of the rather inefficient fact that, in humans, the food hole and the air hole start at the same place and then branch off in two directions. When food goes down the wrong pipe, a short expulsion of air is the best thing the human body could come up with for expelling it. Some lizards can walk on water, dolphins have built-in sonar, and chameleons can change the color of their skin. Humans can cough.

CRAMPS Intense waves of abdominal pain during a woman's menstrual period, right up there on the Fairness Scale with earning seventy-nine cents to every dude's dollar. Some ladies find relief through strategically placed heating pads or by gulping down Midol. Others simply curl up in a ball and wish for a quick death. The intelligent lady smoker obliterates her cramps with the healing power of weed. In addition to neutralizing physical pain, marijuana also evens out the hormonal highs and lows that a menstruating woman might be suffering and provides her with another very good reason to eat all those potato chips.

CREAM SODA SURPRISE A pot smoker's treat, created when vanilla ice cream and flat vanilla cream soda are combined. After they're mixed together, one sip cures the marijuana user's cotton mouth with a rush of vanilla sweetness. The flat soda creates a smooth texture, enticing the drinker

for a second glass. The process of making the concoction—flattening soda, scooping, and stirring—brings a healthy balance of work and reward to the experience. The surprise is that only stoners seem to like it.

CREATIVITY The ability to produce innovative bursts of genius ranging from works of art to technological advancements. While some humans are inherently more creative than others, this ability can be temporarily enhanced through the ingestion of marijuana. Once high, obscure concepts and abstract ideas will suddenly begin to make sense. Because the sensation is temporary, one should use the brief time to scribble feverishly in a sketchbook or attempt to outline the next great American novel in a journal. If, after sobering up, one is dissatisfied with the quality of the work, simply toke up and check again. It should revert back to its previous level of genius. **See also artistic smoker**

CREEPER Marijuana that has a tendency to sneak up on the user. The individual will smoke a reasonable amount of pot or eat an entire brownie but not feel the effects right away. This can be especially problematic if the user attempts to remedy the situation by smoking more weed instead of waiting patiently for the high to kick in.

CROSS, DAVID (BORN APRIL 4, 1964) A stand-up comedian and actor who has worked on such classics as *Mr. Show with Bob and David* and *Arrested Development*. Both shows used absurdist and confidently contrarian humor and appealed in the most profound ways to the weed-inclined. Cross is as funny as it gets, but his appeal to pot smokers may lie as much in his humor as his look. Cross seems to have started going bald as a first-grader. He's got a gangly slacker appeal and sound. And seeing him wear a moustache as Dr. Tobias Fünke will make any pot-smoking viewer fall into hysterics before briefly considering growing one himself. **See also Arrested Development**

CRUNKED The process of being both on chronic and drunk. High plus drunk equals crunked. The term gained widespread recognition thanks to former *The Simpsons* writer and late-night martyr Conan O'Brien, who, along with cohost Andy Richter, used the phrase as a way to get around the censors, e.g., "That is crunked up!" Part of the story is also that Ice-T, a guest on Conan's show that night, fed the late-night host the word beforehand.

CURING An often overlooked but essential step in the smoking process that allows the natural flavors and fragrances of the marijuana to come through and reduces some of the harshness of the smoke. Once the buds have been harvested and dried, they are then placed in sealed jars to begin the curing process. Similar to fruit, marijuana continues to "ripen" after it has been harvested as natural sugars and chlorophyll begin to break down inside the jar. After a few weeks, as long as one has opened the jar every now and then to replenish the oxygen inside, the result will be the finest sticky icky on the block. The shelf life of marijuana that has been properly cured is unknown, as nobody has ever been able to resist smoking it for more than a few days. ▶

CUSTOMS Governmentally appointed authorities charged with the enforcement of laws pertaining to the transport of goods over international borders. Whether importing seeds for some DIY botany or simply trying to get back into America with some souvenirs from Amsterdam, a less-than-savvy pot smoker's encounters with customs often prove to be unfortunate experiences. Fortunately, most casual smokers are smart enough to keep their toking confined to national borders.

CYPRESS HILL An American West Coast hip-hop group that gained mainstream success in the early 1990s with such tracks as "I Wanna Get High," "Hits from the Bong," and "Legalize It," causing thirteen-year-olds everywhere to mindlessly sing along to those songs and parents everywhere to freak out. Cypress Hill is outspoken in both their marijuana use and their desire to see it legalized. Recently, the group announced the release of their own line of cannabis products called Cypress Hill Bhang. Member B-Real opened his own dispensary in California in 2018, and partnered with Driven Deliveries, Inc., which provides on-demand cannabis deliveries to select locations. Kind of like Uber Eats…for pot smokers.

CZECH REPUBLIC A former communist country that has since become a prolific pot-smoking country in Europe. A recent survey found 19.3 percent of fifteen- to thirty-four-year-olds had smoked bud in 2017. The Czech Republic has decriminalized marijuana use and possession, but only medical marijuana has been legalized. Also decriminalized in the Czech Republic: up to forty pieces of magic mushrooms, five tablets of LSD, four tablets of ecstasy, and one gram of coke, making it the number one vacation destination for weeklong benders. **See also Amsterdam ▼**

Dd

DABS Highly concentrated doses of cannabis that are known for giving an extremely potent high. One who does dabs is said to be "dabbing." **See also concentrate; rig**

DANCING The rhythmic moving of legs, arms, body, and neck by humans listening to music. Dancing is an art form that can be studied and perfected, as in the ballet, tango, line, swing, and salsa schools, among others. However, most pot smokers don't enjoy dancing, except when alone and listening to music, at which point they mostly just sit and nod their heads to the rhythm. **See also music**

DANDY WARHOLS, THE An indie rock band whose outspoken opposition of marijuana laws is perfectly reasonable once double-named lead singer Courtney Taylor-Taylor explains why: "We have a lot of stoners in our band, so to have marijuana still be illegal is ridiculous." Damn right. The Dandy Warhols played a show at the Playboy Mansion in support of overturning current US pot laws in 2009. Added Taylor-Taylor: "There are a lot of countries where it's perfectly legal, and they get along better than America. Plus it may be our only chance to go to the Playboy Mansion and hang out." Which is as good a reason as any to overturn pot laws.

DANK Pot that has been deemed to be of especially high quality. While there are no universal criteria for grading marijuana, dank weed is generally slightly sticky to the touch, riddled with brownish-red hairs, carries a pleasantly skunky odor, and is extremely potent. Inexperienced smokers should refrain from using this term, as it is rather embarrassing to declare low-grade schwag as being "dank" simply because one lacks a basis for proper comparison. **See also bomb; headie; ill; skunk**

D.A.R.E. (DRUG ABUSE RESISTANCE EDUCATION) An organization founded in Los Angeles, California, in 1983 that preaches the wonders of a substance-free lifestyle to schoolchildren. The program put police officers in the classroom and broke down barriers between cops and students through honest, open discussions about drug use. Yet, shockingly, science has repeatedly shown that the original D.A.R.E program really doesn't work. Instead, they adopted the "keepin' it REAL" program, which is somehow even less cool than the original (and still not particularly effective). However, the iconic black-and-red D.A.R.E. T-shirts are still 100 percent badass.

See also clean; cops ▶

DARK ALLEY A narrow strip of land located between two closely placed buildings whose proximity and height blocks city lights from reaching the ground. Dark alleys are desirable locations for crime, superhero justice, police car chases, fence jumping, garbage disposal, stray cats, and marijuana smoking.

DARK SIDE OF THE RAINBOW A phrase referencing the fact that when one smokes an outrageous amount of pot and listens to Pink Floyd's eighth album, *The Dark Side of the Moon*, while at the same time watching the family film *The Wizard of Oz*, certain elements of the film line up perfectly with the lyrics and tempo of the album. Sort of. This phenomenon is high-exclusive, meaning it can be observed only while under the influence of cannabis. Members of the band have repeatedly insisted the synchronization is pure coincidence, but the evidence is pretty difficult to dispute. One example includes "Eclipse," the last song on the album, concluding with the sound of a heartbeat just as Dorothy puts her hand to the Tin Man's chest. There are only two possible explanations: The members of Pink Floyd were so high that they synched their album to a popular children's movie and then completely forgot about it, or aliens, greatly dissatisfied with the movie's original soundtrack, beamed down to the studio, directed the members of Pink Floyd to create an alternate score to their favorite film, and then erased their memories. Frankly, the two are equally plausible. **See also highdea; movies; music; Pink Floyd**

DAVE MATTHEWS BAND The eponymously named alternative rock band whose concerts cannot be attended without at least a dozen wafts of marijuana smoke passing before an onlooker's face. DMB appeals to the hippie-styled pot smoker. For one thing, it's not uncommon for the band to break into extended, twenty-minute jams at concerts, the perfect music to lie down to and stare at the sky. Dave is also incomprehensible to anyone at his concerts who is not high. Trying to understand what Dave says to the audience between songs is totally impossible to do, unless one is Dave Matthews. Not to worry though—if you didn't bring any pot yourself, the secondhand high will do the trick. **See also concerts; second-hand smoke**

DAVIDSON, TOMMY (BORN NOVEMBER 10, 1963) A stand-up and character comic who has appeared in such films as *Booty Call*, *Juwanna Mann* (as a pimp named Puff Smokey Smoke), and *Strictly Business*. Davidson's big break came as part of the ensemble

on the classic sketch-comedy show *In Living Color* in the early 1990s, and it led to his appearance in fellow *In Living Color* alum Jim Carrey's *Ace Ventura: When Nature Calls*. Davidson's antics are minimally humorous. However, when high, the viewer enjoys Davidson's quick-talking, overly energetic character-making skills.

DAZED AND CONFUSED A 1993 film, the title of which is derived from a Led Zeppelin song of the same name. The movie takes place in and around a high school in Texas during the last few days of classes as a band of youths on the cusp of freshmandom try to evade fledgling seniors. Meanwhile, several members of the football team try their best to get drunk and stoned while simultaneously struggling with the moral and ethical implications of signing an agreement with their coach stating they will not take drugs during the summer. After an evening of general debauchery, the film culminates with several of the main characters smoking pot on the 50-yard line of the football field and driving to score Aerosmith tickets. Proving once and for all that, no matter how epic the evening, it is not truly complete until a joint is lit. **See also 50-yard line**

DEA (DRUG ENFORCEMENT ADMINISTRATION) A government agency established in 1973 during the Nixon administration with the express purpose of combating illegal drug use and trafficking within the United States of America. Members of the DEA are more than five times more likely to have been tattletales as children, and almost none of them were ever invited to parties in high school. **See also cops; narc**

DEALERS Good Samaritans who risk fines, community service, and potential incarceration to supply the world's pot smokers with a steady stream of marijuana. They come from all walks of life and represent every gender, creed, and sexual orientation on the planet, so identifying one can be difficult. Some signs to look for are loose-fitting clothing, preferences for poorly lit areas, unwavering fear of and disdain for police, and ownership of a digital scale. **See also connect; dark alley; drug deal; scale**

DECARBOXYLATE Step number one for making cannabutter. Also known as "decarbing," this process involves heating the marijuana so that psychoactive components are released. This is essentially what's already happening when you smoke cannabis, so this is an important first step for good-quality pot butter. It sounds tricky, but you can actually just go ahead and use your oven—no fancy tools required. **See also cannabutter; edibles; pot butter; pot oil**

DECRIMINALIZATION A legal term whereby something (in this case, the possession and use of marijuana and associated paraphernalia) is no longer treated as a crime. That would mean that all criminal penalties for drug law violations are removed. To those in the know, this is also step one in marijuanaphiles's grand plan to destroy the youth and take over the world. The plan goes as follows: Step 1: Decriminalization. Step 2: Legalization. Step 3: Destroy youth. Step 4: World domination. Easy! Opponents of decriminalization are hip to the agenda and therefore oppose it at all costs. **See also legalization**

DEEP FRYER The pot smoker's best friend. This cooking device heats oil up to between 300 and 450° F so that the hungry user can infuse food items like chicken wings, potatoes, mozzarella sticks, pickles, and even ice cream and candy bars with delicious oil. The appliance creates a paradox, wherein it is an essential tool for creating the majority of munchie staples, but it is arguably the most dangerous tool known to man to attempt to operate when high. For this reason, it is always wise to have a nonsmoking friend act as chef for the evening. This person can also act as a sober liaison should somebody need to talk to the police or other authority figures for any reason. ▼

DÉJÀ VU The semi-mystical feeling that encompasses one's person when it inexplicably seems that the current moment or experience has happened to the individual before, even if he or she can't place where or when exactly. Déjà vu is an oft-studied phenomenon but little understood. In pot-smoking circles, it describes the experience of hearing someone tell the same joke or story over multiple smoking sessions without remorse, recollection, or shame.

DELIVERY The process by which food is prepared at a restaurant and then brought directly to the customer, usually because the consumer of said food is too lazy or too high (or both) to come pick it up. This can be an invaluable service for times when everyone in the smoking circle neglected to purchase munchies or a preplanned cooking session becomes far too risky a venture. Generally there is a premium for this service in the form of politeness and a tip for the underpaid teenager who handles the delivery. **See also drive-through**

DENVER The most populous city of the state of Colorado, home of the Broncos, Rocky Mountains, 16th Street Mall, and the first city in America to make marijuana downright legal. In 2005, Denver lived up to its nickname as the Mile High City, passing a city initiative making the private use of marijuana by adults twenty-one and older A-OK. The initiative did not usurp state law, which treated marijuana possession like a speeding ticket, with a fine and no jail time. However, stoners did use the city initiative successfully as a defense. In 2010, *The Denver Post* reported that marijuana dispensaries grew to outnumber liquor stores, Starbucks coffee shops, or public schools in Denver. Frappuccino sales at Starbucks, however, skyrocketed. And, to round off an already excellent track record, Colorado became the first state to legalize recreational marijuana in 2014.

DEODORANT A spray, powder, or solid stick used to mask the unpleasant stench of the human body. Given its inherent ability to repress odors, a stick of deodorant can be the ideal hiding place for someone looking to stash exceptionally skunky weed. To unlock its hidden potential, one simply twists the stick until the solid bar falls out, shaves off a section of similar volume to the pot that will be concealed, rolls the weed in plastic wrap and secures it in the now-empty plastic applicator, returns the solid stick, and replaces the cap. While this method is unlikely to fool drug-sniffing dogs or border patrol police, it will generally outsmart snooping family and friends. **See also cereal box**

DESPERATION A feeling that sets in when one is without a proper method for smoking pot or, worse, completely bereft of any smokable marijuana to begin with. When faced with the former situation, pot smokers are capable of extreme acts of ingenuity and genius, creating such devices as apple pipes. Unfortunately, if one is completely out of pot, no amount of desperation can help one create pot from thin air. **See also apple pipe**

DICKINSON, EMILY (DECEMBER 10, 1830–MAY 15, 1886) An American poet who was considered a bit eccentric but was also incredibly prolific. Although unconfirmed, some people attribute her odd behavior to partaking in the occasional joint. After all, you'd be hard pressed to find a more dramatic description of marijuana than "the yearning soul of fire, burning up fall leaves and lost memories, under the midnight stars a'twinkle." **See also artistic smoker; creativity**

DIME BAG A slang term used to describe a small plastic bag filled with approximately $10 worth of marijuana. While considered a mere pittance of pot in the current smoking society, older smokers will often reminisce that a dime bag used to be "a decent amount of weed." **See also eighth; gram; nickel bag** ▼

DISPENSARY A magical location where one can legally purchase marijuana and related products for both medicinal and recreational use. More like a traditional storefront than Amsterdam's coffeeshops, dispensaries are regulated by local government. As of 2016, there are state-regulated marijuana dispensaries in 16 states (and Washington, DC) in the United States. **See also Amsterdam; budtender**

DONNIE DARKO A 2001 dark comedy starring Jake and Maggie Gyllenhaal, Drew Barrymore, and a giant invisible bunny. The movie involves love, time travel, alternate realities, several real and unreal deaths, and a school flooding. It's weird, scary, and, upon first viewing,

nonsensical, making it an instant classic for pot smokers. The film also popularized the phrase "cellar door," which Drew Barrymore's character explains is an example of what some people consider the most beautiful-sounding phrase in the English language. When asked what their favorite movies are, about 25 percent of college pot smokers will place *Donnie Darko* at the top of their list. That percentage hovers around whatever the unemployment rate happens to be post-college.

DOOB A slang term for a marijuana cigarette, which is merely a shortening of another popular term, "doobie." The term is almost universally understood to be a wildly uncool way to refer to a joint. However, it is so uncool that evoking it can actually come around full circle to make one sound cool again. A similar phenomenon exists with several breeds of dogs (e.g., pugs, Mexican hairless, and Boston terriers) that go so far down the ugly spectrum that they come back around to being cute. **See also joint**

DOORS, THE An American band born in the time of psychedelia, led by popular 1960s icon Jim Morrison. The band was formed in Los Angeles, and instead of a bass player, they had a keyboardist, which helped create their unique sound. Because of Morrison's poetic lyrics and erratic stage persona, the band was considered one of the strangest and most controversial music groups of their time. Obviously influenced by marijuana and other drugs, songs like "Light My Fire" and "Break On Through (To the Other Side)" have become anthems for pot smokers around the world.

DOPE A derogatory term common among teachers, parents, and police officers to refer to marijuana and various other drugs like cocaine and heroin. The term is also common in public service announcements that generally involve one or more characters who smoke pot before doing something stupid and end with the line "There's a reason they call it dope." Cue eye rolls here.

DR. DRE (BORN FEBRUARY 18, 1965) A rapper/producer responsible for perfecting the West Coast G-Funk rap style and a record company executive responsible for unleashing Eminem, 50 Cent, and Snoop Dogg on the universe. His first solo album was entitled *The Chronic*. So linked is Dre to chronic it's almost impossible to believe he's the same guy from NWA's "Express Yourself." Several of his other songs have also included drug references, including "Kush," which featured Snoop Dogg and Akon, and "My Life (Smoking Weed for Hours)." With all those references, it's really no surprise to anyone that Dr. Dre's album *Detox* was never released. **See also chronic; Eminem; Snoop Dogg**

DRAG A single pull of a joint or blunt that can last for as long as it has to. Subjects place the unlit end into their mouths and inhale, continuing to do so until they have had enough or a coughing fit sets in, whichever comes first. **See also controlled breathing; inhaling; puff; pull; toke**

DREADLOCKS A hairstyle most commonly associated with the Rastafarian movement characterized by multiple strands of hair twisted together to form long, matted ropes. They can be used as a not-so-subtle means of conveying one's 420 status without the use of words since a person who wears dreadlocks but doesn't smoke pot is more difficult to find than Bigfoot.

DRINKABLES Exactly what it sounds like, a.k.a. a drink infused with pot. **See also edibles**

DRIVE-THROUGH A popular feature ubiquitous to fast-food restaurants that allows customers to pull their cars up alongside the restaurant, yell their order at a menu with a microphone, and pay for their food and pick it up at a window farther down the line. This is especially useful for pot smokers, as it eliminates much of the troublesome in-person interaction that can be difficult to accomplish with a straight face while high. ▼

DRUG Any chemical, plant, food, mineral, gas, or currently undiscovered substance that alters the normal function of the human body. The definition is so broad that it can literally apply to anything. A pencil, for example, if ground up and snorted would sure as hell have a negative effect on one's sense of smell and taste. Does that make it a drug? Also, if one

were to smoke so much pot that being high literally became the normal state of being, would breathable air become a drug by default? And wouldn't pot then cease to be a drug for that person? Unfortunately, the folks making antidrug laws were not nearly high enough during their meetings to travel down this obscure way of thinking. Otherwise, the list of illegal drugs would simply be an infinity symbol. See also D.A.R.E.

DRUG DEAL A scenario where a dealer meets with a client for the purpose of exchanging some form of drug (e.g., cocaine, marijuana, heroin, PCP, etc.) for money, goods, or services. Preferably money. Because of the illegal nature of these meetings, they are usually staged in areas where it is unlikely any law enforcement agents will be in attendance, such as dark alleys, rundown apartment complexes, public bathrooms, and quiet side streets. See also connect; dark alley; dealers

DRUG-SNIFFING DOGS The Judases of the canine world who shun the title of man's best friend and opt instead to pursue a career in professional tattle-telling. The dogs are brought into public situations and trained to alert their handlers when they detect the presence of drugs like marijuana, heroin, or cocaine. There is currently no explanation for why these dogs have turned on their former human companions, although it might have something to do with all the times humans got high and thought it would be really funny to make them wear silly hats and sweaters. ▼

DRUG TEST Any method used to determine whether or not an individual has indulged in a chemical substance not normally found in the human body, such as cocaine, heroin, steroids, marijuana, or PCP. This can range from sophisticated methods like examining blood and urine samples in a laboratory to the far less invasive, and far less conclusive, method of simply asking the subject if he or she has ever done drugs. **See also drug** ▼

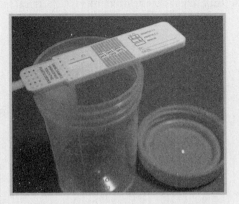

DRY An undesirable state of being, wherein the subject is completely bereft of any smokable or edible marijuana and is unable to obtain any in a timely fashion. It is believed the term is derived from the expression "the well is dry," which is used to declare that a local source of water has been depleted of all its life-giving resources. However, the term could also be in reference to the state of the subject's eyes after hours of crying over a depleted stash. **See also buzzkill**

DUDE One of a pot smoker's favorite four-letter words, along with "cool," "nice," and "food." Dude is unique in English usage in that it is typically an unnecessary word that precedes an unnecessary statement. It is routinely overused by pot smokers, who can conduct full conversations using only the word "dude." **See also cool;** *Dude, Where's My Car?*

DUDE, WHERE'S MY CAR? A 2000 film starring Ashton Kutcher and Seann William Scott as two friends who wake up one morning to a refrigerator full of chocolate pudding, a living room full of undelivered pizzas, an angry boss, even angrier girlfriends, little to no recollection of what happened the night before, and no sign of their car. The ensuing mishmash of fruitless backtracking, pot-addled dialogue, and multiple alien fight scenes was met with mixed reviews, with *USA TODAY* going so far as to write, "Any civilization that can produce a movie this stupid probably deserves to be hit by famine and pestilence." Perhaps the folks at *USA TODAY* would have enjoyed it more if they were as high during the viewing as the folks who made it must have been during its creation.

DUFFLE BAG A rectangular- or oval-shaped gym bag that can be utilized as a carry-on bag on an airplane or a makeshift briefcase in an emergency. Duffle bags are also a convenient and inconspicuous way to store large amounts of weed. While they seem convenient and can be a loyal companion for many years, they are also the number one choice of the dealer who gets found out, as almost all police-bust photos involve weed overflowing from a duffle bag. Intelligent smokers know ahead of time: If their dealer uses a duffle bag, it's best to find another dealer. **See also dealers**

DUGOUT A case used for storing marijuana containing a small chamber to house the pot and another compartment just large enough for a one-hitter, affectionately referred to as the "bat." This piece of paraphernalia is ideal for the smoker on the go, because it allows them to discreetly pack a bowl, take a hit, and disappear like a ninja in a cloud of smoke long before bystanders even realize what's happened. **See also one-hitter**

DURBAN POISON A highly potent strain of marijuana grown in the very hot regions of South Africa, including the coastal area of KwaZulu-Natal. The bud smells like candy and is about as common there, especially in the city where it gets its namesake. Pot tourists travel to the country for this strain specifically; they acquire it from black market pushers on the streets since it's technically still illegal there despite its widespread use. It's no surprise the Zulu people consider themselves "people of heaven," as they surround themselves with vast swaths of untouched weed, which is what most serious weedophiles consider heaven to be anyway.

DUTCH MASTER An inexpensive brand of cigar, the contents of which are commonly discarded so they can be replaced with a far superior filling: marijuana. The flavor profile and distinct aroma of an unaltered Dutch Master have been documented only in lab settings, as no member of the general public has ever smoked one without some degree of enhancement. **See also blunt; cigar** ▼

DYLAN, BOB (BORN MAY 24, 1941) A seminal American folksinger, counterculture hero, and longtime pot user. Dylan's adversarial relationship with the mainstream press, his cryptic quotes, and his stoic voice have made him a mesmerizing figure for pot smokers from the 1960s to today. Dylan, whose birth name is Robert Zimmerman, once explained his name change by saying he never viewed himself "as a Robert Zimmerman," causing weedophiles everywhere to nod along and say, "I so get that." Dylan is also a pioneer in the drug culture, turning The Beatles on to marijuana on their first US visit and also littering his songs with pot references. **See also Beatles, The**

Ee

EASY RIDER A marijuana variety designed to be as easy to grow as it is to smoke. A hybrid strain of part sativa and part indica, easy rider can be grown indoors or out, by experienced growers or novices. It grows to about two feet tall and has about a 12 to 15 percent THC level, making it ideal for clandestine, high-yield pot growing. **See also hybrid**

EDIBLES A cannabis-infused foodstuff. Think pot brownies or cookies —treats that look innocent to the naked eye but are actually going to get the consumer high. **See also drinkables; pot butter; pot brownies; pot cake; pot oil ▼**

EIGHTH A denomination in which marijuana is generally sold, in reference to an eighth of an ounce. Eighths cost anywhere from $30 to $70, depending on the grade of weed, geographic location, and general weed climate. As the well dries up, prices rise. Supply-and-demand economics. Eighths of pot last about a month when not properly stored before the plant begins to dry out and the grade drops. This leads to more eighths purchases, which in turn leads to more weed smoking, and the vicious, beautiful cycle continues forever. **See also gram; ounce**

EMINEM (BORN OCTOBER 17, 1972) A controversy-loving rapper, *8 Mile* heartthrob, and the Real Slim Shady whose ex-wife, Kim, daughter, Hailie, and mother, Debbie, provide about two-thirds of his lyrical content. The other third is mostly reserved for self-loathing, pot, and women who aren't related to him. Eminem is an unapologetic, violence-laden, rather homophobic poet who refuses to use the N-word and always raps about the way-too-personal. He started off rapping about drugs, including marijuana, in songs like "Must Be the Ganja." However, Eminem struggled with addiction to prescription drugs. He has now been sober for more than ten years.

EMOTIONS Feelings that manifest out of basic human wants and desires. For example, hunger can make people feel irritable. Sleepiness can make people feel frustrated. And marijuana (categorically a basic human need of the pot smoker) makes people feel happy. Emotions are accentuated when high, and it's not uncommon for an emotional smoker to tell those in the smoking circle he or she loves them all.

ENGLAND America's former landlord, closest ally, and bottomless reservoir of actors who come to America to play butlers or superhero villains in movies. England is still trailing a bit behind when it comes to the cannabis industry. The country decriminalized the herb years ago, and though it's still illegal, British officials have almost completely stopped arresting those who smoke for private use. It wasn't until 2018 that medical marijuana

was legalized—but only when prescribed by a physician. Oddly enough, despite stricter rules within the country, England has become the largest exporter of legal marijuana due to biotech company GW Pharmaceuticals. Quite the contradiction! **See also decriminalization** ▼

ENHANCEMENT SMOKER A breed of pot smoker succinctly portrayed by comedian Jon Stewart in the film *Half Baked*. Enhancement smokers have convinced themselves that every activity is infinitely better after one has consumed marijuana. To them, going to the zoo is okay, but going to the zoo on weed is simply a much more worthwhile adventure. A little toke here and there to liven up certain activities is fine. However, if the response when asked if one would like to go smoke a joint is, "Hold on, let me smoke a bowl first," one might have crossed the line into enhancement smoker territory. **See also active smoker; antisocial smoker; artistic smoker; social smoker; talkative smoker**

ENO, BRIAN (BORN MAY 15, 1948) An English record producer and musician who has worked with rock acts such as David Bowie, U2, Talking Heads, Coldplay, and many others. Eno's own works have been groundbreaking pieces of ambient music, stuff to put on in the background when silence is too deafening but real music is too distracting. This would include the 1975 masterpiece album *Another Green World*, a quiet, reflective album whose strength is grounded in subtlety, texture, and atmospherics, making it a great album to listen to while smoking a joint. *Another Green World* usually takes several listens before it's "understood," not including the times a pot smoker falls asleep, leaves the room, or doesn't pay attention while it's playing.

ENTOURAGE An HBO series documenting the rise and stardom of Vincent Chase and the antics of he and his childhood friends E, Turtle, and Drama, as well as Vince's agent, Ari. The show is based on the rise of executive producer Mark "Marky Mark" Wahlberg and deals with several after-school-special kind of issues, like sex, alcohol, and drugs. However, it does so in a more realistic way and has thus gained favor with an older, more mature viewing audience. Pot turns up a lot in the show. Turtle, in particular, is a character who seems to enjoy getting high, and Drama joins a medical marijuana club for an episode. *Entourage* teaches America's youth an important, life-affirming lesson: If one gets high all day and leeches off one's friends, one can have an enjoyable, fulfilling life.

EUPHEMISMS The use of more polite-sounding words or phrases to describe things that are undesirable or better left unsaid. Examples include: "hooked up," "in between jobs," "big-boned," etc. Clever smokers employ euphemisms when they run into authority figures in the hopes that they can elicit laughter among their friends while keeping the fact that they're high quiet. The response to a question like "Are you high?" could result in the following euphemism: "No, we were just bobbin' the

Marley." The authority figure will respond: "What?" and the smoker will say, "You know, just exploring the atmosphere, suckin' the succor, puffin' the magic dragon." Upon completion of this sentence, the smoker will flash an ear-to-ear smile at his friends, who will have missed it because they've already started running.

EUPHORIA A state of general content-edness that can be achieved through positive thinking, proper diet, and meditation. Or one can take a shortcut and smoke pot. When in this state, one feels on top of the world, as if absolutely nothing could possibly go wrong. This is usually followed by something going wrong such as an unexpected encounter with law enforcement. Once the dust has settled, this often results in the subject smoking addi-tional pot to get back to the euphoric state. And so the cycle begins again…

EURO STYLE A method for con-suming marijuana wherein smokers take several long hits until they are satisfied with the amount they have smoked before passing it to the next person. This method runs contrary to the regimented style employed in the United States where participants take precisely two hits before passing the smoking apparatus to their neighbor. When smoking Euro style, one should adhere to the self-imposed rules one might follow at an all-you-can-eat buffet. Just because one is allowed to eat seven plates of crab cakes in a single sitting does not mean that one should. **See also puff, puff, pass**

EXHALING The means by which smoke that has been inhaled into the lungs can be expelled from the body. This exercise should be attempted only once the smoke has had a chance to permeate the lungs and harness the THC's mind-altering powers. If one is so stoned that one forgets to perform this necessary maneuver, never fear—one's body will figure it out in due time. **See also inhaling**

EYE DROPS An (often) over-the-counter medical product that one puts in the eyes to create artificial tears for dry eyes, reduce allergy symptoms, or, most importantly, reduce redness. A notorious side effect of smoking too much pot is bloodshot eyes, which can be a dead giveaway as to how one has been spending one's spare time. It's best to keep a small bottle of eye drops on hand whenever possible to avoid unwanted questions. **See also bloodshot eyes**

Ff

FACEBOOK A social networking site, one of the most popular sites on the Internet, and a force that may in fact take over the world. In fact, it may already have. *Facebook* remembers everything its users have ever done or said, from awkward status updates and inappropriate political views to weird teenage interests and the be-all end-all: pictures. Some are benign vacation photos and family portraits. However, more damning images often include pot smokers with their mouths in a bong, exhaling smoke, smoking a joint, or holding their new baggie with a thumbs up. These photos are likely to resurface at exactly the most inopportune moments, like when the pot smoker is looking for a job, running for office, or after accidentally accepting their grandmother's friend request. **See also *Twitter; YouTube***

FACES The front area of the human head that depicts the individual's mug: nose, mouth, eyes, cheeks, freckles, pimples, and facial hair. Faces are the primary source by which people identify other people. When high, inebriated smokers are inclined to stare at their own face in the mirror and wonder, "Why do I look so weird?" This will result in the smoker poking at, mushing, and massaging the face in the hopes that it will somehow turn normal looking.

FAKE INHALE A sneaky trick employed by individuals who do not actually want to smoke pot but still want to fit in with their social group. When it is their turn to take a hit, they will take the smoke into their mouths similar to their friends, but they will not actually inhale the smoke. Instead, they will merely open their mouths and expel the smoke, giving the appearance that they have inhaled. Not only is this an embarrassing display that is unlikely to fool anyone but it is also a waste of perfectly good weed. **See also inhaling**

FAMILY GUY A Fox animated sitcom that follows the Griffin family in its travails in Quahog, Rhode Island. *Family Guy* is in equal parts loved and reviled by the culture, sometimes by the same individual. The main complaint levied against *Family Guy* is that its jokes are random, long-winded, nonsensical references to American consumer culture past. Oddly, this same property is what makes viewers consider the show fresh, unique, and humorous. For some, smoking weed is an essential part of finding *Family Guy* jokes funny, and many critics have been swayed by the use of the drug. It's the only kind of thing that can make an unexplained two-minute fight between main character Peter Griffin and a giant chicken funny. And the only kind of thing that can make it hilarious when they do it a second time.

FAN A mechanical device that utilizes several spinning blades to circulate air around a room. If situated in a window facing out, it can be used to force incriminating marijuana smoke from inside of a room to the relative safety of the outdoors. **See also smoke**

FATTY A large, plump, delectable marijuana cigarette. A fatty is rolled with 100 percent all-natural marijuana and should never contain additives like tobacco, cocaine, or PCP. **See also joint**

FEAR AND LOATHING IN LAS VEGAS A 1972 novel of gonzo journalism by Hunter S. Thompson that blends the real with the fictional and details the exploits of journalist Raoul Duke and his attorney Dr. Gonzo as they cover the Mint 400 motorcycle race and a police narcotics conference in Las Vegas, all while engaging in excessive use of marijuana, LSD, mescaline, and cocaine. The book is subtitled *A Savage Journey to the Heart of the American Dream*, and the book espouses on American culture and being a part of the wave of drug use that had swept the country around that time. It also includes hallucinations of desert animals, trashing hotel rooms, and frequent use of the phrase, "As your attorney, I advise you…" The book is a favorite of yuppie pot-smoker types who find the book's ability to capture the post-1960s counterculture, its references to excessive drug use, and its anti-pristine prose and presentation as the perfect combination of literary function. **See also Thompson, Hunter S.**

FEY, TINA (BORN MAY 18, 1970) A librarian glasses–wearing funny lady who wrote for *Saturday Night Live* and starred on NBC's *30 Rock*. Fey inherited the throne to the comedy-writing kingdom after penning and starring in the movie *Mean Girls* and becoming the only saving grace on *SNL* after Will Ferrell left (and later for her impersonation of politician Sarah Palin). Until 2013, she worked on the popular TV show *30 Rock*, which earned 103 Emmy Award nominations. The show is full of bizarre humor that requires a step outside the completely logical to fully appreciate. As a result, Fey and *30 Rock* are favorites among pot smokers and nonsmokers alike, making *30 Rock* the ideal show to watch in mixed company.

FIENDING A state of being characterized by an extreme desire to locate, purchase, and smoke some form of marijuana. Headies, mids, schwag—it doesn't matter. While studies have shown that marijuana is not physically addictive, weedophiles who have been unable to obtain smokable weed during an extended period of time will often exhibit symptoms such as irritability, anxiety, depression, and an insatiable desire to search their rooms for misplaced pot. The only known cure for this ailment is 100 ccs of weed—stat.

FIRE An extremely hot entity created when a substance in an oxygen-rich environment is heated to a given temperature known as its flash point. It is an essential ingredient in the equation "marijuana plus fire equals high." Fire can easily be created with the help of a lighter or matches. When safely controlled, fire can be more entertaining to a pot smoker than music, TV, and philosophy combined. **See also ash; lighter; matches; smoke ▶**

FISHER, CARRIE (OCTOBER 21, 1956–DECEMBER 27, 2016) Actress and writer most famous for portraying the cinnamon bun–haired Princess Leia in the beloved Star Wars movies. Fisher was known to get high between takes on the first movie, and she quickly moved on to more powerful drugs as she made the successive movies. This culminated in her appearance in the universally derided *Star Wars Holiday Special* in 1978. The two-hour program was so haphazardly put together, it included extended scenes of Chewbacca's family communicating strictly in his native tongue of unintelligible roars and a loose plot revolving around the celebration of the nondenominational holiday Life Day. Perhaps there is no more enjoyable experience than seeing Fisher, portraying Princess Leia, at the end of the special singing a slowed-down version of the Star Wars theme song, with lyrics. Her facial expressions suggest she's high on something, and it ain't Life Day.

FIVE-O A slang term derived from the cop series *Hawaii Five-O* used to describe the po-po, fuzz, cops, and police. It remains one of the most enduring, culturally relevant aspects of the show. Five-O is the natural enemy of the marijuana smoker and can be uniformed or undercover. A simple, sudden "Five-O! Five-O!" means "put the blunt out, toss the baggie, and run." **See also cops**

FLOWER The smokable part of a female cannabis plant. Basically just another slang term for marijuana. **See also bud; herb; nugs** ▼

FOOD Caloric intake meant to sustain the bodily functions of life, including fruit, pasta, peanut butter, ice cream, pizza, etc. Food is one of the best things about getting high. How food tastes increases exponentially once inebriated. As a result, pre-smoking rituals may include trips to local grocery stores to stock up on snacks. **See also munchies**

FORGETFULNESS A controversial side effect associated with long-term marijuana use. Those who don't smoke pot often claim the drug causes their loved ones who do get high to have trouble remembering important things like birthdays, anniversaries, and to walk the dog. The truth of the matter is that pot smokers are perfectly capable of remembering these minor details. However, they would just much rather smoke a bowl than take out the trash or pick someone up from the airport. **See also long-term memory loss; short-term memory loss**

FORMULA 420 A line of cleaning products designed specifically for removing tar, resin, ash, odor, and general griminess that can accumulate inside of anything used for smoking pot. Simply pour the solution into the piece, cover the openings, shake for one minute, and rinse to restore the paraphernalia to a state similar to how it looked before it contained more resin than glass. **See also stoke**

FREAKS AND GEEKS A poorly rated, critically acclaimed cult-classic TV show and among the first incarnations of future cannabis-friendly crew Judd Apatow, Seth Rogen, James Franco, Jason Segel, and Paul Feig. The show follows Lindsay and Sam Weir and their friends in Chippewa, Michigan, as they experience life on the bottom rung of William McKinley High School. While only eighteen episodes of the show were made, a fan-led campaign got the show to air the final six episodes and release the entire series, with all the original music intact, on DVD. *Freaks and Geeks* then became one of the most frequent shows to watch the entirety of while smoking a joint. Probably because pot smokers get to re-experience all their foibles and misadventures through the characters in the show…without all the parts that actually sucked about being in high school. **See also Apatow, Judd**

FREE-RANGE WEED A term used to refer to pot that has been planted in a secluded stretch of forest, a hidden trail in a local park, or an unused plot in a community garden and left to grow on its own without the aid of fertilizer, artificial sunlight, or pesticides. This hands-off style of farming offers all the benefits of growing one's own pot with far less risk of legal ramifications. While it may be impossible to prevent thieves from pilfering the budding plants, at least the grower has plausible deniability should anyone start wondering why the local rabbit population has suddenly taken to rolling on their backs and staring at the clouds for hours at a time.

FRENCH FRIES Potatoes that have been cut into thin strips and fried in oil to produce a crisp, golden-brown finger food perfect for dipping into various flavor enhancers like ketchup, barbecue sauce, milkshakes, and (in some forward-thinking countries) mayonnaise. Making them from scratch can be wildly dangerous in the best of circumstances, so it is usually advised that those in search of a French fry fix seek out their nearest fast-food restaurant or super-market freezer section in advance. ▸

FRENCH INHALE A parlor trick wherein smoke is released from the mouth and simultaneously inhaled through the nose, creating an unbro-ken chain of smoke. Although there is little to no practical application of the technique, it is very popular at parties and will often elicit godlike reverence from onlookers who have not yet fig-ured out how to perform the maneu-ver themselves. The far less impressive Norwegian inhale, in which the smoker exhales into a jar and seals the lid for later use, has yet to catch on.

FRIDAY A 1995 comedy starring Ice Cube and Chris Tucker about two weedophiles who need to pay a drug dealer $200 in sixteen hours or face death. The movie is about weed, and therefore it can be watched while on weed and summarily enjoyed.

The story moves seamlessly from lighthearted and fun to serious and dramatic, as the two friends fight and nearly kill each other in the process of attempting to find the money.

FRIED A state of complete and utter bakedness. The subject is so high, he or she can do little more than slump over on the couch and stare off into space while occasionally eat-ing a few cookies. While the subject could be contemplating very deep, thought-provoking concepts, it is far more likely that he or she is simply wondering if it's possible to overdose on marijuana. **See also baked; half-baked; high; stoned; wasted**

FRIENDS Individuals with whom one generally associates, shares com-mon interests, and likes. Friends are broken down into three categories: best friends, general friends, frenemies. The definitions are distinct in the pot world. For example, frenemies are those friends who always leech off one's weed supply. General friends are those with whom one will frequently get high. And best friends are the ones who, when one is craving a joint at a party, pulls one out of a back pocket, along with a lighter. All three inhabit a smoker's world at any given moment, and it's certain that the best friend will be a best man or bridesmaid at the wedding. Everyone else gets usher status.

FROZEN CHICKEN NUGGETS Fun-sized breaded chicken portions designed for easy home preparation. These scrumptious poultry snacks were developed in the 1950s as part of an academic project undertaken by a food scientist at Cornell University. If the project was to find the ultimate method of simultaneously enticing and infuriating a nation of starving pot smokers, one can only assume the scientist in question received an A with a smiley face next to it. Frozen chicken nuggets represent the cutting edge of delayed gratification. Factoring in oven preheat time, cooking the nuggets can be a bit more than

someone with a bad case of the munchies can handle. But the flavor is worth the wait…and when you add in dipping sauce? The deliciousness quotient is off the scale. It's, therefore, recommended that one initiate nugget prep prior to smoking up.

FROZEN RASPBERRIES Small, squishy, red fruit stored at a temperature below 32°F for the purposes of storage, transportation, and consumption. Frozen raspberries are one of a handful of fruits designed for the naturalist smoker, the vegan smoker, or the health-conscious smoker. Once they're tried, they become the best munchie available. They're tasty, interesting, sweet, and fairly healthy. Regrettably their caloric value is very low, meaning that even after going through three bags of frozen raspberries, the smoker is still looking for food. And there's one other problem: While delicious in nature, frozen raspberries leave eaters with red-stained fingers, which in turn leads to a red-stained shirt, couch, remote control, and face.

FULL MOON PARTY The international smoker's haven for all things beach, party, and beach party. Held on the beautiful and crowded beaches of the town of Haad Rin on the Thai island of Kho Pha Ngan, the Full Moon Party happens once each month when the moon is full (go figure). The rager attracts pot smokers from around the world for its infamous buckets of booze, fire dancers, and tasty Thai herb. Haad Rin beach bars stay open all night to serve the 20,000–30,000 Full Moon Partiers, who dance to drum and bass, house, and reggae music—and smoke till sunrise. Attendees don't have to speak Thai, but it helps if they know what a Thai stick is. **See also Thai stick**

FUNNY BEFORE FEELINGS An understanding reached among members of the smoking community that the mental well-being of any individual is secondary to saying something the rest of the group will find amusing, at least while everyone in a group is high. This philosophy is not universally understood, however, so it is best to test the waters with a minor putdown before graduating to "your mama" jokes and accusations of bed-wetting.

G g

G-13 A strain of pot of such urban legend it may have been briefly considered as the subject of an Indiana Jones movie. Allegedly, the US government genetically engineered G-13 while developing strains of marijuana at the University of Mississippi in the 1970s. Its THC level apparently reaches 28 percent, which is among the highest of any known strain. There's no evidence to support the claims that G-13 exists, but dealers who want to earn an extra buck on an eighth may claim to have the G-13 stuff, and smokers who want to think they're smoking G-13 may knowingly go along with the ruse. **See also** *American Beauty*

GALIFIANAKIS, ZACH (BORN OCTOBER 1, 1969) A bearded stand-up alternative comedian who starred in the comedy *The Hangover* and whose act consists mostly of delivering one-liners while intermittently playing piano. Galifianakis also plays different characters (a word he sometimes pronounces with the "ch" sound, like "charcoal"), including his brother Seth Galifianakis and the awkward, disinterested host on the show *Between Two Ferns with Zach Galifianakis* on *Funny or Die*. He's also been featured in some mainstream children's films, including *Puss in Boots*, *A Wrinkle in Time*, and *The Lego Batman Movie*. As should go without saying, Galifianakis's humor is designed to appeal to only kids or pot smokers.

GANJA The Sanskrit word for hemp that has been adapted by English-speaking pot smokers as another slang term for the drug. The word is more typically used in West Indian countries. When being spoken in America, it works most aptly with a crowd listening to reggae music or anything with a sitar.

GARCIA, JERRY (AUGUST 1, 1942– AUGUST 9, 1995) The enduring guitarist of original jam band the Grateful Dead and ranked by

Rolling Stone as the No. 13 greatest guitarist of all time. Garcia played extended soulful guitar riffs, and concerts sometimes saw the band extend into twenty-minute jam sessions. Garcia smoked so much pot and inspired so many smokers to reach temporary enlightenment that he even now remains a pivotal, emotional part of many smokers' experiences. **See also Grateful Dead, The;** *Half Baked*

GATEWAY DRUG A term used to describe marijuana by the antidrug crowd amongst a larger argument about the ill effects of legalizing or decriminalizing the herb. The idea is that marijuana, while not harmful in and of itself, is the first drug users will take en route to more dangerous drugs. The argument is propagated by the news, talk show guests, eighth-grade health teachers, and concerned parents. It is an argument that has been largely debunked by scientific evaluation. A twelve-year University of Pittsburgh study found that any number of sequences can take place in where marijuana falls in a user's drug progression, and that it does not indicate whether a user will move on to stronger drugs. Welcome relief for pot smokers

everywhere! **See also Anslinger, Harry J.; drug**

GENERATION JOINT A marijuana cigarette that has been imbued with the concentrated potency of five or six older joints that have been reduced to roaches. Once the generation joint has been smoked to near completion, it can then be saved for later use as the base for a third-generation joint, several of which can then be saved up for a fourth-generation joint, and so on. In order to create a ninth-generation joint, one would need to first create 1,953,125 roaches. Better get started. **See also roach**

GERMINATION The process by which a seed splits and the plant or fungus inside emerges and begins to form. Germination is an important process for the home marijuana grower and involves placing the seeds in a moist environment for twenty-four hours to help the seed crack before planting. The biggest obstacle to germinating the seeds is remembering to check on them after a day. Sometimes pot smokers lose their short-term memory and come across the seeds in the back of their closet two weeks later, dried out and unusable. Alarms and reminders on your smartphone are always helpful. **See also paper towel germination** ▼

GHOST HIT A rare phenomenon where, during the course of a smoking session, one of the participants manages to hold in a single hit of marijuana for so long that little to no visible smoke escapes when he or she exhales. To the untrained eye it may appear as if the subject has not actually inhaled any smoke at all. This is not the case, however. In truth, the smoke has merely been absorbed by the body or is temporarily trapped behind a pocket of bong resin that has built up in the lungs. There is the slight possibility that an actual ghost has possessed the body of the subject and taken the hit for himself. This possibility is especially troubling, as it would indicate that all of the wonders of the afterlife and benefits of complete spiritual enlightenment still pale in comparison to a single bong rip.

GINGRICH, NEWT (BORN JUNE 17, 1943) The amphibiously named former Speaker of the House whose superhip political positions include promoting fiscal conservatism, closing America's borders, and legalizing waterboarding. Radical. Gingrich is sort of a schizophrenic on marijuana issues though. Not only has he admitted to smoking it, but in the 1980s he supported the legalization of medical marijuana. Later, however, he totally changed his stance and started promoting the death penalty for drug smugglers. Gingrich was always good for a stoned laugh, though, when he was interviewed on a news channel, not because he's particularly (intentionally) funny, but because his fake moral outrage is so transparent and insincere the pot-smoking viewer can't help but see right through it. **See also politics**

GINSBERG, ALLEN (JUNE 3, 1926– APRIL 5, 1997) A prominent American poet, member of the infamous New York Beats, and author of the drug-and-sex-soaked poem "Howl," which serves as a preamble for any discussion of the Beats. Ginsberg palled around with several prominent Beat writers like William S. Burroughs, John Holmes, and Jack Kerouac,

Gg

sharing ideas, advice, and an occasional joint here and there. Like many prominent writers of his generation, Ginsberg experimented heavily with drugs in order to expand his mind and allow for more creative thought, and he was a vocal proponent of LSD and marijuana use. His advocacy for legalization, while admirable, can mostly be attributed to the fact that his poetry cannot fully be appreciated unless under the influence. **See also Burroughs, William S.; "Howl"; Kerouac, Jack**

GLOBAL MARIJUANA MARCH A worldwide demonstration of marijuana smokers' power in numbers and the number one social event of a smoker's year. The march usually takes place on the first weekend in May, or somewhere around there, or whenever they get around to it. It involves more than six hundred cities around the world, as well as all the typical suspects, including but not limited to the guy with a pot leaf shaved into his hair, the woman dressed as a giant bong, the dude with the "Free Hugs" poster, and the lady handing out hemp-styled leis. The march's intention is to celebrate marijuana as a personal choice and to have public perception move in that direction,

but, like most pro-marijuana demonstrations, it remains more of a hippie mixer than a seriously taken political statement.

GOD BUD A strain of marijuana that is intoxicatingly delicious and perhaps the first and most popular use of marketing in advertising when it comes to strains. God bud is a great, award-winning strain. It is dense, the high is very satisfying, and it has one of the most alluring names in all of weed. Anyone who hears the name God bud wants that stuff immediately—even atheists.

GOLDBERG, WHOOPI (BORN NOVEMBER 13, 1955) An actor, comedian, and TV personality best known for her appearances in films like *The Color Purple, Ghost*, and *Sister Act*, as well as her long-standing role as a moderator on the talk show *The View*. Goldberg is also a proponent of the healing properties of marijuana. Her company, Whoopi and Maya, offers a line of edibles, tinctures, rubs, and even a bath soak, all specifically designed to help women with menstrual cramps. For Whoopi Goldberg, it's not about getting high but instead about giving women access to products that might actually help them manage severe pain. We'll smoke to that. **See also cramps; edibles; tincture**

GONDRY, MICHEL (BORN MAY 8, 1963) A French music video and motion picture director who has worked on films such as *Eternal Sunshine of the Spotless Mind*, *The Science of Sleep*, *Dave Chappelle's Block Party*, *Be Kind Rewind*, *The Thorn in the Heart*, *The Green Hornet*, and *The We and the I* and directed the White Stripes's LEGOs video for "Fell in Love with a Girl." Gondry's visuals are brightly colored and charmingly dreamlike and thus appeal to any pot smoker. In *The Science of Sleep*, he shoots scenes that literally take place in someone's subconscious, blowing the minds of pot smokers everywhere.

GOOGLE The most powerful and precise search engine, as well as a mail, map, directions, recipe service, news aggregator, and one-stop shop for most everything on the Internet. Google has helped users find the most obscure and hard-to-find information, and it is theorized that Google contains every bit of knowledge available. If the meaning of life exists, it is likely stored somewhere on Google. With such endless information, Google is a key partner for all sorts of marijuana-friendly activities. Google searches can yield plenty of practical pot-related advice: the best food to eat while high, how to plant seeds, where to buy seeds, the best food to eat while high, how to roll a joint, the differences between specific strains, fun things to do while high, and, oh yeah, did we mention the best food to eat while high? ▼

GORE, AL (BORN MARCH 31, 1948) A Frankenstein-like robot engineered to sound as droning and boring as possible. A former vice president and presidential candidate, Gore is usually considered an unserious caricature whose autospeak setting is stuck on "global warming." Still, Gore is a member of the growing list of prominent politicians who have admitted to smoking weed. Unfortunately for progressives, he's also among the list of prominent politicians who no longer holds formal office. These days he's mostly sticking to his environmentalism gig and keeping his thoughts on marijuana to himself.

GRAM A unit of mass in the metric system defined as the weight of one cubic centimeter of water. The gram is also a standard unit of measure in the world of marijuana, and 3½ grams equals ⅛ ounce is the standard conversion between the English and metric marijuana systems. Grams of weed generally cost between $15 and $20 and can be reserved for either smokers who want higher-grade stuff to keep costs low or the less-consistent smoker to keep the weed fresh. Grams can usually provide for two to three joints, or about ten small bowls. ▼

GRANDMA'S BOY A 2006 film produced by Adam Sandler starring Allen Covert as walking, talking, pot-smoking cliché Alex. When the thirty-six-year-old video game tester is evicted from his apartment after his roommate spends their rent money on Filipino hookers, he is forced to move in with his grandmother and two of her elderly friends. The film is fairly formulaic, although it does contain one groundbreaking moment. While Alex is out of the house, the three geriatric women mistake his stash of marijuana for tea and get high off their asses. While the movie itself is mediocre, the opportunity to witness an old woman insisting she can hear her hair growing is well worth the time.

GRASS (FILM) A 1999 Canadian documentary starring old archival footage and the voice of Woody Harrelson detailing the history of marijuana law and illegality through the twentieth century. The movie takes a pro-marijuana stance and, as such, has become a favorite of the 420 subculture. However, it does very little to truly explore the reasons people don't want the drug legalized. As a result, upon viewing, every weedophile will declare it required viewing to prove that marijuana should be legalized, and it will be summarily dismissed by anyone who doesn't smoke as propaganda. Both sides will retire to their respective bunkers and think the other side is full of assholes. **See also Harrelson, Woody**

GRASS (PLANT) A slang term for marijuana likely stemming from the mild similarities in color and appearance between graminoids, the most prevalent plant on Earth, and *Cannabis sativa*, the most prevalent plant in college dorm rooms. ▼

GRASS IS GREENER A Netflix documentary that explores society's complicated relationship with marijuana in the United States, especially when it comes to race. The criminalization of weed has had a drastic impact on black and Latino communities, even with growing support for legalization. Worth watching if only for interviews with key pot-supporting celebrities like Snoop Dogg, B-Real, and more. **See also Netflix**

GRASSROOTS ORGANIZING The act of bringing together large groups of relatively powerless people in an effort to take on an entrenched powerful political entity or structure. The relatively powerless people largely consist of the immediate circle of people suffering from the injustice, friends and family, bored college students, and professional protesters. Because most of the planning for grassroots efforts is done under the influence of marijuana, the majority of grassroots efforts end with the entrenched political entity victorious. Unsurprisingly, the movement to get marijuana legalized is a grassroots effort, as it's the only issue pot smokers are motivated enough to do something about.

GRATEFUL DEAD, THE A San Francisco–based jam band whose styles ran from electric blues to psychedelia and space rock. The band performed for thirty years before the death of guitarist Jerry Garcia. Fans of the Dead are known as Deadheads, a term that reflects both their fascination with the band and their current mental state. To become a Deadhead, one must consume a minimum of 100 hours of Garcia solos, smoke weed daily while wearing a tie-dye shirt and bandana, and grow one's hair down to at least armpit length. Deadheads are also required to allow at least a three-second gap between someone calling their name and them responding. **See also Garcia, Jerry**

GRAVITY BONG A variety of smoking device, usually homemade, that consists of a plastic jug or bottle with the bottom removed and a bowl head inserted into the cap. The makeshift bong is then inserted into a tub of water, marijuana is placed into the bowl and lit, and the bong is slowly drawn upward to pull smoke inside. Finally, the cap is unscrewed and the smoker places his or her mouth over the opening and pushes the bong back down, rapidly filling the lungs to capacity with an intense hit of smoke.

The existence of the gravity bong is indisputable evidence that smokers are far more intelligent and inventive than one could ever possibly imagine. **See also apple pipe; bong ▼**

GREAT MIDWEST MARIJUANA HARVEST FESTIVAL A hippie jam fest sponsored by Madison (Wisconsin) NORML featuring, as all hippie jam fests do, bands, speakers, and political ambition. GMMHF is more locally focused in its agenda though. It specifically wants to enact the Jacki Rickert Medical Marijuana Act, which would grant Wisconsinites the same medical marijuana rights as neighbor Michigan. While legislative entanglements continue to hold up its passage, every year organizers hope that one more music festival may be enough to put the bill over the top. **See also medical marijuana; NORML**

GREEN One of the three primary colors that can be seen in American money, leprechauns, and various forms of vegetation, most notably marijuana. The term has been adopted by the pot-smoking community as a euphemism for the drug itself as well as for money.

GREEN DRAGON, THE A drink made when mixing vodka and marijuana. When boiling bud in some vodka, a green liquid will form, thus creating a not-so-tasty drink that will get the subject high as a kite and drunk as a hobo, all at the same time. Obviously the best way to get crunked, it is best to strain all weed out of the vodka before imbibing to create a smooth and pleasurable experience. **See also crunked; drinkables**

GREEN HIT The first hit of a freshly packed bowl of marijuana, so named because the color of the weed has not yet turned an ashen gray. Marijuana connoisseurs prize the first hit due to its crisp, clean flavor. It is considered good etiquette to offer it to other members of the circle when packing a bowl. Tragically, it is also considered good etiquette not to be greedy and accept the green hit for oneself, thus creating a never-ending cycle of generous offers and respectful declinations that can carry on for anywhere from several awkward seconds to several awkward hours before somebody finally caves. **See also cornering**

GREEN LEAFY SUBSTANCE A euphemism employed by various law enforcement agencies and journalists to refer to any piece of plant matter that is most certainly marijuana but cannot be referred to as such until a battery of tests can be performed to confirm the obvious. Its use perpetuates the absurd belief that there are actually groups of people in the world who walk around the streets carrying baggies of oregano in the event they get a hankering for pizza and, alas, the restaurant is fresh out. **See also cannabis ▼**

GREENHOUSE A man-made structure used for the cultivation of plant life. The building sports a transparent glass or plastic ceiling, which allows solar radiation to enter the enclosure to maintain a steady, warm temperature. Vegetation grown in a greenhouse, like marijuana, for example, is usually of especially high quality because the grower has complete control over the cultivation process. He or she can adjust the temperature, mineral content of the soil, and amount of water provided to the plants. For all intents and purposes, the owner of a greenhouse is God—minus the omnipotence and legions of worshippers. **See also aeroponics; hydroponics** ▼

GRILLED CHEESE A common snack enjoyed when one is spontaneously hit with the munchies, perhaps because all of the ingredients (butter, cheese, and white bread) are usually on hand. This can easily be made into a 420-friendly variation by cooking the weed in butter before sautéing the bread. Be forewarned: Doing so may bring on more munchies instead of curing the original onset.

GRINDER A circular contraption that consists of two interlocking hollow halves with small protrusions sticking out from the inside of each half. It is an essential tool when rolling joints, as it does exactly what its name implies—it grinds. One places pot in between the two halves, closes them together, and twists in opposing directions to transform large nugs into a relatively uniform consistency that burns more evenly. One could also use scissors or one's hands for this purpose, but the grinder is more fun. **See also nugs** ▼

GRONKOWSKI, ROB (BORN MAY 14, 1989) A former football player for the New England Patriots, who's best known by his imaginative nickname "Gronk." Gronk is a three-time Super Bowl champion and the five-time number one ranked tight end in the NFL Top 100 Players list. Post-retirement, however, Gronk has taken a slightly different path. As of 2019, Gronk has partnered with medical marijuana company CBD Medic and plans to advocate for CBD products as a valid treatment for sports players. It's almost worth taking up football to support such an important message… almost. **See also CBD; sports**

GUITAR HERO A video game series that recreates the experience of playing in a rock band by giving the player a plastic guitar, video crowd, and false sense of finally living out a long-lost dream. Guitar Hero's obvious appeal to pot smokers is its musical aspect, but it's the hand-eye coordination required to time the racing-forward, multicolored disks that makes Guitar Hero the ultimate challenge. While most of a high Guitar Hero session will consist of clanking missed notes, every now and then the inebriated player will achieve true Guitar Hero nirvana and feel one with the song. It's important to congratulate Guitar Hero players after a particularly good showing, as their entire self-image depends on it.

GYM A large, warehouse-like space with weights, stair-climbers, tread-mills, bikes, swimming pools, and squash courts. The gym is a fantastic place to spend some time after smoking a joint. Not only does the sight of oversized macho men flexing in front of a mirror trigger automatic hilarity, but it's also a more productive way to spend time than just sitting on a couch at home. Instead, smokers can sit in a whirlpool with strangers. **See also active smoker**

Hh

H.R. PUFNSTUF A 1970s children's entertainment program whose multiple marijuana references subliminally raised a generation of unknowing soon-to-be pot smokers. While the producers deny the program had any intentional references to drugs, the evidence is pretty overwhelming. The show's plot involves a young boy trapped on an island in which the imagery is multicolored and psychedelic, and every plant and animal can talk. Also, the title character often used phrases like "Whoa, dude," or "Far out," which any Five-O knows only comes out of the mouths of pot smokers. Theories are that *H.R. Pufnstuf* is short for hand-rolled puffin' stuff. The producers also later produced a show called *Lidsville*. "Lid" was 1970s slang for an ounce of marijuana.

HALF-BAKED (CONCEPT) A state of being for pot smokers wherein one is not completely high but most certainly at least a little buzzed. It gets its name from a half-baked cookie, which is still a little soft and gooey on the inside, which is how a half-baked smoker would describe him or herself as feeling. Similar to the cookie, the smoker need but fire up the oven (read: light joint) in order to reach the proper level of bakedness. **See also baked; high**

HALF BAKED (FILM) A 1998 film starring infamous pothead/comedian Dave Chappelle. The film follows a group of friends as they attempt to bail out their buddy Kenny to protect him from a particularly intimidating inmate, Nasty Nate. The crew turns to stealing pot from a local laboratory and selling it on the streets to every variety of pot smoker ranging from the "you should have been there smoker" who loves recounting pot stories from days gone by to the "enhancement smoker" who thinks everything is better while under the influence. Spoiler alert: The group gets high (constantly), makes (and loses) tons of cash, and Kenny makes it out of jail without issue. **See also Chappelle, Dave**

HALLUCINATIONS Tricks of the mind often experienced while under the influence of hallucinogenic drugs like LSD, mushrooms, and certain strains of marijuana. They can manifest as mild alterations to common household items, like a potted plant transforming into a bird, to imagined auditory sensations like hearing voices or music. While they can seem frightening at first, hallucinations are nothing to be afraid of as long as one reminds oneself that they are not real. The ghost of Jim Morrison has better things to do than drop in on random smoking sessions to tell participants to hurry up and pass the bowl already. ▸

HALO A first-person shooter science fiction video game series, commonly played by pot-smoking males in their teens to early twenties. The game is set in a fantasy universe inhabited by the technologically enhanced Master Chief and various aliens he kills with guns, high-tech swords, and his bare hands. The campaign mode is fairly decent, but the game's full potential can be realized only by smoking large quantities of ganja. The pinpoint accuracy needed to snipe a jumping opponent from several hundred yards can be achieved with a high dose of pot and years of having nothing better to do but practice. **See also video games**

HAMMOCK A single piece of canvas that is suspended between two sturdy points to create a makeshift bed. They can also be constructed of an amalgamation of several pieces of fabric or rope. Popular among those living in tropical paradises, they are common places for carefree individuals to smoke a joint, drink out of a coconut, and waste away the day. When a person lies in one, the hammock wraps itself around the user like a cocoon. This is especially appealing while high, as the increased sensitivity to touch makes the envelopment feel like a giant hug.

HANDY SMOKER A type of smoker who is capable of building paraphernalia with nearly any combination of items. Need to smoke in an open field with only a plastic bag, a car battery, and a hunting knife? He's got it covered. **See also active smoker; intellectual smoker; social smoker; talkative smoker**

HANFPARADE A marijuana legalization demonstration that takes place each August and is one of the largest marches of its kind in Europe, attracting between five thousand and ten thousand people each year. The parade takes place in Berlin, which has several annual demonstrations. In addition to Hanfparade, Berliners annually hosted the Berlin Motor Show until 2002, which allowed manufacturers to showcase their new car models, as well as the Berliner Festwochen, celebrating German classical music. Berliners can be forgiven for hosting such unimaginative leftover parades: Their Love Parade and Fuck Parade, both actual real-life events, were discontinued after the government found they had no practical political purpose. **See also legalization**

HAROLD AND KUMAR ESCAPE FROM GUANTANAMO BAY The 2008 sequel to the film *Harold and Kumar Go to White Castle*. The sequel picks up where the original left off, but instead of delicious White Castle hamburgers

the duo is now in search of Harold's second passion in life, his hot neighbor Maria. Coincidentally, Maria is vacationing in Amsterdam, a.k.a. the pot capital of the world, which may or may not have influenced their decision to follow her. Their dreams of John Hughesesque romance and hash cookies are dashed when they are mistaken for terrorists and incarcerated in Guantanamo Bay. The film follows the tried-and-true formula of the first—lots of pot smoking leading to an increasingly unfortunate series of events—but this time with more nudity, more NPH (Neil Patrick Harris), and slightly less funny. **See also *Harold and Kumar Go to White Castle***

HAROLD AND KUMAR GO TO WHITE CASTLE A 2004 film that gives new meaning to the concept of a literal title. Shortly after the film begins, the title characters smoke pot and get an insatiable craving for White Castle sliders. The two battle New Jersey state troopers, campus security, a disturbed tow truck operator, several wild animals, and NPH (Neil Patrick Harris) on their quest for the perfect late-night munchie. A person's reaction to the film can be a very good indicator of his or her experience with marijuana, as anyone who responds with "Why didn't they just give up and go home?" has clearly never been high. **See also** *Harold and Kumar Escape from Guantanamo Bay*; munchies

HARRELSON, WOODY (BORN JULY 23, 1961) An actor famous for his part as Woody the bartender in *Cheers* and for his roles in films such as *White Men Can't Jump*, *Natural Born Killers*, *Kingpin*, *No Country for Old Men*, and more recently *Zombieland*, *The Hunger Games*, *War for the Planet of the Apes*, and *Solo: A Star Wars Story*. Harrelson is also one of the most outspoken marijuana enthusiasts in the country. His pot resume includes narrating the pro-marijuana film *Grass*, serving on the board of directors for NORML, and conducting interviews while high. In 1996 he symbolically planted four hemp seeds in Kentucky with cameras rolling to challenge the state laws, which did not distinguish between industrial hemp and marijuana. Harrelson won the case, briefly causing a "Harrelson for President" campaign that came to a screeching halt once *EDtv* was released to a wide audience. In 2016, he was one of the first people to apply to open a medical marijuana dispensary in Hawaii, although, unfortunately, his request

was denied. Instead, he decided to briefly quit smoking…although after a two-year stint of sobriety, Willie Nelson finally convinced him to start smoking like normal again. **See also** *Grass*; Nelson, Willie; NORML

HASH BAR A term originally used to refer to a coffeehouse in the Netherlands (although they're starting to spread in the United States as well) where it is perfectly legal to buy, sell, and consume marijuana in small quantities. In other words, weed heaven. Cannabis purchased from these locales is generally of a higher quality than that purchased on the street, and because they are not technically illegal they attract visitors from all across the world searching for a way to get high without having to buy pot from a shady character in a dark alley. The laws surrounding the coffeeshops (apparently spelling it as one word eliminates the possibility of confusion with a traditional coffee shop) can be extremely confusing and contradictory at times. For example, it is legal to sell marijuana there, but it is not necessarily legal for suppliers to sell their products to the shops. Also, the coffeeshops are technically not allowed to advertise their status as purveyors of pot, but the billowing smoke coming from the exits is generally a dead giveaway. **See also Amsterdam ▼**

HASH BASH An annual gathering in early April of pot smokers on the University of Michigan campus whose purpose is generally to oppose state marijuana laws, even though Michigan has some of the most lenient laws in America and Ann Arbor has decriminalized the drug. The event culminates at high noon, when students gather around the quad and sit around high. Hash Bash organizers warn students to pregame and not to get high at the event, which makes Hash Bash day just like every other day, only with speakers and entertainment. **See also legalization; protests**

HASHISH A processed form of marijuana that takes all the best, most potent parts of the cannabis plant, shaves them off, compresses them, and creates a new sort of super marijuana. Hashish is made up mostly of trichomes, which are fine hair-like appendages that grow off the plant and are rich in THC. Through various heating and cooling methods, the resin from the plant's trichomes is bricked and solidified. Essentially hashish is like slicing only the frosting off the best cakes and putting it together to make one super frosting-only cake, which incidentally makes a great companion to any hash-smoking experience. **See also kief; trichomes ▼**

HAWAII The fiftieth US state, vacation getaway, and tropical paradise America strong-armed away from natives in the late nineteenth century. Hawaii has since become an important part of American history. Hawaii bore witness to the attacks on Pearl Harbor in 1941, bringing the United States into World War II. It is also the birthplace of both President

Barack Obama and the Hawaiian shirt craze. Most important, however, Hawaii was one of the first states to approve the use of medical marijuana. As Hawaii has sandy beaches, fruit smoothies, leis, ukuleles, and boatloads of sun for marijuana plants to grow, it's an ideal place to fake sick so a doctor can prescribe some medical marijuana. Sadly, they have not yet legalized recreational marijuana, although they're finally moving in the right direction with decriminalization starting in 2020. **See also medical marijuana**

HEAD SHOP A store where one can purchase an assortment of smoking paraphernalia, including simple rolling papers, pipes, elaborate bongs, and more. In the United States, the legality of such establishments falls into a hazy gray area, as many of the products they carry can be sold only for use with tobacco products or other legal herbal products. However, the vast majority of customers purchase them exclusively for use with substances that are (in some states) still illegal. This paradox necessitates a pathetic song-and-dance routine between the customer and salesperson wherein both are perfectly aware what the products are

actually used for, but the two of them must act as if they have never even heard of a substance called marijuana, let alone the fact that it can be smoked out of one of the intricate structures on display. For many, their efforts to legalize marijuana are based solely on the desire to end these embarrassing displays permanently. **See also paraphernalia** ▼

HEADIE Top-quality bud with the ability to give smokers a "heady" high. What's a "heady" high? No one can be sure, of course, as all experience is purely subjective and prone to individual interpretation. Its effects are so unique to each individual that headies to one person can be something completely different to someone else. And how can it even be known that smokers get high? Maybe the sober state is really being high and being high is really being sober? How can people even know they exist anyway? Does anyone else feel a huge déjà vu feeling right now? Yeah, that's what headies do. **See also mids; schwag**

HEDBERG, MITCH (FEBRUARY 24, 1968–MARCH 29, 2005) A stand-up comedian who died tragically in the spring of 2005 as a result of "multiple drug toxicity." His blend of comedy was easily recognizable thanks to the slow, methodical delivery he employed that is also commonly associated with pot smokers. Hedberg was far from shy about his drug use, often openly admitting to it during his shows. During performances, Hedberg would occasionally lose track of a joke and screw up the ending or forget the punch line entirely, but these gaffes often received bigger laughs than jokes that went according to plan…proving once again that marijuana is an effective humor-enhancing drug.

HEMP A jack-of-all-trades plant whose industrial uses include food, medicine, water purification, and fuel, and whose recreational purposes include getting really high. The difference between industrial hemp and recreational hemp is subtle but profound. For example, industrial hemp's THC content is about 0.05 percent, whereas marijuana contains anywhere from 5 to 20 percent THC levels on average. This means it would require about twenty tightly rolled joints of industrial hemp smoked in a very short period of time to experience even a mild high. ▼

Hemp (*Cannabis sativa*). 1, 2 Flowering shoots, 1 of Staminate, 2 of Pistillate Plant ; 3 Staminate Flower ; 4 Pistillate Flower ; 5 Fruit.

HENDRIX, JIMI (NOVEMBER 27, 1942–SEPTEMBER 18, 1970) An electric blues-rocker widely considered the greatest guitarist ever to live. He rose to fame after his performance at the 1967 Monterey Pop Festival, which he concluded by setting his guitar on fire and then smashing it to pieces. This act of wanton destruction led to his rise in stardom in the United States, where he eventually headlined Woodstock and played his iconic rendition of "The Star-Spangled Banner." Hendrix is a guitarist who sounds excellent sober and even better when the listener has just smoked a joint. Hendrix is also the subject of a widely circulated but completely fabricated rumor that when he was nine or so, he was deciding whether to play guitar or trumpet and went to the guitar store solely because it had a Coke machine and the trumpet store had a Pepsi machine. It's completely untrue, but that story still manages to blow a smoker's mind every time he or she hears it.

HENRY An obscure piece of pot slang that requires an absurd series of mental leaps and a general understanding of world history in order to comprehend. See, Henry is short for Henry VIII, an English monarch who ruled the country from 1509 to 1547. The V in his name is actually the Roman numeral for five, and each I is the Roman numeral for the number one. Add them together and one gets eight, or eighth. This in turn is a universal pot term representing an eighth of an ounce of marijuana. So, in theory, asking somebody for a Henry is equivalent to asking somebody for an eighth of weed. Please never use this slang.

HERB A slang term for marijuana likely stemming from its resemblance, especially when ground, to various kitchen staples like basil,

parsley, oregano, and thyme. To the untrained eye, marijuana is so similar to various herbs that many newbies will fall for a common bait-and-switch con in which an unscrupulous dealer sells them a bag partially or entirely filled with dried herbs instead of pot. ▼

HICKS, BILL (DECEMBER 16, 1961– FEBRUARY 26, 1994) A stand-up comedian whose sarcastic wit and observational humor made him a popular act in the 1980s and early 1990s. Many of Hicks's routines centered on past drug use. Much to the surprise of the audience, he would claim that despite giving up drugs earlier in life, he had nothing against them and was a proponent of legalizing marijuana. If a man experiencing road rage were leaning on his horn in traffic, Hicks proposed he should be forced to take a hit of a joint to calm his nerves. Unfortunately, Hicks died of pancreatic cancer before his dream of mandatory weed could be realized.

HIGH A state of sublime, subconscious self-awareness induced by marijuana. While attempts to describe what it feels like to be high are varied and incomplete, some descriptions can help peel away the mystery. Some people claim it's like one's mind is flying. Others, while high, say it's like floating in space. Others say it's a state of pure contentedness that makes music, TV, food, conversation, and everything else around the smoker better. **See also every entry in this book ▼**

HIGH MAINTENANCE A comedy-drama series featured on HBO that follows The Guy, an unnamed cannabis deliveryman, as he makes his deliveries around New York City. Playing with various stereotypes and clichés, all of The Guy's clients are unforgettable and often very relatable. Seasoned pot smokers will recognize the hippies, the assholes, the free spirits, and many more.

HIGH TIMES *The New York Times* of weed consumption and go-to pop culture reference for any mainstream marijuana reference. *High Times* has been parodied on *The Simpsons* (Homer reads a *Pie Times* magazine) and *SNL* (Jack Black plays an investigative reporter for *High Times*), and it pops up in movies or songs routinely. *High Times* is a strong advocate for legalization and a leading purveyor of decriminalization literature. The magazine has also created a sort of revolutionary guard called the High Times Freedom Fighters, who marched in legalization demonstrations wearing psychedelic Revolutionary War garb and playing drums. Over the years, the magazine has nabbed interviews with unlikely sources: Noam Chomsky, Arnold Schwarzenegger, and Al Gore. It's also gotten some of the biggest names in the pot world: Bob Marley, Bob Dylan, and Mick Jagger. As of 2018, they acquired cannabis media company Green Rush Daily

Inc....so it's safe to say, we can only expect their reach to get bigger from here. **See also** *Cannabis Culture* **magazine; 420 Magazine**

HIGH YOGA Yoga + marijuana = high yoga. On its own, yoga is a practice that combines breath control, meditation, movement, and specific poses that are useful for health, relaxation, and spirituality. Adding in cannabis simply takes it to the next level since smoking a joint basically has the same effect anyway. Participants partake in whatever form of marijuana consumption they prefer (although a medical marijuana card might be required for some classes) before going about their practice as usual. Some people love it, some people (a.k.a. buzzkills) think it takes away from the power of the yoga practice, but one thing is for sure: A great way to get your pot-smoking friends to head to an 8 a.m. yoga class on a Saturday is to promise them a fat joint when they get there. **See also buzzkill**

HIGHDEA A groundbreaking, earth-shattering idea, the awesomeness of which is eclipsed only by its monumental lack of any practical application. Some examples include the recliner with a built-in toilet and Da Vinci's aerial screw (nonfunctioning helicopter). The term can also be attributed more generally to any moment of inspiration one is struck with while under the influence of marijuana that requires the clarifying statement, "Well it sounded like a good idea when I was high." ▼

HIPPIES Members of a subculture that emerged in the 1960s, largely around the use of marijuana and LSD. Hippies were instrumental in Woodstock, the sexual revolution, the civil rights movement, and protesting the war. Though the Vietnam War ended more than four decades ago and there is no draft, hippies remain a vibrant part of college campuses. Modern hippies have embraced a lifestyle that revolves around long hair, sandals, acoustic guitars, sing-alongs, Eastern religions, and anti-corporatism. They are mostly a derided and disrespected group, though they remain firmly committed to their legitimacy and sincerity. This commitment lasts until about three months after graduation, when hippies realize they need to cut their hair, buy a suit, and land a job if they're ever going to move out of their parents' basement. **See also Woodstock** ▼

HIPSTERS Urban, middle-class young adults whose primary interests reside outside of mainstream culture, including but not limited to alternative music, thrift-store finds, hand-rolled cigarettes, messenger bags, Chuck Taylors, piercings, incorporating one's nipples into a tattoo, PBR, hoodies, veganism, and of course, smoking pot. Hipsters have set up armies in three American locations: Cambridge,

Massachusetts; San Francisco, California; and Portland, Oregon.

HIT A subjective slang term used by pot smokers to describe a single serving of marijuana inhaled from a joint, bowl, pipe, bong, hookah, or modified common household object. A hit is generally understood as a single inhalation. However, variations in lung capacity, tolerance to smoke, and overall level of selfishness vary from smoker to smoker, making it nearly impossible to set a universal definition for the term. **See also drag; puff; pull; toke**

HOLDING IT FOR A FRIEND What everyone in possession of marijuana is doing, until they smoke it.

HOODIE A garment of cotton clothing worn on the upper body with long sleeves; a heavy, insulated fabric; a hood; and a general feeling of warmth and comfort. Hoodies are a frequent clothing choice of pot smokers, though the reasons remain mysterious. Some theories: Body temperature drops while stoned, and hoodies help smokers maintain a proper warmth level; the pouch that often accompanies hoodies can be used to store bowls, baggies, joints, or lighters; and perhaps most important, because all the cool smokers are wearing them. ▼

to smoke to their heart's content without interruption. ▼

HOOKAH A large, elaborate structure used to smoke tobacco that can also be employed for use with marijuana. The contraption consists of a base filled with water to cool the smoke, a bowl to house the tobacco, and a hose from which to pull the smoke. Many hookahs come with several hoses attached to the base, allowing multiple smokers to enjoy the experience simultaneously. This can cause immense confusion among smokers trained in the puff, puff, pass method of smoking, and it is not uncommon for first-time users to cry from the sheer joy of being able

HOTBOX A recreational activity wherein a group of stoners enters a confined space, lights up, and recycles the air among themselves so as not to waste any precious THC-laden smoke. Common locales include bathrooms, automobiles, refrigerator boxes, dorm rooms, abandoned train cars, and large closets. **See also contact high**

HOUSTON, WHITNEY (AUGUST 9, 1963–FEBRUARY 11, 2012) A troubled pop diva and actress whose marriage to Bobby Brown and repeated drug use led to her becoming a tabloid phenomenon and caused her to utter her now-famous phrase "Crack is wack" after accusations arose that she used the drug. For Houston, though, pot was not wack. She said she increasingly used it, along with cocaine, after her performance in the 1992 romance movie *The Bodyguard*. Despite being detained at an airport in Hawaii for possession of marijuana, she *literally* walked away from the incident and all criminal charges were dropped. Pot smokers everywhere are jealous. Houston said she would stare at a TV screen and space out for weeks on end. She also claimed that she and ex-husband Brown hardly spoke during that time, because they were so high. Houston gives pot smokers a bad name because staring at a TV screen and spacing out is only recommended for days, not weeks, on end. **See also Brown, Bobby**

HOW HIGH A 2001 film starring Method Man and Redman as two Harvard students who are accepted to the college after they ace their THCs (Testing for Higher Credentials) thanks to the help of their recently deceased friend Ivory, whose spirit is conjured whenever the pair smoke special pot that was grown from soil mixed with his ashes. Seriously, that's the plot. The film's baffling success can be explained by one simple fact:

Pot makes everything funny. **See also Method Man**

"HOWL" An iconic poem penned by Allen Ginsberg in his 1956 work *Howl and Other Poems*. The 2,902-word opus stands as a direct insight into the mind of the average 1950s young man. That is if one assumes the average 1950s young man is a pot-smoking, free-loving, angst-ridden Beat who is dissatisfied with society and seeks an outlet through mind-altering drugs and philosophical discussion. **See also Ginsberg, Allen**

HUMBOLDT COUNTY A veritable pot smoker's paradise located in the northeast corner of one of America's most forward-thinking states, California. Thanks to Proposition 215, a note from one's doctor in this magical land translated into the right to grow ninety-nine marijuana plants in a space of 100 square feet or less. A pot grower was not necessarily required to grow that many, but why would he or she grow less? There's been some debate about the helpfulness of Proposition 64 to Humboldt County growers. Passed in 2016, Proposition 64 legalized recreational marijuana, which has actually made business harder for some growers. **See also** *Murder Mountain*; **Proposition 215**

HUMMUS A popular munchie among hipster pot smokers, the basic version of which consists of ground-up chickpeas mixed with garlic, tahini, and olive oil. It is prized for its versatility, as it can be spread on bread, pita chips, bagels, fruit, or vegetables, or simply eaten raw by dipping one's fingers into the tub and licking them clean. The last option is disgusting and should be employed only when nobody else involved in the smoking session is in a position to observe and subsequently judge.

HUNGER A sensation that occurs in the human body when the stomach increases the levels of the hormone ghrelin found in its lining to alert the hands that it's time to make a sandwich. Certain activities can stimulate this reaction, such as fasting, exercising, smoking marijuana, and standing downwind of bakeries.

HUNGRY SMOKER Most smokers are susceptible to the munchies. This breed of pot enthusiast, however, is at the mercy of food. In general, they like to have a stockpile of all the munchies they plan to consume before smoking commences. As there is no telling what foodstuffs they will find appealing after a session, they often pick several varieties from every major smoker food group: salty, sweet, deep-fried, sour, and frozen. Once high, they will devour anything and everything that is not tied down. Because of this, they are invited into few private homes. **See also antisocial smoker; lazy smoker; paranoid smoker; quiet smoker; social smoker** ▼

HYBRID A cannabis plant bred using parents from two different strains. In the same way that one can, say, breed a lion with an eagle to make a griffin, different types of cannabis plants can be strategically crossbred to create new strains of marijuana that boast different traits of the parents. Hybrids can be created either from two different types of cannabis plants (e.g., a sativa/indica hybrid) or from two different strains of the same type of plant (e.g., an indica/indica hybrid). Sometimes, hybrids are created in order to increase harvest productivity, as crossing a fast-growing indica plant with a slower-growing sativa plant will yield a moderately fast-growing hybrid plant. Other times, hybrids are created to produce varying types of highs. Carmelicious, for example, is an indica/sativa hybrid that boasts a light, consistently headier high, whereas Big Bud, another indica/sativa hybrid, offers a TKO hypnotic-regression-therapy-is-necessary-to-recover-all-memories type high. **See also Carmelicious; indica; sativa**

HYDROPONICS A method of cultivating plant life that allows the plant to grow in nutrient-rich water instead of more traditional soil, thus spitting

in the face of nature and conventional wisdom. Marijuana that is grown using this method is generally superior to pot grown naturally, as it allows for greater control over the entire cultivation process. **See also aeroponics; greenhouse ▼**

Ii

I LOVE YOU, MAN A movie in an up-and-coming genre of film known as the "bromantic comedy." While some bromantic comedies try to pass themselves off as regular comedies that just happen to center around the relationship between two male leads, *I Love You, Man* embraces the bromance element; the movie actually sends the main character, Peter (Paul Rudd), off on a series of man dates in the hopes of finding a partner in crime. After a disappointing search, he eventually meets Sydney (Jason Segel), a messy, under-motivated musician with a passion for the band Rush (read: pot smoker) to serve as his heterosexual lifemate. If the premise seems trite and contrived, that's because it is. However, this is nothing a few bong hits can't fix.

ICE A strain of marijuana that ranks among the most potent in America and the most artistic looking as well. Seeing an Ice strain makes it easy to understand where the name came from since it looks like fine, untouched icicles. Ice pot has tentacles and fuzzy white trichomes pointing out of it, giving it a light greenish-white hue. It looks as if it was grown in a snow globe and makes the pot look angelic and innocent. As consumers quickly discover, the strain is neither.

ICE CREAM A combination of dairy products and natural or artificial flavorings that, when combined and frozen, create a magical, heavenly experience. Frequently consumed as a post-smoking munchie, its cooling properties are especially useful for combating the negative effects hot marijuana smoke can have on the human mouth. If allowed to melt in the mouth before swallowing, it can help alleviate cotton mouth. Also, it is a necessary ingredient in other popular munchie concoctions like toast cream and milkshakes. **See also ice-cream shop; milkshake; toast cream**

ICE-CREAM SHOP A store where one can often acquire marijuana on the sly. Oh yeah, and it also sells ice cream. There are some places that one would pay more for a product than others. For example, one wouldn't normally pay $15 for a hot dog and beer, but if one is at a baseball game, one might. Economists call this a "total rip-off," but they also call it a "captive market." In this example, one is totally high and willing to pay $4 for a scoop of ice cream plus another $2 to throw some crushed Snickers on top. Behind the counter at the local ice-cream store, a community college dropout is happy to sell one a scoop of Chunky Monkey. But he really wants one to come into the back room so he can sell one an eighth of Super Skunk. Just don't forget to order some ice cream before leaving. With Snickers. **See also ice cream**

ICE HITS An elaborate method of smoking marijuana in which the smoker chills a mug in the freezer for several hours, takes a hit, exhales into the bottom of the cup, lets it sit there for a moment, shows off the display to his or her friends, and then "drinks" the smoke from the mug. Its existence is further evidence that pot smokers are some of the most ambitious members of society. They simply refuse to put their knowledge to good use and instead spend their time brainstorming new, wildly impractical yet indisputably awesome ways to get high.

IDEA BOOK A blank notebook kept in a smoker's apartment alongside a pen. The idea book is kept within reach in case an idea or worthwhile thought occurs to the person while under the influence. These ideas are usually not worthy of writing down, as they can often include wayward movie plots or seemingly hilarious albeit completely nonsensical practical jokes. Still, the idea book has value in itself, in that it tracks the story of the smoker's experience. It is also a reference tool for the bet that inevitably takes place between pot-smoking friends: Which member of the group gets stupider when they get high? There is never a winner in such an argument. **See also highdea**

ILL A term widely used among the pot-smoking community to refer to anything that possesses the quality of being really, really awesome. This stands in direct opposition to the traditional definition of the word, which is used in the medical community to denote a patient who is suffering from some sort of malady and is thus not well. This phenomenon can be found elsewhere in a pot smoker's vernacular with words like "bad" (awesome), "wicked" (awesome), and "dope" (awesome). As it turns out, marijuana has a unique ability to allow the definition of any word to be temporarily changed to "awesome."

"ILLEGAL SMILE" A song written and performed by country music singer John Prine. The song begins with a character whose day is going so poorly he loses a staring contest to his bowl of oatmeal. Then something happens that is not explained, and he is suddenly wearing an "illegal smile" and things begin looking up. While it is not revealed precisely what caused the change in mood, whatever it was is fairly inexpensive, lasts quite some time, and leaves the character hiding in a closet wondering if the cops can hear his thoughts. Someday perhaps musicians will be able to stop hiding behind euphemisms and Prine will officially be able to change the name of the song to "My Day Really Sucked, So I Smoked Some Pot and Now It's Awesome."

IN PLAIN SIGHT The ideal location to hide illicit substances such as marijuana. This is not to say that one should simply leave it lying around. However, one should not waste his or her time sneaking through ventilation ducts, hollowing out the leg of a table, or prying up floorboards in an attempt to find the ideal hiding place. Instead, slide it into a boxed set of the series *Friends*, inside of a soda can, or simply at the bottom of a tissue box. KISS: Keep It Simple Stupid. **See also stash can** ▶

INCENSE An organic substance that, when lit, gives off what some describe as a pleasant, soothing odor (results may vary). It is commonly employed in religious ceremonies and by pot smokers attempting to mask the smell of a recent pot-smoking session. When using incense for the latter purpose, one must weigh the benefits of masking the odor of skunky weed with the risk of one's room smelling like a combination of gasoline and burned hair. ▾

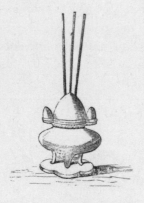

INCREASED ATTENTION SPAN One of the side effects of smoking marijuana that appears beneficial at first but can actually be rather troublesome in practice. It's all well and good when one is able to smoke a joint and watch the entire Lord of the Rings trilogy without stopping. However, when there is nothing specific to pay attention to, the smoker can become confused and disoriented. For example, imagine what might happen if one were to get high, enter a toy store, and pick up a kaleidoscope. An entire day could go by before one even realized he or she was still in the store.

INDICA One of the two meta-categorizations for marijuana, along with sativa. Indica is a slightly different type of plant, however. Its leaves are shorter and stubbier than sativa, and its consumption leaves smokers in more of a lethargy than sativa. Indica is noted for not being as tall, typically growing only six to eight feet, making it ideal for the home-grower. Also making it ideal for the home-grower: It is great in the stress-relief, zoned-out, kind of couch-locked high that employed smokers enjoy to unwind at night. Indica is helpful in the treatment of insomnia too. **See also sativa**

INHALING The act of pulling air from the outside world into the lungs so oxygen can then enter the bloodstream and permeate throughout the body. In a happy coincidence, this same process also allows THC to permeate the body if one chooses to inhale marijuana smoke instead of air. The human body is not technically designed to inhale much other than normal air, so it might attempt to reject the smoke through uncontrollable spasms called "coughing." Some lucky humans have evolved beyond this unfortunate shortcoming to a point where their body actually prefers weed smoke to ordinary air. **See also controlled breathing; coughing; exhaling**

INTELLECTUAL SMOKER A variety of marijuana enthusiast who, upon smoking the leafy green substance, proceeds to spark up literary discussions, spirited political and philosophical debates, and any manner of intelligent discourse with unsuspecting individuals in the immediate vicinity. Sometimes their rants and tirades are well-researched and quite coherent, other times not so much. The intellectual smoker has mastered one important aspect of human interaction: If one says anything quickly and with authority, it is universally believed to be true. **See also active smoker; artistic smoker; casual smoker; social smoker; talkative smoker**

INTERSTATE 420 The designation of two never-built auxiliary highways that would have been built around Atlanta, Georgia, and Monroe, Louisiana, both of which would have allowed commuters to avoid the major cities through which I-20 passes. Neither road was ultimately built, however. The plan to build the road around Atlanta was derailed after communities in its path objected. Monroe's auxiliary highway was shelved after the state agreed to invest in a different highway. The proposals would have cost each state about ten times as much as their proposed budget, as every weedophile in a 100-mile circumference would have jacked the signs and hung them in their bedrooms.

INTROSPECTION The act of inward-focused thought performed by individuals seeking a greater understanding of the self that is often achieved by smoking large quantities of marijuana and assuming a contemplative position (e.g., lying in bed, sitting on a couch, or in a field on one's back looking up at the clouds). This can range from the trivial "Why did I order a ham sandwich?" to deeper questions like "Where is my life going?" While it can be an enlightening experience, any insight gained is temporary, usually fading proportionally as the effects of the marijuana begin to wear off. **See also antisocial smoker** ▾

ISRAEL The Holy Land. While mostly a strip of desert, Israel still pulls primo weed, mostly importing from neighboring Lebanon and Egypt, as well as producing some decent homegrown stuff. The country has (mostly) decriminalized marijuana, legalized medical marijuana, and boasts its own pro-legalization political party as well. And, despite the delay in legalizing recreational use, Israel is well-positioned to become a major leader in the medical marijuana industry due to its pleasant climate, extensive research programs, and large-scale, controlled growing spaces.

IZZARD, EDDIE (BORN FEBRUARY 7, 1962) A British transgender comedian who has a number of televised specials to his credit and starred in the FX show *The Riches*. He has appeared in several popular films including *Ocean's Twelve*, *Across the Universe*, *Cars 2*, and *The Lego Batman Movie*, as well as several unpopular films including *Mystery Men* and *The Cat's Meow*. During his show *Circle*, he calls for the creation of a "stoned Olympics" where athletes compete in leisurely versions of popular events like the long jump where, instead of leaping over a pit of sand, these Olympians fall into it. Best shape wins. Immediately after the show aired, hordes of hopeful pot smokers began training for the events, mistakenly assuming they had finally found a practical use for their badass Guitar Hero skills. **See also Guitar Hero**

Jj

JAMAICA An island nation in the Caribbean Sea where Americans vacation in order to "feel all right." Jamaica is just as much of a tropical paradise as it's depicted in pop culture, just with more crime and poverty. Cannabis was decriminalized in 2015, so possession is now considered only a petty offence and even tourists can apply for permits for small amounts of medical marijuana. The first legal medical marijuana dispensary opened in 2018. As the home of Bob Marley, Jamaica is socially obligated to offer visitors their choice of weed, and it does. The best of the original Jamaican weed is called Jamaican Haze, and it's not uncommon to see vendors selling sticks of marijuana on buses or in the streets like they're churros. If that doesn't work, the guy standing on a street corner smoking a cigar of weed can probably lend a hit. And if he's too selfish, the guy next to him can. Or the guy next to him. It's pretty much everywhere.

JAY A shortened slang term used in place of the slang term "joint," which itself is already plenty short enough as it is. Its existence can be seen as evidence that pot smokers are gradually evolving beyond the need for human speech and could progress (or regress if one wants to be a jerk about it) to a point where they could communicate solely through grunts and gestures. This evolutionary leap is a necessary move if smokers are ever to solve the pesky problem of deciding whether to articulate the awesome thought they had or to just take their turn on the blunt. **See also joint** ▼

JAY-Z (BORN DECEMBER 4, 1969)
Entrepreneur, creator of Rocawear,
self-proclaimed "best rapper alive"
and "the Sinatra of my day," and
perhaps most importantly, Beyoncé's
husband. Jay started off as a crack
dealer before meeting rappers like
Jaz-O (partly where he derives his
stage name) and Big Daddy Kane,
working his way onto some tracks
and eventually releasing his first
album, *Reasonable Doubt*, in 1996.
Jay's released thirteen albums to date
and has the ability to tell his audience how great his life is—including
how often he gets high on weed—in
many new and fresh ways. As of
2019, he's entered the cannabis
industry as the chief brand strate-
gist for California-based company
Caliva.

JAY AND SILENT BOB STRIKE BACK
A 2001 film following the popular
drug-dealing duo Jay (Jason Mewes)
and Silent Bob (Kevin Smith) as they
venture to Hollywood to prevent the
release of a film based on the Bluntman and Chronic comic series that is
itself based on the pair. The film takes
place in Kevin Smith's imaginary
View Askewniverse, and many popular (and unpopular) characters and
actors make appearances. The most
notable cameo comes during a bong
saber battle between the heroes and
Mark Hamill, former Jedi Knight and
savior of a galaxy far, far away, as the
evil enemy of the fictional Bluntman
and Chronic. Hamill's willingness to
participate in the film makes perfect
sense because it is unlikely he would
have been able to tolerate the presence of Ewoks in the original Star
Wars films without the benefit of
marijuana. **See also Mewes, Jason;
Smith, Kevin; View Askewniverse**

JOINT A slang term for a marijuana
cigarette that is one of the most com-
monplace throughout the smoking
culture. The word itself comes to the
English language from the French
word "joindre" (to join). While it is
possible its use in reference to pot is
related to the fact that various nefarious establishments such as opium
dens were often called "joints," anyone who has ever smoked one knows
full well that few things can join a

group of people together as a smoking session does. ▼

JONZE, SPIKE (BORN OCTOBER 22, 1969) Music video and motion picture director who has made many of the pot smoker's favorite films, including *Being John Malkovich*, *Adaptation*, and *Where the Wild Things Are*, as well as directed the timeless Weezer video for "Buddy Holly," which took place at Arnold's Restaurant from the classic TV show *Happy Days*. He's also known for his work on the Jackass films, which really requires no further explanation. Along with Michel Gondry, Jonze is among the crossover directors who have gone from music video to movie directing and the rare kind of director who will get pot smokers to pay to see any movie he makes. Attending a Jonze film is like attending a DMB concert...meaning there are usually wafts of marijuana smoke hovering above the audience at all times. Behind all that, however, is usually a great film. **See also Dave Matthews Band**

Kk

K2 A synthetic compound that simulates the high of marijuana but whose side effects also include hallucinations, nausea, and vomiting. K2 is known as "fake weed" because of its similarities and because it's actually legal to obtain and smoke. It was created in a lab in the 1990s by a chemist who studies cannabinoid receptors, and it is used as a plant-growth stimulant. While K2 is apparently ten times as potent as THC in marijuana and can get users very high while smoking only a small amount, its wider array of side effects make it a slightly less reliable drug. Smokers of K2 are prone to have "bad trips" more than pot smokers. Best to stick with things that grow in the ground.

KB A term used to describe any high-grade weed, usually some with visible THC crystals, but more commonly specific to seedless strains of incredibly potent pot. KB is short for "kine bud," which is often misspoken as "kind bud," a pet peeve of the pretentious smoker. In fact the term "kine" derives from the Hawaiian word for "excellent" and was likely misinterpreted once the term hit the continental forty-eight.

KEROUAC, JACK (MARCH 12, 1922– OCTOBER 21, 1969) An iconoclastic American novelist whose prose, along with Allen Ginsberg and William S. Burroughs, is primarily associated with the Beat movement. Kerouac's magnum opus is the Great American Novel *On the Road*, but he also wrote *The Dharma Bums*, *Mexico City Blues*, *The Subterraneans*, and *Visions of Cody*. The subject matter of these books often dealt with youth, travel, drugs, drinking, women, jazz clubs, transience, boxcars, and bummery. The stories are based on Kerouac's travels, and the author dabbled in drugs as a youth. Still, his first love was the drink, and he sadly died at age forty-seven from cirrhosis of the liver. Nevertheless, every pot smoker, upon reading *On the Road*, dreams of living

Kerouac's life. Some even bundle their clothes into a hamper, affix it to the end of a stick, and hop on the next train that stops in their town. They usually make it about six miles before realizing that's not how trains work anymore and they'd rather be on their couch at home. **See also *On the Road***

KICKED A state of being for a bowl or bong wherein the pot that has been loaded into the head has been smoked to completion, leaving nothing but ash and disappointment in its wake. Similar to the effect that occurs when one sees a sign reading "wet paint" and touches the bench just to be sure, one smoker will never take the word of another when the declaration has been made that the bowl is kicked. Once confirmation has been made that the bowl or bong is in fact kicked, a smoker needs merely to refill the piece of paraphernalia to return it to its preferred state of being.

KID CUDI (BORN JANUARY 30, 1984) A rapper and actor who is recognized by his thick-rimmed glasses and is part of the alternative hip-hop scene that Kanye West has so dominated. Cudi was featured on West's 2008 album *808s & Heart-break*, gaining songwriting credits on

"Heartless" and "Paranoid." Cudi's fame skyrocketed after the release of his debut album, *Man on the Moon: The End of Day*, a concept album that sold one hundred thousand copies its first week. One of the album's tracks, "Day 'n' Night," features a protagonist called the Lonely Stoner who gets high at night and never makes the human connections he desires. Cudi has explained that the song describes a time in his life when he would "cop bud, listen to Ratatat for hours and hours on end, and just fuckin' write songs by myself, and just smoke," proving to basement-dwelling, unemployed pot smokers everywhere that smoking tons of weed always pays off in the end. Cudi has said that he quit smoking marijuana, successfully confusing all of his fans when he released his song "Marijuana," which he humbly called "the best smoking song ever made."

KIDS IN THE HALL: BRAIN CANDY
A 1996 movie starring the Canadian comedy quartet playing multiple main and peripheral characters in a plot revolving around a superdrug that seems to cure depression. The drug freezes patients in their happiest memory and makes their depression go away. While only mildly amusing

sober, the movie has attained cult-classic status as a result of its appeal to watch while high. It's wacky and offbeat, involves some heady ideas about mind control and repressed homosexuality, and features dark musical numbers and Lorne Michaels impressions. Seriously, nobody should watch it sober.

KIEF A fine powdery substance that is the closest thing nature has to pure THC. Consisting primarily of loose trichomes harvested from dried cannabis buds, kief is the basis for hash but can also be smoked directly or sprinkled on top of lower-quality bud as a high enhancer. Sort of like squirting chocolate syrup on boring vanilla ice cream. **See also trichomes** ▼

KLOSTERMAN, CHUCK (BORN JUNE 5, 1972) A pot-smoking slacker, hipster, and pop-culture writer who has written for *Esquire*, ESPN, and *GQ*, penned ten books, and whose purposely ironic wordplay and contrast allow the author to sound profound while saying absolutely nothing. An example of a potential Klosterman line: "Gus at the gas station informs me my tire is flat, and this, I think, is not good for my hair." Or, "Amber is one of the few attractive women at this venue, so I approach her with trepidation, nervous energy, and the hopes that she can explain to me why Sam Worthington would be the best choice to play the next RoboCop." Or, "Andy orders a whiskey straight and launches into a story about the last time he lassoed a pit bull for money, and this is the moment when I realize I should not have worn cologne to this bar." Klosterman remains a prominent voice of this generation.

KNOCKED UP A 2007 film starring Seth Rogen as an enterprising young pot smoker who, thanks to a combination of celestial alignment, boyish charm, and large quantities of alcohol, hits it off with an infinitely more attractive E! Entertainment reporter, played by Katherine Heigl. As had likely been foretold by their respective middle school health teachers, the ensuing one-night stand results in an unexpected pregnancy.

The career-driven mother-to-be and incompetent but affable future father attempt to paste together a meaningful relationship for the good of their unborn child. The two fail miserably at first but reconcile at the end of the film much to the surprise of absolutely no one. **See also Apatow, Judd**

KUSH A term often misused in reference to any variety of marijuana that is of particularly high quality. The term actually refers to a potent strain of marijuana that gets its name from the Hindu Kush mountain range located near countries in which it is grown, like India and Afghanistan. The real stuff carries a THC content of around 20 percent, so it is best to smoke genuine kush in moderation and savor the experience. There is no telling when or if one will have the opportunity again. **See also Afghan Kush ▼**

Ll

L The twelfth letter of the alphabet and also a slang term used to describe a blunt or marijuana cigarette. Some use the term indiscriminately, but the proper usage is in reference to a specific kind of joint rolled with two perpendicular rolling papers. The resulting product is longer than a traditional joint and has a tapered shape instead of the ubiquitous uniform cylinder. Some benefits to rolling Ls include a longer burn time, more room to fit extra pot, a feeling of accomplishment, and a dramatic increase in respect among one's smoking circle. **See also joint**

LAUGHTER A spontaneous reaction to witnessing, hearing, or thinking something funny that is characterized by an audible response as well as physical signs like knee-slapping, tearing up, and falling on the floor. Laughter is a common side effect associated with smoking marijuana, although it is far more welcomed than some of the less desirable ones like cotton mouth and bloodshot eyes. Because of their penchant for laughter, many smokers have a skewed sense of what is and what is not funny. This is why it is important to avoid watching any of the following when sober: *Half Baked*, *Pineapple Express*, and any film starring Jack Black.

LAVA LAMP A novelty lighting device that is only really cool to get as an eleven-year-old. The various blobs of what one can only assume is molten lava rise and fall at a steady pace and are usually lighted by a colored light bulb. Lava lamps can be stared at for hours by the marijuana user, during which time he or she will develop emotional attachments to each bulbous glob as it passes slowly in and out of existence.

LAWNMOWER BAG A large canvas container attached to a lawnmower that serves as a receptacle for grass clippings as well as an obscure hiding place for marijuana. In theory, the smell of freshly trimmed grass will mask the odor of the pot. This is an extremely desperate (and probably unnecessary) measure, since attempting to actually find the stash of weed in the grass clippings when one wants to smoke it is like looking for a needle in a stack of needles.

LAZY SMOKER The most common breed of pot smoker. The lazy smoker lacks the motivation to do anything more strenuous than stumbling into the kitchen to microwave a plate of nachos. They are a paradoxical breed in that they often have very ambitious plans for things they will accomplish in the future but they almost never put any of them into practice. When they run out of weed, however, they are considered to be one of the fastest beings on planet Earth. **See also antisocial smoker; handy smoker; hungry smoker; quiet smoker; social smoker**

LEAF The universal symbol for marijuana that can be found adorning hats, backpacks, T-shirts, water bottles, pants, and more. Regardless of one's age, country of origin, or religious beliefs, the pot leaf is a universal symbol of 420 friendliness. Unless of course it is encased in a red circle with a slash through it. Avoid those people at all costs. ▾

LEAP (LAW ENFORCEMENT AGAINST PROHIBITION) A pro-regulation, anti-prohibition group comprising current and former law enforcement officials who speak out about the financial and human cost of conducting the War on Drugs. The group is an important vehicle for the pro-legalization movement, which can use some authoritative voices besides Cheech and Chong. More important, though, is learning the group's secret handshake. In case a stoner gets caught, he or she can try the handshake on the officer in the hopes of getting off the hook. **See also decriminalization; legalization; NORML; War on Drugs**

LEARY, TIMOTHY (OCTOBER 22, 1920–MAY 31, 1996) A psychologist, philosopher, and counterculture icon who openly promoted the regular use of hallucinogenic drugs and coined the phrase "Turn on, tune in, drop out." Although best known for espousing the physical and emotional benefits of LSD, Leary was instrumental to the 1970 repeal of the 1937 Marijuana Tax Act. He also used the symptoms of a classic pot high as an example of how drugs expand the human consciousness and prepare that consciousness for the next stage of human evolution: life in space.

LEECH A negative slang term used to describe a person who never has any marijuana of his or her own but is always looking to smoke someone else's stash. They are often the first ones in a group to suggest a smoking session and are frequently guilty of bogarting. Similar to the animal that shares their name, pot leeches should be avoided at all costs. **See also bogart ▼**

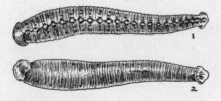

FIG. 119.—Blood-sucker, *Macrobdella decora:* 1, dorsal; 2, ventral.

LEGALIZATION The holy grail of the pot-smoking community, a concept where buying and smoking a joint would be just as benevolent as purchasing an ice-cream cone or a stick of gum. Although several states have now legalized both recreational and medical marijuana, states that have only decriminalized the drug still impose fines and possible prison time if one is found in possession of excessive amounts of marijuana. While the current strategy of hosting jam festivals and smoke-ins does not seem to be swaying political opinion, it is at least resulting in a really good time being had by the pot smokers who participate in them. And that's really the important thing. **See also decriminalization**

LIFE AQUATIC WITH STEVE ZISSOU, THE Director Wes Anderson's fourth film, a dramatic comedy about the travails of a washed-up Cousteau-esque documentarian (Bill Murray) and his Melvilleian quest to find and destroy the shark that killed his best friend. Bearing all the trademarks of Anderson's past work—elaborate sets, an eccentric ensemble cast, a classic-pop soundtrack—*The Life Aquatic* still manages to be Anderson's strangest live-action film, mixing the director's requisite preciousness and tongue-in-cheek melodrama with violent action sequences and beautiful stop-motion creature effects. Never before has the triumphant sadness of an existential angst-dulling jay hit been captured as accurately as it is in the scene where Bill Murray gets high on a boat while David Bowie's "Life on Mars?" swells in the background.

LIFTED Another way to describe the feeling of euphoria associated with marijuana use that is more commonly referred to as being "high." Similar to the more popular term, lifted implies general upness, which is in direct contrast to the downness associated with not smoking pot. The term first came into the public consciousness after it was used by the rapper Sir Smoke-a-Lot in the film *Half Baked*. It pretty much left the stoner lexicon immediately after. **See also *Half Baked***

LIGHT OF JAH A strain of marijuana known for its euphoric, sativa-like high and its tendency to grow in the shape of a Christmas tree. Pot smokers who take a toke of the Light of Jah after smoking only decent weed for a while may notice the high lasting longer than normal. That's because

it's a stronger strain than most. Light of Jah is a favorite among wake and bake pot smokers because it keeps the user functional while high and there is minimal post-high haze.

LIGHT UP A slang term used to describe the process of getting high. The phrase comes from the act of igniting the marijuana combined with the fact that getting high is synonymous with being "up." Despite the term's practicality, it is not especially welcome in the pot-smoking community. Pot smokers prefer terms that make no logical sense with what they mean, such as ill, bogart, and shibby.

LIGHTER A plastic or metal device that utilizes the wonders of physics to take a flammable liquid and combine it with a spark to create fire, a necessary component for smoking marijuana. Unlike a match, a lighter can be used multiple times in succession, making it ideal for smoking from devices that rarely stay lit, like bowls and bongs. One would assume that the lighter would be a common commodity among pot smokers. However, despite their portability, some smokers seem incapable of keeping them in their possession for any extended length of time. **See also fire; lighter gnomes; matches; spark** ▼

LIGHTER GNOMES Small creatures who have an inexplicable affinity for unattended lighters. Lighter gnomes are sadistic creatures, and their single greatest pleasure is to spy on pot smokers, wait until they have finished packing a bowl or rolling a joint, and then strike with lightning speed to steal the lighter for their own sinister purposes. While they will occasionally steal expensive lighters, the gnomes actually prefer cheaper disposable models, perhaps counting on the fact that the owner would sooner purchase a new one than spend much time searching for the stolen item. **See also lighter**

LIT A slang term used to describe someone who is fairly to moderately stoned. They are most certainly high, but they are not quite baked and are definitely not yet wasted.

LOBSTER WITH BUD BUTTER A bottom-dwelling crustacean most commonly boiled, steamed, or grilled and then dipped in butter that has been infused with the mind-expanding powers of the cannabis plant. Lobster can be quite expensive, as can the process of making pot butter, so this combination is generally reserved for pot smokers with more expensive tastes. Those with limited means should avoid this extravagant meal at all costs, as indulging even once could instantly take all the joy out of eating humbler treats like pot brownies. **See also cannabutter; pot brownies; pot butter** ▼

LOCK, STOCK AND TWO SMOKING BARRELS A 1998 British heist film following a crew of inexperienced criminal masterminds who, in an attempt to settle a gambling debt, plot to steal a cache of marijuana from a group of far more experienced thieves who have already stolen it from a local dealer. Utilizing the element of surprise along with two antique shotguns that may or may not actually work, the crew ambushes the more experienced thieves and makes off with the loot. Unfortunately the entire plan falls apart when their potential buyer turns out to be none other than one of the very people it was originally stolen from, albeit tangentially.

LONG-TERM MEMORY LOSS A mental impairment associated with extensive marijuana use that causes users to lose track of rather important life events. Unlike short-term memory loss wherein one might forget where one has left one's car keys, long-term memory loss might find the subject forgetting that one even owned a car to begin with. **See also short-term memory loss**

LOST A TV show that makes no sense—unless one is high.

LYNCH, DAVID (BORN JANUARY 20, 1946) An American visual artist best known for his feature films, which combine traditional narrative storytelling with surreal visuals evoking dreams, nightmares, and other aspects of the human subconscious. Even Lynch's straightforward works, like the historical biopic *The Elephant Man*, contain abstract dreamscape sequences and disquieting, atonal sound. So his nonlinear films? Nutty beyond the limits of even the highest pot smoker's capacity for thinking something completely bughouse insane actually makes sense. See 1997's *Lost Highway* and 2001's *Mulholland Drive* for examples. Every David Lynch film screening will end with lots of deep, head-nodding conversations through which all participants will gain a revelatory intellectual understanding of the film's themes and meaning. Unfortunately, all one will remember the next day is that *Mulholland Drive* was about girls making out, and *Blue Velvet* had that dude from *Showgirls*.

Mm

MACRAMÉ A form of decorative folk art that employs knotted fibers, beads, shells, and bones to create jewelry, wall hangings, or other displayable crafts. Having most likely originated among thirteenth-century Arab weavers, who used various artistic knotting methods to clean up the fringed edges of hand-loomed fabric, the technique eventually spread throughout Europe. In modern times, the art has been taken up by artistically inclined pot smokers who, through the liberal employment of shiny beads and mesmerizing patterns, popularized the knotted hemp jewelry that gives away weedophiles as halos give away angels. ▾

MAHER, BILL (BORN JANUARY 20, 1956) Outspoken political comedian whose strong stances and riffs on politicians and religion have earned him a place among the most self-righteous talking heads on TV. Maher is an outspoken supporter of drug legalization, with a certain "fuck you" attitude toward anyone who presumes to tell others it is wrong to get high. Maher also starred in a 2008 documentary called *Religulous* in which he travels to Amsterdam and interviews the head of some religion whose main pursuit is to get high and be spiritual. Maher doesn't take to the religious aspect, but he does smoke a joint with the guy before the guy's hair literally catches on fire. The scene serves as a public service announcement: Friends don't let friends with long hair smoke marijuana near candles. In 2016, Maher sparked some additional controversy by apparently lighting up a "real" joint during a live broadcast of his show *Real Time with Bill Maher*. Despite

Maher's insistence that the joint was real, the lack of FCC response has pot smokers everywhere feeling a bit skeptical.

MALL, THE An acres-wide structure populated by many large, well-known consumer goods stores. Although sometimes overwhelming, the mall is a destination location for stoners, who often find themselves indulging in a meal of stoner delicacies—French fries, pizza, soda, and more—at the food court.

MANNERS Rules of etiquette that are associated with decency, politeness, and propriety. Simple manners include things like not eating with one's mouth open and covering one's mouth when burping. However, manners are of no issue to an inebriated pot smoker, who can turn from the most honorable and deserving gentleman or gentlewoman into a boorish, disrespectful brute. This can include picking their noses, scratching themselves inappropriately, wolfing down whatever edible crumbs are within sight, and generally disgusting all nonsmokers in eyeshot.

MARIJUANA The common name for a humble little plant that has found uses in everything from religious ceremonies to medicine to music festivals. Cannabis, as it is known in the scientific community, has been used by humans for millennia and was particularly popular among ancient Hindus who smoked it to attain spiritual enlightenment. For thousands of years it was a sacred herb that carried no negative connotations, and then all of a sudden it became a substance that was banned in the majority of the world. **See also every entry in this book ▶**

Male (1) and Female (2) Plants of Hemp (*Cannabis sativa*). — *a*, male flower; *b*, female flower; *c*, embryo.

MARIJUANA ANONYMOUS An addiction and counseling organization modeled after Alcoholics Anonymous that includes the legendary twelve-step program to help those who wish to refrain from marijuana control their urges.

MARIJUANA, INC. A 2009 CNBC documentary about Northern California's Mendocino County, which details the exploding underground marijuana black market. The scene had existed for more than thirty years when the film was released, since the California climate is perfect for growing primo bud. The documentary claims Mendocino County was, at the time, responsible for about 10 percent of the national drug market and that marijuana accounted for two-thirds of the local economy. The documentary examined the situation from the perspective of the growers, the dealers, the community, the Drug Enforcement Agency, and, of course, the children. It also aired about six times a weekend, every weekend. Pot smokers who were alone at home at 3 a.m. looking for something to watch undoubtedly got sucked in by the title and watched for about thirty minutes before realizing the documentary is boring, overdramatic, uninteresting, and a complete buzzkill.

MARIJUANA POLICY PROJECT An advocacy group that supports the legalization of marijuana, honest education, and positive, non-punitive treatment programs for problematic smokers. MPP has claimed many victories in terms of medical marijuana laws, decriminalization efforts, and ballot initiatives. It is also overrun with internship applications each summer from young pot smokers who are eager to dedicate their lives, both personally and professionally, to marijuana, and to find an internship that doesn't require a drug test.

MARIJUANA TAX ACT OF 1937 A landmark piece of legislation that, while not formally criminalizing marijuana, served as a significant deterrent in its dealing and led to the drug's eventual illegality. The act imposed a $1 fine on anyone who possessed or used the drug, and it laid out strict regulations by which manufacturers and producers of the drug needed to comply. The initiative was passed based on various hearings and testimony, some of which included the belief that marijuana caused madness, criminal behavior, and even murder.

Other things people believed in 1937: Typewriters are practical, vinyl records are the wave of the future, "basketball" should be spelled as two words, and it's totally safe to dump all trash into the local lake.

MARIO KART 64 An installment in Nintendo's popular video game racing series designed for the Nintendo 64. The game saw a resurgence in popularity in a downloadable format playable on the wildly popular Wii gaming system. Unlike some video games where getting high would be detrimental to one's performance, smoking pot before playing the game is essential to ultimate mastery of the various courses. Without the benefit of a pot-addled brain, a clearheaded player is incapable of the out-of-the-box thinking necessary to defeat the other players.

MARLEY, BOB (FEBRUARY 6, 1945– MAY 11, 1981) A Jamaican reggae star and the most widely featured musician on weedophiles' posters. Marley is a symbol of the pot smoker, and the pot smoker finds a common cause with Marley. His laid-back musical stylings, Rastafarian heritage, and unabashed and much publicized marijuana use have caused more smokers to dreadlock their hair than any ever should. Marley himself smoked pot up to his death in 1981 and, per his wishes, was buried with a marijuana bud. His ghost is probably getting high to this very day. **See also posters**

MARTHA AND SNOOP'S POTLUCK DINNER PARTY A popular TV show featuring unlikely duo of Snoop Dogg, beloved rapping weedophile, and Martha Stewart, lifestyle expert and party planning extraordinaire (who's not as unfamiliar with cannabis culture as one might have thought). Together they team up to redefine the potluck, whip up some delicious (and sometimes 420-friendly) snacks and drinks, and host a series of celebrities, including Seth Rogen, Post Malone, Bella Thorne, Kathy Griffin, Ice Cube, and more. **See also Rogen, Seth; Snoop Dogg**

MARY JANE A common name for human females, the popularity of which probably peaked around May 15, 1970 (nine months after Woodstock). In Spanish-speaking cultures, the name is written as "maria juana," which might explain why it has become synonymous with pot. If one chooses to name his or her daughter Mary Jane, one immediately waives all rights to complain when she expresses an unwavering devotion to the Grateful Dead, an insatiable appetite for toast cream, and an inexplicable fascination with hollow household objects that don't burn easily.

MASSACHUSETTS One of three commonwealths in the United States of America and the place of landing for the Pilgrims all the way back thousands of years ago or some time around then. Despite its importance in America's founding, Massachusetts serves as a political punch line for conservatives, who often refer to the state derisively as Taxachusetts (though the state has no tax on food or clothing). The state decriminalized marijuana in 2008, legalized medical marijuana in 2012, and legalized recreational marijuana in 2016. This has led to a precipitous rise in Cambridge hipsters hand-rolling spliffs and joints instead of just free-range tobacco cigarettes. The state's first recreational marijuana retail shops opened in November 2018 and boasted over $2 million in sales within a week, as hundreds of pot smokers stood in line for enough weed to get them through the upcoming Thanksgiving holiday. **See also Boston Freedom Rally; hipsters**

MATCHES A primitive method of creating fire invented in sixth-century China that is only slightly more effective than rubbing two sticks together or waiting for lightning to strike a tree. They consist of a flammable stick (usually paper or wood) and a combustible head, which ignites when friction is applied. Although not ideal, a match can be used for lighting certain objects, including joints. **See also fire; lighter ▶**

MATHEMATICS An educational pursuit involving patterns of numbers that follow a set of defined rules. For example, one plus one will always equal two. For some smokers, however, these universal rules do not apply, such as when a smoker takes his or her turn on a joint in the "puff, puff, pass" manner of smoking. In this scenario, sometimes one plus one can equal one or even zero, resulting in the subject taking several more hits than originally allotted. This breakdown in the fundamental principles governing the universe can mean only one of two things: Either pot has mystical powers that interrupt the space-time continuum, or it has very unmagical powers that reduce the functionality of the adult brain to that of a three-year-old. Pick whichever helps the reader sleep better at night.

MAUI WOWIE Potent, sticky, bright green marijuana born in the tropical paradise that is Hawaii. Coveted by pot smokers the world over, the weed is regrettably found in a state consisting of a series of islands, thus making it difficult for those without flippers or wings to obtain the genuine article without purchasing an expensive plane ticket or paying a premium for an imported stash. One could try to replicate the tropical experience by lighting a few tiki torches, rolling a joint of the best local pot, and toking up to a recording of ukulele music while eating a pineapple. However, this is a surefire recipe for disappointment. **See also Hawaii**

MAYER, JOHN (BORN OCTOBER 16, 1977) A pop musician and multi-platinum-selling artist who is known for radio hits "Your Body is a Wonderland," "No Such Thing," and "Waiting on the World to Change." Mayer serves as a conundrum to the pot smoker, on par with the stars, the space-time continuum, and Liza Minnelli. Mayer is both a jerk and cool. He's both a sellout and talented. He's both annoying and funny. His music both sucks and is catchy. How can this be? Scientists have been studying the phenomenon since *Room for Squares* was released with mixed results. To sustain the highest level of mental health, it's best not to care about John Mayer one iota. However, he did announce in 2017 that he'd given up drinking and replaced it with a cannabis habit—so maybe there's hope for him still.

MCCONAUGHEY, MATTHEW (BORN NOVEMBER 4, 1969) Golden-locked

Southern gentleman and thespian whose works include his critically lauded performances in *The Wedding Planner*, *How to Lose a Guy in 10 Days*, *Failure to Launch*, *Magic Mike*, and *Dallas Buyers Club*. Pot smokers will best recognize McConaughey as postgrad David Wooderson, the pot-smoking, smooth-talking former football star who still chases high school girls in *Dazed and Confused*. While the role secured McConaughey's placement as a credible pot smoker, the story of his October 1999 arrest made him a legend. McConaughey was arrested in his Texas home for possession of pot and paraphernalia after police officers came to his house due to noise complaints. The noise they were complaining about? A naked Matthew McConaughey, playing the bongos with his bong at the ready. The story serves as an important lesson for pot smokers: At least put on a pair of pants if the police knock on the door. Most recently, Snoop Dogg accidentally got McConaughey high on the set of their film *The Beach Bum* after he swapped out what McConaughey thought were fake, oregano-stuffed joints. Snoop Dogg claims he was going for authenticity, but regardless, it sounds like

McConaughey was all right, all right, all right. **See also *Dazed and Confused*, Snoop Dogg**

MEDICAL MARIJUANA A term used to describe the use of cannabis as a legitimate treatment for any range of ailments such as glaucoma, depression, nausea, and multiple sclerosis. The drug's hunger-inducing properties have also found a use for patients recovering from chemotherapy. As of 2019, thirty-three states have legalized the use of marijuana for medical purposes. However, that has not stopped a nation of pot smokers from self-medicating to cure a host of unrecognized medical conditions like head-hurts, stomach-owies, lazy legs, poor self-image, and several million raging cases of "boring Friday night in the suburbs." **See also California; Compassionate Investigational New Drug Program; medical marijuana plotlines ▼**

Mm

MEDICAL MARIJUANA PLOT-LINES Storylines used in "edgy" sitcoms describing situations when one of the main characters begins using the drug, typically as a result of a phony illness, a pharmacy mistake, or deliberate effort. Every medical marijuana episode has the same moment: the first time the patient uses the drug and walks cooly down the sidewalk as bass guitar plays in the background. Medical marijuana plotlines are a clear sign that a sitcom is out of ideas, or, if in the third season or earlier, completely unoriginal.

MERSH Weed of subpar quality that often contains an excess of stems, seeds, and shake. While it may not be premium bud, it will certainly get the smoker high when times are tough and no superior pot can be acquired. When smoking mersh, one should keep a bottle of water handy to double as a lubricant to counteract the effects of the harsh smoke as well as a receptacle for the unfinished joint when one gives up and goes back out to buy some decent weed.

METHOD A slang term for weed that is pretty much confined to Staten Island. Luckily, much like the individuals who inhabit that area of New York, the term almost never leaves the borders of Staten Island.

METHOD MAN (BORN MARCH 2, 1971) Actor, musician, frequent subject of photos featuring pot-smoking, and principal emcee of the Wu-Tang Clan whose artistic pursuits have placed him side by side with weed at almost every stop. Method Man played a drug dealer both on *The Wire* and in the movie *The Wackness*, as well as a pot-smoking botany expert in *How High*. His fourth solo album's title, *4:21…The Day After*, is a not-so-subtle tribute to the drug, and the album opens with a rallying cry to "legalize it." Sadly, the forces that be did not heed his call, as Method was arrested the following year for marijuana possession. Method played his album as his defense at the trial, but it was rejected once it was learned the album featured only three tracks that were produced by RZA. Today, he's a strong advocate for marijuana and has been working with rapper Redman on their own legal marijuana brand. **See also *How High***

MEWES, JASON (BORN JUNE 12, 1974) An American actor best known for his portrayal of Jay, a drug dealer in suburban New Jersey who plays second fiddle to his stoic heterosexual lifemate, Silent Bob (Kevin Smith). He has appeared in all of Smith's films, unless one counts *Jersey Girl*, which one never should. Mewes's character Jay stands as a proud antithesis to the stereotypical lazy stoner. Throughout the course of Smith's films, Jay helps sabotage a dating show, becomes the inspiration for the Bluntman and Chronic series, saves an orangutan named Suzanne from imminent death, witnesses a donkey show, travels around the country beating up anonymous Internet users who bad-mouthed him and Silent Bob online, and even plays an integral role in releasing God from a fleshy prison in time to stop two fallen angels from ascending back to heaven due to a loophole in Catholic dogma, thus negating all of existence. To date, he is the world's most productive pothead. Mewes the person is, of course, much different from his character. Despite his struggles with addiction, Mewes claims to have no issues with alcohol or marijuana and continues to be a strong supporter of both. However, since he has not yet saved the world from imminent destruction, he is thus far less interesting to write about.

MEXICO A country just south of the United States that routinely supplies its neighbor to the north with cultural diversity, fresh produce, and a steady stream of illegal drugs (nearly $40 billion worth each year). In 2009 the country passed a law decriminalizing the possession of small amounts of heroin, marijuana, cocaine, and other illicit substances, thus drastically increasing the presence of rowdy college sophomores visiting the country the following year. Limited medical use was legalized in mid-2017. Confusingly, Mexico's Supreme Court ruled that laws prohibiting recreational use of cannabis were unconstitutional, so technically those laws are still in effect but are basically unenforceable. As pot smokers everywhere could explain, the only solution here is legalization. ▶

MICROWAVE A common kitchen appliance invented by Percy Spencer in 1945 used for the cooking of food. The device works by bombarding food molecules with microwave radiation to rapidly heat the food, a process that is probably harmless to humans. The microwave is easy to operate, works in a matter of minutes, and requires absolutely no monitoring on the part of the user. Guess who likes that idea? The pot-smoking community has been using the microwave as the primary means for munchie preparation since its inception, preferring it to more dangerous cooking methods like baking, sautéing, roasting, and anything that involves more thought than hitting buttons and waiting patiently. ▼

MIDNIGHT TOKER An individual who indulges in a hit or two of marijuana just before bed. The term was popularized by the Steve Miller Band in their song "The Joker," in which the singer admits to being, among other things, a sinner, a lover, a smoker, a grinner, and a midnight toker. While some frown upon this practice, it is widely acceptable among the pot-smoking community as the second-best method for falling asleep. The first being to turn on old episodes of *The Joy of Painting* until Bob Ross slowly lulls one into a happy coma. **See also Ross, Bob**

MIDS A level in the arbitrary grading of marijuana used to describe pot that isn't really great but also isn't really all that bad either. As its name implies, it is somewhere in the middle. While it isn't going to help one attain complete spiritual oneness, it is perfectly acceptable weed to smoke if one doesn't want to break the bank in the name of getting high. **See also chronic; headie; KB; kush**

MILKSHAKE A combination of milk and ice cream that is mixed together in a blender, poured into a glass, and slurped through a straw. The milkshake makes for an excellent munchie for several reasons. First and foremost, it is delicious. Second, its deliciousness is increased exponentially by adding any number of common kitchen staples like chocolate syrup, peanut butter, or whipped cream. And last but not least, the fact that it is in liquid form makes it easy to ingest quickly and can also help to alleviate the symptom of cotton mouth. Smokers should take caution while enjoying a milkshake, as there is a slight risk of developing brief but excruciating pain localized within the forehead if ingested too quickly. Of course this can easily be avoided by enjoying the milkshake slowly. However, everyone knows such a feat would be impossible.

MILKY How one might describe a particularly large quantity of smoke accumulated in the chamber of a bong or bubbler. With a fresh bowl, long pull, and experienced bong ripper in control, the smoke can become almost completely opaque and milky in appearance. If a newbie has drawn a particularly milky cloud, a pro should probably be called in to finish off the hit, similar to calling in a pinch hitter in baseball. One doesn't want a rookie at the plate when the bases are loaded in the bottom of the ninth, metaphorically speaking. ▼

MOSS, RANDY (BORN FEBRUARY 13, 1977) A former NFL wide receiver and current frequent marijuana user who successfully navigated the NFL's drug program better than fellow NFL star Ricky Williams before his retirement in 2012. Unlike Williams, who failed numerous drug tests while in the NFL, Moss was never suspended because of a failed drug test. Still, in a 2005 interview with HBO, he admitted to still using the drug. The admission was one of the least surprising statements Moss has ever made. Moss was suspended in college for failing a drug test for marijuana, he was subjected to random drug testing for two years after testing positive for marijuana in an NFL drug test, and he admitted that he took certain plays off when he felt like it, reflecting the attitude of most pot smokers. Moss's talent still surpassed most of the competition, and he seemed to succeed in the NFL without really trying, allowing him to reach the apex of pot smokerdom: the ability to get high and still be a success at the highest level. **See also sports; Williams, Ricky**

MOTIVATION An internal driving force that can be severely altered by smoking pot. In sober humans, this force compels them to do everything from getting out of bed in the morning to balancing their checkbook. While motivation is not completely eliminated after smoking pot, it certainly switches gears. Instead of wanting to clean the house, a weedophile might feel an intense desire to build a miniature house out of the stack of coasters on the coffee table, or watch every episode of *Arrested Development* (including the extended pilot). While these pursuits may not be as "productive" as some others, they are infinitely more gratifying. **See also Arrested Development; lazy smoker**

MOVIES The art of motion pictures. Movies have developed from silent single-shot films to multi-angle narratives, shorts, documentaries, and other storytelling mechanisms. Developed in the late nineteenth century, motion pictures were an outgrowth of the theater and captured the public's imagination in America. The industry now resides primarily in Hollywood. The combination of celebrity culture, loose morals, and plastic surgery has combined to produce epic American pot experiences. Everybody has his or her personal favorite movies, but only a pot smoker can tell you the best movies to watch while high. ▼

MUNCHIES A slang term used to describe both the feeling of insatiable hunger experienced after smoking marijuana as well as the myriad snack foods smokers ingest in futile attempts to satisfy said hunger. The most satisfying foods include but are not limited to potato chips, nachos, cookie dough, pizza, French fries, mozzarella sticks, pickles, popcorn, milkshakes, and toast cream. **See also toast cream**

MURDER MOUNTAIN A true crime documentary that appeared on Netflix in late 2018. Centered around Humboldt County, which is known for its booming marijuana industry, this series unpacks the series of mysterious disappearances and murders that have happened in the area. Although some officials in the Humboldt County area claim the show is one-sided and "highly sensationalized," it's a compelling story…and enough to keep the average pot smoker seeking safer methods of acquiring their bud. **See also Humboldt County, Netflix**

MUSIC The art of sound, typically synthesizing melody, harmony, and groove. Music is a holy grail of pot smokers, who are known to go through stages of musical appreciation in the following order: jam bands, psychedelic rock, classic rock, hip-hop, rap, jazz, blues, and folk. The whole process takes about two years, during which time listeners may insist certain lyrics are so deep and personal to their lives that they can be explained only by divine intervention. ▼

Nn

NACHOS A culinary delight associated with Tex-Mex cuisine. Nachos were originally created from the humble combination of cheese and tortillas but have morphed to include everything from salsa and ground beef to catfish, pickles, sweet potatoes, and pretty much anything that one has lying around. In fact, scientists have yet to discover a food item that does not work with nachos, although they came close with the combination of lamb, ice cream, and rakfisk. They are most commonly enjoyed either as a lunch replacement or in pot-fueled food celebrations. ▼

NARC A member of the human race who has sold his or her soul to the devil in the interest of self-preservation. Usually in exchange for political amnesty, a narc agrees to cooperate with one of several government agencies and provide them with information about friends and acquaintances who engage in the buying or selling of drugs like marijuana.

NELSON, WILLIE (BORN APRIL 29, 1933) Iconic American country singer who saw widespread acclaim and success during the 1970s "outlaw country" movement. At the time, Nashville was interested in using strings and orchestras to accompany popular country music, but Nelson insisted his music could sell itself, leading to the outlaw designation. Nelson's rebellious nature has been seen in other elements of his life as well, as Nelson is an admitted pot smoker and has remained a vibrant part of the pot legalization movement pretty much since he was born in 1933. Now in his eighties, Nelson continues to toke. Nelson had a bit part as an old stoner in *Half Baked*, which was not at all a stretch for him. In January 2010, six members of his band were arrested in North Carolina for possession, and in April 2010, during an appearance on *Larry King Live*, Nelson admitted he had smoked pot earlier in the day, causing Larry King's suspenders to snap. Like many other celebrities, he released his own line of marijuana products in 2015 post-legalization in some states. Nelson is even a member of the NORML Advisory Board and has hosted benefit events to support his pro-marijuana message. Willie Nelson is basically the quintessential pot smoker. **See also NORML** ▼

NEPAL A hot spot for marijuana users and the unofficial second-friendliest country in the world to pot smokers. Nepal is sometimes referred to as the Jamaica of the East, though marijuana remains technically illegal there. Weed is available in the cities and even in the remote regions of the country. ▼

NETFLIX A massively popular streaming service that features movies, beloved TV shows, and original content, including *Stranger Things*, *Big Mouth*, *13 Reasons Why*, *Peaky Blinders*, *You*, and more. Pot smokers (sometimes mistakenly) take the phrase "Netflix and chill" very literally and can easily wile away hours upon hours mindlessly watching everything and anything with nothing but a fat joint to keep them company. **See also Netflix Collection, The**

NETFLIX COLLECTION, THE A collection of ten customized strains inspired by popular TV shows, created through a collaboration with streaming service giant Netflix and Alternative Herbal Health Services. As a promotional event for their show *Disjointed*, Netflix briefly set up a pop-up event in 2017 in Los Angeles, where strains were available to complement shows like *Arrested Development*, *Wet Hot American Summer: Ten Years Later*, *Santa Clarita Diet*, *Orange Is the New Black*, and more. A delightful experience for California-based pot smokers; less fun for everyone else. **See also Netflix**

NEW YORK CITY A city on America's East Coast with a population of over 8 million and host to a number of American landmarks, including the Statue of Liberty, Broadway, Carnegie Hall, and Times Square. Most of the city is covered in pot dealers riding bicycles or pushing in Central Park, which is why it was terrible news when it was revealed that New York is the pot-arrest capital of the world, having booked four hundred thousand people for possession in the previous decade, more than any other city on Earth. The good news is that although cannabis is still illegal for recreational use, law enforcement is stepping back on low-level possession, so hopefully that number will be decreasing drastically in the years to come.

NEW YORK CITY DIESEL A strain of marijuana that carries the namesake of the Big Apple itself. New York City Diesel mysteriously has a grape taste and smell. The high can be described as "exotic," meaning it's very heady and wavy. Seeing all the trichomes on the bud will make users want to lick the bud like a lollipop.

"NEXT EPISODE, THE" A rap song released in the year 1999 by Dr. Dre, Snoop Dogg, Nate Dogg, and Kurupt. In 1992, Snoop had advised his listeners in "Nuthin' But a 'G' Thang" of chilling until the next episode. Nearly ten years of chillin' later, they were rewarded with this homage to weed, ladies, and generally being badass. In the track, Dr. Dre and Snoop recount their adventures enjoying the chronic, hitting up the hottest nightclubs, and finding nice women to party with. **See also chronic**

NICKEL BAG A minuscule amount of marijuana that can be purchased for $5. Many years ago, this was actually a decent amount of pot. However, with the rise of inflation it currently amounts to approximately a single bowl's worth. If one is lucky. If this trend continues, a nickel bag could someday amount to naught but a single trichome stuck to a piece of paper. **See also dime bag; eighth** ▼

NIGHTCAP Named after a warm piece of headgear that one might wear to bed before the advent of central heating, this term now refers to a small sampling of marijuana one indulges in just before retiring for the evening. As it can be difficult to smoke pot in one's sleep, this ritual is essential for anyone attempting to maintain a steady high before it's time for the morning wake and bake. Sort of like a bear storing up fat for winter hibernation, but with less salmon and more smoke. **See also wake and bake**

NORML The National Organization for the Reform of Marijuana Laws, a nonprofit foundation headquartered in Washington, DC, whose mission "is to move public opinion sufficiently to legalize the responsible use of marijuana by adults, and to serve as an advocate for customers to assure they have access to high quality marijuana." With the power of Willie Nelson, a member of the advisory board, NORML has had some important legislative victories…and a few less significant ones as well. For example, when Michael Phelps was dropped by Kellogg's after his weed use was made public, NORML led a boycott of Kellogg's. A nice idea in theory, but the boycott probably would have been more successful if cereal weren't part of most pot smokers' balanced breakfasts. **See also Nelson, Willie; Phelps, Michael**

NORTHERN LIGHTS A strain of marijuana popular among home growers thanks to its rapid growing cycle (about seven weeks from seed to flower) and moderately high potency. It is also rather hardy and difficult to kill, a desirable trait from the perspective of a novice grower. The strain shares its name with the aurora borealis, a celestial phenomenon where waves of greenish light hover in the sky, occurring more frequently as one nears the North Pole. While it has never been documented, there are rumors that smoking Northern Lights while observing the northern lights will create a rift in the space-time continuum resulting in the end of the universe as it is known today. Please don't attempt this—just in case.

NUGS Dried buds from the female flowering *Cannabis sativa* plant. They come in varying shapes and sizes ranging from small round peas to large conical pieces about the size of the palm. In order to be properly smoked, nugs must be delicately broken down into tiny pieces small enough to fit into the bowl of a pipe or bong. If rolling a joint, it is advisable to break the nugs up even more finely with the assistance of a grinder. Their bite-sized appearance may entice the owner to begin popping them into the mouth like bonbons. However, this temptation should be resisted. **See also grinder** ▼

Oo

OBAMA, BARACK (BORN AUGUST 4, 1961) Forty-fourth president of the United States, first black president of the United States, and unabashed White Sox fan. Upon his inauguration, Obama announced that his administration would stop DEA raids of marijuana facilities in states that have approved its medical use, and, although his administration's level of follow-through on that statement is up for debate, Obama's reputation was solidified as an overall cool guy. Before, Obama's coolness was only hinted at. In addition to his smooth, deep voice and delivery, his laid-back demeanor in the face of political havoc, and his referencing Jay-Z's "Dirt Off Your Shoulder" after a preliminary presidential debate, Obama's cool because there's a picture of him from college smoking a joint. Well, the administration claims it's a tobacco cigarette, but Obama's sure holding it like a joint, and his heavy eyelids sure don't help their assertations. Obama has also admitted to smoking weed before and inhaling because "that was the point," causing every pot smoker in America to rationalize their overconsumption of pot by claiming they will make up for it by one day running for president.

OFFICE OF NATIONAL DRUG CONTROL POLICY The Big Kahuna nationally when it comes to deciding what is and is not going to be the stance of the US government when it comes to drug policy, in terms of enforcement, resources, and treatment. The leader of the ONDCP is referred to colloquially as the "Drug Czar," and he is the supreme leader of a monarchy of drug law in America, whereby marijuana is deemed illegal and unsuitable for public consumption. The Drug Czar is a ruthless but fair leader whose limitless power is divinely given and whose ultimate authority cannot be questioned without the perpetrator facing the gallows at the czar's whim and merry. **See also DEA**

OK A simplification of the English word okay that is generally used to say that the status of a particular person, object, or task has been deemed acceptable. The word's full potential can be realized only after one has ingested a fairly large amount of marijuana. Once in the proper state of mind, one should notice that, when written out, the word OK looks exactly like a tiny sideways person. The implications of this discovery will appear groundbreaking at first, but that feeling should diminish exponentially over time. **See also highdea**

ON THE ROAD A semiautobiographical, drug-saturated novel written by Jack Kerouac in 1951 detailing a series of road trips he took in the mid-twentieth century. The two main characters crisscross the North American continent getting high, discussing philosophy, and doing their best to live rootless existences punctuated by brief periods of odd jobs and temporary homes. Kerouac allegedly wrote the original manuscript during a three-week drug-fueled blitz on a single continuous scroll of paper. Kerouac claimed to have indulged in nothing but coffee during said session. However, this is widely regarded as

being about as true as the thought that the word "gullible" is not in the dictionary. **See also Kerouac, Jack**

ONE EGG AND A FRYING PAN According to a 1987 public service announcement sponsored by the Partnership for a Drug-Free America, this equates to one's brain on drugs. Most pot smokers just see breakfast. ▼

ONE-HITTER A small pipe that is usually just large enough to accommodate a single decent hit of marijuana. One-hitters are a handy piece of paraphernalia when privacy is difficult to come by, as they often resemble ordinary cigarettes and don't draw much attention to the smoker. Their small size usually limits them to individual use. **See also apple pipe; can bong**

Oo

ONE-HITTER-QUITTER Marijuana so potent that even the most hardened smokers are high off their asses after but a single puff. When one encounters bud of this quality, it is unwise to tempt fate and attempt a second hit.

ONE-TOKE JOKE An individual who has a very low tolerance for THC and possesses the unique ability to get completely ripped off of a single hit of marijuana. While the name implies a negative connotation, frugal smokers often envy this supernatural power, longing to return to a time when they themselves could pack a single bowl of pot that would get them high for eight nights straight, like a magical marijuana menorah. ▼

ONION, THE A nationwide newspaper whose news stories feature headlines such as "School Administration Reminds Female Students Bulletproof Vest Must Cover Midriff," "Man Overcomes Fear of Public Urination," and "Parent Struggling to Find Good Reason Why 5-Year-Old Shouldn't Be Afraid of Starting School." *The Onion* is originally a satirical paper, but it's expanded to include real content under the name *The A.V. Club*, which offers reviews and stories on music and movies. Most people who work at *The Onion* and *The A.V. Club* are probably pot smokers, and most of the readership probably is too. As a result, since *The Onion* makes all of its content available free online, including its archives, getting high and reading *The Onion* is now one of the most time-consuming, money-saving, and frequent activities for pot smokers everywhere.

ORANGES Citrus fruits that can serve a number of uses for an industrious pot smoker. First and foremost, they are a portable munchie that can be easily carried in a backpack, large pocket, or hand and eaten at the smoker's leisure. The peel also has mystical properties that can turn dried-up pot into sticky icky if one

Oo

tosses peel and weed into a sealed container for a few hours. Unfortunately, its transformative properties apply only to pot. Keeping orange peels in one's room will not improve one's life. It will temporarily make one's room smell like oranges, though, which isn't half bad.

OREGANO A common herb used for culinary applications like seasoning soups, sauces, and meat. In its fresh state, it bears little resemblance to marijuana. However, when dried it could be pot's distant cousin, twice removed. For this reason, many quick-thinking weedophiles will attempt to convince law enforcement that their stash of pot is merely a bag of oregano they keep on hand just in case an uncontrollable urge to make pasta should arise. This is almost never believed by anyone, but it's worth a shot for the one time out of a thousand when the cop actually falls for it. **See also herb** ▼

OUNCE A unit of measure in the imperial system that equates to approximately twenty-eight grams or, to the casual smoker, a pretty decent amount of herb. **See also eighth**

Pp

PAC-MAN An early arcade-style video game in which the player guides a hungry yellow circle (Pac-Man) through a maze of edible food dots while, at the same time, trying to avoid four menacing ghosts. Pac-Man advances to the next map only after every round foodstuff on the current map has been devoured. Pot smokers tend to excel at the game because they can relate to Pac-Man's munchies-stricken state and often view the ghost quartet as family or friends who continuously nag, nag, nag about taking responsibility, cutting their hair, getting a job, and putting on pants.

PACK A BOWL A phrase uttered by pot smokers as a call to action for any other smokers within earshot who are in possession of both a stash of marijuana and a bowl to smoke it out of. The person making the request is often within reach of the tools necessary to make their dream of smoking more pot a reality, but they are occasionally too lazy, high, or both to do so.

PANAMA RED A famous strain of marijuana indigenous to—wait for it—Panama, which has since been picked up and exported to America to take advantage of its desirable high. Panama Red was popular in the 1960s and early 1970s and is known for its high potency, ability to cause intense, psychedelic highs, and for its red, claylike color. The strain is also the inspiration behind the Jerry Garcia and Peter Rowan song "Panama Red," and it was specifically requested by the character Chef in the Vietnam War film *Apocalypse Now*. **See also Garcia, Jerry**

PAPER TOWEL GERMINATION A method for convincing a seed from the *Cannabis sativa* plant that it would be an awesome idea to break out from its hard enclosure and begin growing into a mature, smokable plant. The process goes as so: The grower dampens a paper towel, wraps it around one or more seeds, tucks the towel into a plastic bag, places the bundle in a warm place, and crosses his or her fingers. This method is especially popular among novice growers, as it is essentially idiot-proof. Unfortunately, it is not weedophile-proof, so one should not be surprised if the seeds die after one gets high and forgets about them. ▼

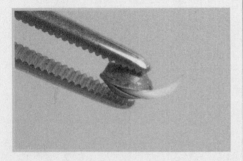

PARADISE BURNING A book written by *High Times* editor Chris Simunek that details his exploits as he travels the world chasing various marijuana stories. These include his interaction with a dirt farmer who grows the finest green south of the Mason-Dixon, his infiltrating a Marijuana Anonymous meeting, and his attendance at the Sturgis Rally and Races for biker dudes and chicks. Not only does the book tend to occupy a visible spot on a pot smoker's bookshelf but it's a great book to casually invite their nonsmoking friends to read in an effort to entice them to try the drug.

This strategy is only occasionally successful, as the friend often just places the book on his own bookshelf hidden from view and inevitably forgets to ever read or return it.

PARADOX A statement or argument that draws upon acceptable premises but leads to a contradiction or a situation that defies intuition. Some examples include: This statement is false. One's mission is not to accept this mission. If nothing is better than eternal bliss and a slice of bread is better than nothing then a slice of bread is better than eternal bliss. Paradoxes are fun little mind teasers, except when pot smokers begin thinking about them too much, at which point they become the ultimate answer to what life is about. If someone is ever concerned his or her friend might be a robot or an alien, get the person high and recite a paradox. Either the alleged person's circuitry will overheat or the human form will melt, revealing a terrifying and confused creature from outer space within. If it's a real human being, the person will just sit there in stunned, blank silence. **See also coincidences**

PARANOIA A feeling that arises when one has consumed either too much bad pot or not enough good pot. Subjects will experience a sudden sense that the world is out to get them and may begin to suspect friends and family of conspiring against them. These feelings are perfectly normal and it is important not to let them interfere with the experience of being high. For example, one should not dwell on the new kid in the smoking circle who definitely looks like a narc and is totally memorizing everyone's face so he can provide accurate descriptions to the DEA officer who is absolutely waiting outside in his car right now. **See also paranoid smoker**

PARANOID SMOKER An irritating variety of pot smoker who spends the majority of his or her time worrying out loud about the possibility of getting caught smoking pot. Every car with a roof rack that passes by is instantly assumed to be a cop. Each gust of wind is his or her nonsmoking roommates coming to bust the session. While some level of paranoia can be a good thing, it is best to leave this type of smoker at home hiding in the closet where it's safe. **See also antisocial smoker; enhancement smoker; hungry smoker; lazy smoker; paranoia; social smoker; talkative smoker; violent smoker**

PARAPHERNALIA A term used to describe various apparatuses used in conjunction with any number of different types of drugs. The DEA defines it as "any equipment, product, or material of any kind that is primarily intended or designed for use in manufacturing, compounding, converting, concealing, producing, processing, preparing, injecting, ingesting, inhaling, or otherwise introducing into the human body a controlled substance," which includes marijuana, hashish, and hashish oil, among other drugs. In practical terms, this can apply to literally anything. Pick up the closest object to this book. Under the right circumstances, it could be considered paraphernalia. Especially if it is hollow. **See also piece** ▶

PARIS The capital of France and a famously bohemian city that generally tolerates single-portion marijuana consumption and possession. A historic home away from home for literary American expats like Ernest Hemingway, Gertrude Stein, and Sherwood Anderson, Paris holds a special place in its resin-varnished heart for wandering artists and intellectuals looking to subdue their demons and stoke their creative fires with a few hits of reefer. While pot remains illegal throughout France (with limited legality for medical products), police and other officials tend to look the other way, assuming the smoker/buyer isn't making an obnoxious show of illicit drug activity. It doesn't hurt that the clouds of cigarette smoke surrounding most Parisian bars and cafés are thick enough to conceal the Riddler's escape.

PARSEC A unit of measure that is equal to approximately 3.26 light years. Despite what some film directors would like to believe, it cannot be used to measure time. So the phrase, "You've never heard of the Millennium Falcon? She's the ship that made the Kessel Run in less than twelve parsecs," is the equivalent of saying, "I'm going to run down to the store to get some rolling papers. It should take me about two miles. But if I'm not back in thirty inches, just smoke without me."

PARTY BONG A bong of exceptional height and girth that frequently contains several chambers and/or hoses, allowing for multiple users to smoke simultaneously. Party bongs can range from several feet to several stories in height, can be constructed out of any number of materials, and are ideal for—you guessed it—parties.

PARTY FOUL An act of stupidity, incompetence, or general rudeness that negatively affects the well-being of every person in the near vicinity and transcends the level of mere buzzkill. Some examples include spilling bong water, volcanoing, eating all the munchies, losing the lighter, and vomiting anywhere other than a toilet or garbage can. Although the term implies there must be a large number of people present for a party foul to occur, this is a common misconception. When one drops a freshly packed bowl and watches it shatter into a hundred pieces, whether there were four witnesses or four hundred, one is still guilty of committing a party foul. **See also buzzkill; volcano**

PASSING OUT The act of losing consciousness due to an excessive amount of drug ingestion, usually taking place on a couch. Passing out is a time-honored tradition usually resulting from the body's overwhelming desire to sleep and rid itself of the toxins that the drug user has pumped into his or her body. While usually harmless in one's own bed, passing out with friends still in one's presence is an invitation to have the passer-outer's body covered in inappropriate Sharpie drawings and insults, having pictures taken of such drawings on the person's body, and having said pictures posted to social media. ▶

PCU A 1994 comedy starring Jeremy Piven as Droz, an aging super super senior at the world's most politically correct institute of higher learning, Port Chester University. Droz's contempt for his cause-loving fellow students is eclipsed only by his intense desire for them to lighten up and have a beer (or seven) together. Piven is at his irreverent finest in *PCU*. However, it is Jon Favreau's portrayal of perma-burned sidekick Gutter that really steals the show. On his way to acquire beer for a kegger, he is presented with the opportunity for a quick toke and must make an important decision. The solution: "Just one hit, then I got to go." With just a few short words, Favreau completely nails the eternal struggle that exists within every weed-ophile: smoke pot, or do something useful. When in doubt, always bet on pot. **See also perma-burned**

PEANUT BUTTER A creamy delight made of ground peanuts, salt, and other stuff, and the main ingredient in nutcrackers, a beloved marijuana snack made by spreading peanut butter between two crackers, then sprinkling it with weed before making it into a sandwich.

PEARL JAM A grunge band from the 1990s that achieved widespread acclaim and success with its debut album *Ten* and is most known for the singles "Alive," "Even Flow," and

"Jeremy," as well as for lead singer Eddie Vedder, whose deep baritone voice and long surfer-dude hair have served as an iconic image of the grunge era. Pearl Jam has spent the better part of its career eschewing traditional means of achieving fame. In addition to refusing to make music videos, the band led a boycott of Ticketmaster and fought for cheaper concert ticket prices. Such a stance makes Pearl Jam an anti-corporatist, semi-hippie-like group within the music industry. As such, the band appeals to the revolutionary side of pot-smoking musicians with dreams of someday becoming rock stars. Since Pearl Jam remains a popular group that has achieved success without selling out, Pearl Jam has cemented its legacy as the type of band every young pot smoker coming up on the scene ever wants to be in.

PERMA-BURNED A state of being that results from an extended period of steady marijuana use. The subject will often exhibit the telltale signs of smoking lots of pot (lethargy, intense relaxation, euphoria, introspective thoughts, and insatiable hunger) but may not have actually smoked pot in several days, months, or even years. Those outside the smoking community often look down upon those suffering from this common affliction. However, many smokers actually strive for this state of being. It's like attaining spiritual oneness without the religious overtones and false sense of superiority.

PHELPS, MICHAEL (BORN JUNE 30, 1985) An American Olympic swimmer, possibly the greatest of all time, and definitely the most accomplished pot-smoking athlete of all time. He has won twenty-three gold medals, broken world records that nobody even knew existed, and has starred in commercials for everything from Speedo swimsuits to Subway sandwiches. In 2009, a British tabloid published a photo of Phelps taking a hit from a bong, which caused the public to briefly question its fanatical support of the swimmer. That is until the public collectively realized that it didn't care enough about swimming in the first place to mind whether or not Phelps smoked pot.

PHILOSOPHY A means for analyzing important questions like "Is there a God?," "What is the answer to the ultimate question?," and "Is it possible to smoke so much pot that one becomes sober again?" Philosophy advocates for thinking things out logically in order to come to a reasonable conclusion. When pot smokers adhere to this school of thought, the answers to the previous questions are: "No, because God couldn't create a rock so heavy that even he couldn't lift it," "Forty-two," and "There's only one way to find out." **See also highdea** ▼

PHISH The ultimate jam band of the modern era. Phish was formed in 1983 at the University of Vermont and comprises members Trey Anastasio and three other guys no one really knows. The group played together for twenty years before a breakup in 2004 and has since reunited. Though Phish receives little radio airplay, it has a devoted following. Fans, colloquially known as Phishheads, are known to download every Phish show ever, or, if financially capable, follow Phish on the road and see every concert. This is usually done during college and with heavy amounts of marijuana consumption, as listeners can hear any given Phish song only once when they're sober before losing interest. This is known as the Phish Law, a mathematical imperative proved in 1993 by a pioneering group of straightedge college students at DeVry University. The Phish Law has helped the CIA break down enemy combatants at Guantanamo Bay, and forced listening to Phish while sober is now a violation of the Geneva Conventions. **See also Grateful Dead, The; straightedge; Vermont**

PICKLES A condiment, snack, or meal, depending on how high one is. Pickles begin life as humble cucumbers but achieve their true flavor potential with the help of vinegar, salt, garlic, dill, and time. Pickles come in a number of varieties ranging from crisp, garlicky kosher dills to sweet-and-sour bread and butter chips. Similar to pairings of various foods with wine, some believe the type of pickle one should enjoy varies depending on the type of pot being smoked. Gherkins, for example, are best enjoyed with a gram of Northern Lights. **See also Northern Lights**

PICKLE JUICE A liquid compound found almost exclusively inside of pickle jars that is rumored to have magical properties. Many people believe that, when ingested in large quantities, it erases any evidence of recent drug use should the drinker be subjected to several forms of drug testing, both random and anticipated. Many people also believe in Santa Claus.

PIECE A generic term used to refer to any structure used for smoking marijuana that can be used multiple times. This can include bongs, bowls, pipes, hookahs, and anything that one would be proud to whip out during a session. For this reason, a piece of foil one has folded into the shape of a pipe does not qualify, regardless of how long it took the creator to produce. **See also paraphernalia ▼**

PINEAPPLE EXPRESS A 2008 bromantic film following a pot smoker (Seth Rogen) and his dealer (James Franco) fleeing from a corrupt police officer after the smoker witnesses a murder and leaves behind an incriminating piece of evidence—a roach filled with a rare and potent strain of pot called Pineapple Express. As a result, the pair is forced to sleep in the woods, engage a good friend in battle, steal a police car, and escape from an underground pot lair. The series of events would be difficult to navigate with a clear head, but the two manage to muddle through despite being high out of their minds for the duration of the film. Which could explain why, despite being shot, burned, and battered, the duo, along with their friend, can still be found munching away at a local diner at the end of the film. **See also Apatow, Judd; Rogen, Seth**

PINK FLOYD An English rock band noted for its development from psychedelic rock to prog rock and for its lyrics and audio experimentation. Pink Floyd plays a major role in any adolescent pot smoker's life, as songs from *The Wall* like "Mother," "Young Lust," and "Another Brick in the Wall: Part 2" appeal to their angsty tendencies. "Another Brick in the Wall: Part 2" is also one of the first songs many pot smokers will learn to play on guitar. Other Pink Floyd albums are equally interesting to listen to: *Animals*, *The Piper at the Gates of Dawn*, and *The Dark Side of the Moon*. *The Dark Side of the Moon*, of course, was made with the sole intention of one day having a pot smoker somehow listen to that album while simultaneously watching *The Wizard of Oz* and noting that the sonic elements eerily coincide with the on-screen action. Less known is that if *A Momentary Lapse of Reason* is played simultaneously with Tim Allen's *The Santa Clause*, sleep can be induced in even the most insomniac viewer within twenty seconds. **See also Dark Side of the Rainbow**

PINNER A very small, tightly wrapped marijuana cigarette that frequently contains more paper than actual weed. One generally rolls a pinner only when one is not in possession of enough pot to roll a respectable joint or pack a bowl but would still like the experience of inhaling smoke from a burning piece of paraphernalia. By itself, a pinner is not enough to get the average smoker very high, but it can make for an excellent appetizer before a main course of bong hits or blunts and also doubles as a delightful nightcap. Its existence reminds the world that it is not the size of the joint that matters, but what one does with it. **See also vegetarian joint**

PIPE A device used for smoking marijuana that is often used synonymously with a bowl. In some cultures, a pipe is slightly different from a bowl in that there is no carb present to allow air to circulate when inhaling. They are prized for their portability, versatility, and inexpensive cost of ownership. ▼

PIPE WEED A type of herb smoked by hobbits and various other races in the Middle Earth realm of J.R.R. Tolkien's *The Lord of the Rings*. There are a number of varieties available throughout the land. However, no self-respecting hobbit would smoke anything other than Longbottom Leaf. Unless of course it was just after second breakfast and somebody else was offering.

PITT, BRAD (BORN DECEMBER 18, 1963) American film actor whose roles include stints in *Seven*, *12 Monkeys*, *Inglourious Basterds*, *Sleepers*, *Fight Club*, *Ocean's Eleven* (and its sequels), *Mr. & Mrs. Smith*, and more. However, his dashing good looks and personal life have dominated his public image. Everyone knows about Pitt's past relationship with Jennifer Aniston and subsequent relationship with Angelina Jolie (which some sources suggest might have ended because of his weed habit). But more relevantly, Pitt was outed as a pot smoker by trendy Los Angeles head shop owner Craig Rudin, who said Pitt used to come into the shop and buy decorative bongs for his coworkers and "it seemed like all he wanted to do was smoke weed, make movies, and go to the beach." Pitt was also outed when he appeared on comedian Bill Maher's show. Maher claimed Pitt rolled the most perfect joints at a party the two attended years earlier. Handsome, talented, rich, and an expert joint roller. No wonder he's still the hunkiest hunk around.

PIZZA Possibly the greatest food ever invented. Pizza consists of bread, tomato sauce, and cheese, with any choice of toppings for an additional fee. Pizza is the rare food that can be delivered, picked up, or baked at home. It also tastes good, from low-end brands to the highest delicacy. While pizza is obviously a staple of the smoker's experience, so too are pizza boxes. On rare occasions, a post-slumber smoker may wander into the kitchen craving just one more piece. When the marijuana gods are smiling, the smoker will hopefully open the pizza box cover and, as if a golden light beams out from inside, find one last piece remaining. That last piece, cold, stale, and lifeless, is still the greatest-tasting single piece of pizza in history. **See also pizza sandwich** ▼

PIZZA SANDWICH Arguably one of the least creative munchies ever developed. The pizza sandwich is simply two pieces of pizza stacked on top of one another to create a superslice. Twice as filling as a single slice and 25 percent more portable, the resulting sandwich is the perfect marriage of ingenuity and a false sense of accomplishment. **See also highdea; pizza**

PLANET EARTH A landmark eleven-part BBC nature documentary featuring high-definition footage of a vast array of the world's ecosystems. Whether watching the David Attenborough–narrated BBC version or the Sigourney Weaver–narrated Discovery one, the soothing voiceover is guaranteed to lull one's pot-addled mind into a Thoreau-like state of natural contemplation. With each environment given its own individual episode, the series has something to offer all of one's smoke-hazed headspaces. For that checked-out, meditative high, there's episode six, "Ice Worlds." For that dazzled-by-shiny-things high, there's episode eight, "Jungles." And for that laughing-endlessly-at-weird-looking-crap high, there's episode eleven, "Ocean Deep."

POCKETS Small crevices woven into pants, shirts, hoodies, and jackets that can be used to store small amounts of marijuana and associated paraphernalia. They can also be used to store cell phones, money, and hands (when not in use). They may not seem like much,

but one would be wise to remember that it would be next to impossible to smoke pot without them. If one does not believe this, try turning them inside out and get ready to go smoke pot at a friend's house. Not so easy, is it? ▼

POGO STICKS About three-foot-tall artificial jumping devices that contain pressurized springs, two steps, and a handle. To operate, they require balance, agility, and confidence. Pogo sticks are typically used by pre-pot-smoking-aged youngsters, meaning they usually disappear into the back of the garage. All of which makes the time-honored tradition of rummaging through the garage while high that much more enjoyable when the childhood pogo stick is found. This will lead to an impromptu decision by the heavily inebriated smoker to retest the pogo stick. After four successful jumps, the stoner will scream "I'm so high!" and revel in his clever use of the phrase before falling helplessly to the ground. Any observers should feel free to share video evidence on social media for full impact. **See also trampolines**

POKER (DEVICE) An essential instrument when smoking from a bong that does exactly what its name implies—it pokes things. Specifically, it pokes ash, resin, and stray pieces of dust through the bowl head and into the chamber of the bong so that it can be later flushed away the next time the owner decides to get off his or her lazy ass and clean the bong. While there are dedicated pokers specifically built for this function, a paper clip, safety pin, or any long and thin apparatus will suffice. **See also stoke**

POKER (GAME) A card game of chance and skill played for money in many different formats but whose most popular incarnation in America is Texas Hold'em. To begin the game, each player receives two cards face down. The dealer then places five cards face up in the middle that are community cards available to all players. The best five-card hand then takes the pot, with betting in between each round. High poker is a slightly different variety. In high poker, the players smoke a joint before the game is played. Then, hits are required any time a player lands a full house or higher, knocks another player out of the game entirely, or sucks out on a hand.

POLICE STATION The place where, according to every movie in which a police station is depicted, there is a long line of cubicles, phones constantly ringing, reports being filed, people walking around with guns in holsters, and detectives playing cat-and-mouse with suspects. It's also the location where the police bring all the marijuana they ever confiscate. **See also cops; Super Troopers** ▶

POLITICS A once-noble pursuit undertaken by some of the smartest, most selfless individuals in the country that has devolved into name-calling, finger-pointing, and temper tantrums better suited for a kindergarten classroom than the US Capitol. In some countries, politics is a mere formality as the same person always wins. In the United States, however, belonging to a particular political party is roughly equivalent to rooting for the Red Sox instead of the Yankees. While normally immune to such fanaticism, pot smokers are arguably the most susceptible to political affiliation. This could have something to do with the fact that legalization is, at its heart, a political issue. However, it is more likely because only pot smokers have the patience and concentration to allow them to watch CNN twenty hours a day.

POLLINATOR A type of multi-tiered grinder that contains a fine mesh screen above the bottom level that can be used to filter out all smokable plant material, leaving behind the THC-bloated trichomes. If one has a lot of time, patience, and the proper equipment, one can use these harvested trichomes to create hashish. However, if one is like most smokers, one can simply sprinkle the trichomes on top of the weed about to be smoked, thus negating the entire reason for purchasing a pollinator. **See also grinder**

POP The correct way to refer to any carbonated drink that isn't seltzer or tonic water if one is from one part of a country, and a really stupid way to refer to any carbonated drink that isn't seltzer or tonic water if one is from some other part of the country. Pop is an essential item to have on hand when smoking large quantities of marijuana, as it can be used to alleviate cotton mouth or stave off an impending coughing fit. It also happens to be delicious, but this fact often goes unnoticed by particularly wasted smokers who are just chugging it faster than their taste buds can register the potpourri of flavors.

POPCORN Regular corn that can achieve its full potential only after the application of heat and artificial butter topping. It is an exceptionally popular food among pot smokers because it meets all of the necessary munchie requirements: It's salty, delicious, there's lots of it, and it's microwavable. The only proper method for consuming popcorn is to take large fistfuls and shove them into one's mouth hole repeatedly.

POPEYE THE SAILOR MAN World-renowned cartoon sailor man created in 1929 who is strong to the finish because he eats his spinach. Popeye has some instantly recognizable and unique traits: his tumor-sized forearms, his tattoos, his white sailor cap, his undying affection for Olive Oyl, a pipe that seems to switch sides in his mouth based on which way his head is turned, and his penchant for eating spinach. Popeye has become the subject of speculation that he was a pothead, as questions have been raised: What's in his pipe? What is that spinach really? Why does it give him super strength? Some scholars have speculated that spinach is a not-so-subtle reference to marijuana (spinach was used as a euphemism for pot within jazz circles in the 1920s and 1930s), and one 1980s Popeye strip showed him and Wimpy picking up "pure Bolivian spinach." The strip has gone through many animators and writers over the years, so in all likelihood some writers infused explicit pot references to Popeye and others paid no attention to it. Nevertheless, the more credibility this theory gains, the quicker Popeye becomes the coolest nonagenarian in the world to pot smokers, next to Noam Chomsky. **See also euphemisms**

POSTERS Mass-produced decorative wall hangings marketed toward teenagers and young adults who generally cannot afford to purchase expensive works of art to adorn their walls. They generally fall into one of a few different categories, including bands, celebrities, and snarky references to drugs and alcohol. The final category is most popular among the pot-smoking community, as it allows the owner to express his or her 420-friendly status by taping a 32" × 32" marijuana leaf on the door or placing a replica of the *Mona Lisa* smoking a joint over the bed. Bonus points if it is black-light sensitive. **See also clichés**

POT A slang term used to refer to marijuana, the popularity of which rivals that of the euphemism "weed." The word is probably a shortening of a Spanish word for marijuana, "potiguaya." A few people believe it is in reference to how the drug affects the human mind and body, in that it makes the user feel like an inanimate cooking utensil. There is little to no evidence to defend this theory, but it certainly sounds plausible.

POT BROWNIES A popular baked good that has been prepared with a secret ingredient that, given the name of the dessert, is not a secret at all. Often called "special" brownies, the treat is made by following a traditional recipe for brownies but substituting pot butter in place of regular butter. Once finished, the confection appears identical to a normal brownie to the naked eye. Any differences will not be discovered until about a half hour or so after one has ingested the brownie. When consuming pot brownies it is very important to have additional munchies on hand that do not contain any marijuana. Otherwise, the temptation to consume more brownies could be unbearable. **See also edibles; pot butter; pot oil ▼**

POT BUTTER An essential ingredient when cooking with cannabis that consists of ordinary butter that has been infused with the mind-enhancing substance THC through the application of heat, time, and grim determination. When baked into snacks like cookies and brownies, the time it takes for the THC to be absorbed in the stomach and then permeate the blood stream can be significantly longer than when pot is smoked. If one does not feel the effects within thirty minutes of consumption, it is wise to be patient and resist the urge to continue eating them. The experience is worth the wait. **See also edibles; pot oil**

POT CAKE Simply put, cake with pot in it. While this application may seem like an ingenious idea for a pot smoker's birthday party, it can be difficult to section the finished product into uniform individual servings. In theory, each person should get a single slice of cake, but how does one define a slice? Most people would judge it as two slanted cuts meeting at a single point to create a piece that is approximately two inches wide at the end, but what if one's friend pulls a Garfield, cuts a thin sliver out, and bogarts the rest of the cake? Better to avoid the problem entirely and stick with cupcakes. **See also edibles; pot butter; pot oil**

POT OIL Similar to pot butter, but made instead with any type of edible oil. THC is fat-soluble, so oils with higher fat contents like coconut and palm are better suited for this culinary adventure. In its most basic form, pot oil is created by heating oil and sautéing the desired amount of bud in said oil for an extended period of time (usually from thirty minutes to an hour). Once strained, the resulting oil can be drizzled on pasta, bread, or directly into the mouth. However, only two of these applications could be considered "good" ideas. **See also edibles; pot butter**

POTATO CHIPS A munchie staple consisting of paper-thin potato slices that have been deep-fried and coated with salt or a number of other flavorings like garlic, pepper, sour cream, vinegar, and various herbs. The invention of the delicacy is generally attributed to Saratoga chef George Crum who, in the mid-1800s, served them to a disgruntled customer complaining his French fries were too thick. While this fanciful tale makes for a good story, it is far more likely that Crum just got high one evening and started throwing different foods into the deep fryer to see what would happen.

POTHEAD A derogatory term directed toward people who smoke marijuana to excess. While many nonsmokers use this term as a blanket descriptor for all people who smoke weed, this is a misconception. A pothead smokes at least five times a day and has given up on all life pursuits that are not directly related to the acquisition and subsequent smoking of weed. In the late 1970s, a simple test was developed to determine if someone is in fact a pothead, and it can still be used today. A small amount of pot is placed on a table next to a lighter and a crisp $100 bill in an empty room. If the subject pockets the money and leaves, the subject is a square. If the subject pockets the money first and then the pot, the subject is your average casual pot smoker. If the subject scans the scene, uses the money to roll a joint, and lights up, he or she is most certainly a pothead. ▸

POTTERY The art of creating vases, bowls, cups, flower pots, paperweights, and other assorted ceramic ware by using wet clay, a potter's wheel, and one's own hands to shape the creation before heating it in a kiln to cause permanent change. Only the dumbest smokers attend pottery classes in hopes that they are, in fact, classes on how to grow pot. **See also sculpture**

POWER HIT A single hit of marijuana that defies the ordinary limits of the human body. When a smoker takes a power hit, he or she proceeds to exhale clouds of smoke as onlookers watch in horror as a thick gray cloud continues to billow out long after the threshold of human lung capacity has been exceeded. Witnessing this event is a cause of celebration, however, as it is believed to indicate that 420 will come early that particular year. Unless of course the stoner sees his or her shadow, in which case the group must wait until April 20 to celebrate.

PREGNANT A slang term used to refer to a marijuana cigarette that has an unbalanced level of pot sitting in the middle, causing the joint to bulge outward. This is terrible news for someone who will get the joint at the beginning or end of a session. This is joyous news, however, if one happens to be in the middle of the smoking circle. Be wary of someone who offers to roll a joint only under the condition that he or she can choose the smoking order.

PRIMUS An American rock band whose lineup consists of singer and bassist Les Claypool, guitarist Larry "Ler" LaLonde, and drummer Tim "Herb" Alexander. While known mostly to the public at large as the band that wrote the *South Park* intro music, Primus has gained a cult following of fans attracted to their diverse and unique sound and ability to continue to not take themselves too seriously, a perfect combination for pot smokers. Not only has Claypool dubbed his record label "Prawn Song Records" (a reference to the Led Zeppelin song "Swan Song"), but he also encourages fans to shout "Primus Sucks!" at shows, instead of the more typical and expected "Primus rocks!" The opposite day–style slogan has caused widespread confusion among new Primus fans, who are known to out themselves by responding to the proclamation by saying, "Dude, Primus rules!" **See also Sublime**

PRISON A building specifically designed to keep dangerous criminals like rapists, murderers, thieves, and arsonists safely contained and away from law-abiding citizens. Unfortunately, the prisons are also overflowing with individuals who don't really belong there, like scattered overzealous pot smokers who decided it would be a great idea to buy 1.1 ounces of marijuana during a trip to Mexico and bring it back to America. We're working on getting this issue corrected ASAP. **See also decriminalization; legalization** ▼

PROJECT MKULTRA An experiment conducted by the US government from the early 1950s to at least the mid-1960s and the best use of taxpayer dollars in US history. The project served as a way to study the effects of LSD, cocaine, marijuana, and other psychoactive drugs on human behavior. Usually the drugs were administered without the subject's consent or knowledge. American author Ken Kesey was a subject in the experiments, and they shaped the writer's future book *One Flew Over the Cuckoo's Nest*. Today, Project MKUltra is probably best known for its impact on Eleven, a psychokinetic and telepathic protagonist of Netflix series *Stranger Things*. The project is especially important to know for the pot smoker, because if and when someone invents time-travel technology, the smoker should know to go back to 1953 in San Francisco and try to look as shady and forgettable as possible. Such behavior will likely result in getting picked up and given free LSD by the government. **See also *Sometimes a Great Notion*; time travel**

PROPOSITION 215 A landmark win for proponents of medical marijuana and a giant leap toward the dream of legalization. The proposition appeared on the ballot in California in 1996 and, among other things, allowed individuals who had been prescribed

cannabis by a qualified doctor to culti-
vate the plant for personal use. It also
protected them from criminal liability
should they be found in possession
of the drug. The new regulations set
in place by Proposition 215 have
changed since then. However, the
general principles remain as of 2010.
While the drug is generally reserved
for patients with serious diseases like
cancer and AIDS, there's no harm
in going to California and trying to
convince a doctor that one's hangnail
would really feel a lot better with
the proper application of medical
marijuana. **See also medical marijuana**

PROTESTS Events wherein groups of
like-minded individuals gather
together at an appointed place and
time to spread a particular message
with the help of chants, poster board,
Sharpie markers, and warm weather.
Because all protesters really do is
stand around holding signs, pot
smokers often adopt this as their primary means of self-expression, especially when issues of pot are
concerned. At first glance it may
appear very productive. However, little is solved during a protest other
than getting some much-needed sun,
spouting rhetoric, and fighting with
passersby who don't believe legalizing

weed would eliminate the national
debt. ▼

PUBLIC TRANSPORTATION Preferred
method of transport for environmen-
tally conscious and law-abiding pot
smokers. (Law-abiding pot smokers
may seem like an oxymoron, but in
the law-abiding smoker's mind, smoking pot is not a crime, although oper-
ating heavy machinery while smoking
is.) Public transportation is filled
with shady characters, degenerates,
delinquents, weirdos, creeps, pick-
pockets, and maybe murderers. As
such, it is unique in that it is a locale
in which a pothead can exist as one of
the more trustworthy, reliable people

in the immediate vicinity, a feeling the smoker is probably not used to experiencing.

PUFF A word used to denote a single intake of marijuana, which is synonymous with the term "hit." It can also be used in reference to the general experience of smoking marijuana, similar to "toke" or "get high."
See also hit; puff, puff, pass ▼

PUFF, PUFF, PASS A common method of smoking marijuana wherein participants organize themselves in a static configuration, preferably a circle, and take two hits before passing the smoking apparatus of choice to the next person. In general this process has proved to be an effective method of ensuring each smoker receives an equal amount of marijuana. However, a strange phenomenon has been known to occur wherein otherwise intelligent individuals struggle with rudimentary concepts like counting to two, telling time, and differentiating between right and left.

"PUFF THE MAGIC DRAGON" A song based on a poem written by Leonard Lipton and popularized by the band Peter, Paul and Mary about a little boy and his magical dragon who lives in a land called Honah Lee. Or a song based on a poem written by Leonard Lipton and popularized by the band Peter, Paul and Mary all about smoking pot and getting high. The song features a little boy named Jackie Paper (read: rolling papers) and a whimsical dragon named Puff (read: toke, drag, hit). While the song's creators insist it has absolutely nothing to do with Mary Jane, the urban legend has become so pervasive that Ben Stiller cites it as fact in the 2000 film *Meet the Parents*. And as anyone knows, if Ben Stiller says it, then it must be true. **See also euphemisms**

PULL The act of putting one's lips to the end of a smoking apparatus, be it joint, blunt, bong, bowl, or hookah, and sucking smoke into the lungs. While there are plenty of other slang terms used to describe this process, the powers that be felt one more was in order. Similar to the human pyramid, it does not need to exist. But it's nice to know it's there.

PULP FICTION A 1994 Quentin Tarantino film following a menagerie of characters whose lives intertwine throughout the city of Los Angeles. The film stars John Travolta as Vincent Vega and Samuel L. Jackson as Jules Winnfield; these two mobsters spend the greater part of the film trying to deliver a briefcase to their boss without getting shot by deadbeat twenty-somethings or arrested after inadvertently shooting one of said twenty-somethings in the face. They also spend their time talking. A lot. So much so that the film's most memorable scene is a short dialogue between Vince and Jules where Vince details his recent sabbatical in Europe. While explaining the nuanced differences between McDonald's menu items in France and the United States, Vince also enlightens Jules about the

wonders of Amsterdam smoke shops. Add in the fact that several clocks in the movie are discreetly set to 4:20 and a pot smoker has one of the most critically acclaimed cannabis-friendly films of all time. **See also Tarantino, Quentin**

PURPLE HAZE A particularly potent strain of cannabis known for its violet-tinted trichomes and for providing a clean, energetic high. The debate over what came first—the weed or the Hendrix song—is a frequent argument among stoners, though it's most likely that the plant was named after the tune. Despite the musician's repeated denials, many fans believe the song's true inspiration to be a superpotent form of LSD that was served up on purple blotters at the 1967 Monterey Pop Festival, at which Hendrix performed. Absurd urban legends persist that Purple Haze is, itself, laced with a powerful hallucinogenic drug. Not so. It's just that good. **See also Hendrix, Jimi**

Qq

QUALITY A term used to refer to the inherent level of goodness an object possesses. In some instances this can be relatively arbitrary, such as is the case with brands of baking soda. However, items like marijuana have very tangible differences that can be used to assess quality. Weight, color, moisture content, visual evidence of trichomes and crystals, fragrance, and taste can all determine the quality of a sample of weed. **See also schwag; stress**

QUANTITY A term used to refer to how much of a certain item one is currently in possession of, or, in the abstract sense, how much one would like to possess. In the landmark Supreme Court decision of *Quantity v. Quality* (Nashville, December Term, 1926), quantity was in fact ruled to be better than quality. A rather unusual turn of events since, in most situations, it's quality that's more significant.

QUAP A slang term used when purchasing large amounts of marijuana that refers to four ounces, or approximately one quarter of one pound. The average smoker will never purchase this much pot for personal use, so this is a term reserved primarily for dealers and groups of friends buying in bulk. Many weedophiles often dream of purchasing a quap and using it to roll one giant blunt. However, the $1,000 price tag generally deters all but the most dedicated smokers.

QUAYLE, DAN (BORN FEBRUARY 4, 1947) Former vice president and spoiled rich kid who did very little in life besides use his political power and rich family to pull strings for him to dodge the draft and attend law school. Quayle admitted to smoking pot, and drug dealers have come forward about his buying from them, but more relevant are his gems of ridiculous quotes. Read aloud, they are almost impossible not to crack up at, especially while high. On Mars: "Mars is essentially in the same orbit…somewhat the same distance from the sun, which is very important. We have seen pictures where there are canals, we believe, and water. If there is water, that means there is oxygen. If oxygen, that means we can breathe." On the environment: "The best thing about rain forests is they never suffer from drought." If Quayle released a comedy album of his greatest hits, it would be the number one seller in the *420 Magazine* gift shop. **See also *420 Magazine*; Bush, George W.**

QUICK FIX A brand of synthetic urine (yes, really) that can purportedly be used in place of real urine to help one pass a drug test. Each kit comes with a two-ounce container of fake pee, a heat pack, and a temperature strip to ensure the ringer matches the temperature of normal urine. The product works wonders if the user is allowed a private bathroom, but its practicality breaks down when one must urinate under the watchful eye of a lab tech.

QUIET SMOKER A type of pot aficionado whose body chemistry reacts with THC in such a way that he or she becomes completely incapable of human speech immediately after ingesting pot. These smokers will often appear attentive and involved in whatever event or conversation is going on around them. However, they will make no attempt to communicate with anyone in the group. Depending on their normal demeanor, this can be either a welcome break from their loudmouthed persona or simply par for the course with their usual sheepish disposition. **See also antisocial smoker; artistic smoker; enhancement smoker; intellectual smoker; lazy smoker; paranoid smoker**

QUOTING MOVIES A common pastime among pot enthusiasts that requires an encyclopedic knowledge of film dialogue—especially if said film has even a tangential connection to the world of marijuana. To an outsider, it may appear as if individuals engaging in this practice are speaking a foreign language, when in fact they are simply rehashing every single inane piece of dialogue from their favorite movies. The social event almost always begins with one person posing the question: "Has anybody ever seen that movie with Jack Black?" If the answer is yes, the individual will then quote a line and laughter will hopefully ensue. If the answer is no, the individual will meekly respond with, "Oh," and look down at the floor while an awkward moment of silence ensues. **See also movies**

Rr

RADIOHEAD A five-piece English rock band whose layered sound, complex arrangements, and cryptic lyrics make them a favorite of the pot-smoking crowd. In fact, most non-smokers will claim not to get Radiohead. Smokers, however, are at risk for growing so enamored with the band that some, for at least a short time, may claim lead singer Thom Yorke as their personal god. Always attempt to record this and use it against the smoker later. Radiohead's 2007 album *In Rainbows* was released online and the band allowed users to name their own price for its download, an idea Yorke said they came up with while the band was a little high in the studio. Radiohead is unique in pot-smoking circles in that few of their songs contain direct references to getting high, though they're so multi-interpretable it's possible they *all* reference getting high.

RAKFISK A regional dish found in areas of Norway consisting of a fish that has been cured and allowed to ferment for several months. Deemed the anti-munchie by some pot smokers, rakfisk is one of only a handful of foods that the degree to which a person would need to be high in order to crave it exceeds the limitations of the human body. Other examples of such foods include casu marzu (maggot-ridden cheese), balut (partially developed duck or chicken egg), and baby mice wine (exactly what it sounds like).

RAMEN A Japanese soup consisting of noodles, various vegetables, and meat in a flavorful broth. The dish gained popularity in restaurants after World War II. However, it was not perfected until 1958 when Momofuku Ando, founder of Nissin Foods and hero of college students and pot smokers the world over, invented the inexpensive instant version common today. In less time than it takes to pack a bowl and smoke it, one can prepare a delicious snack with enough sodium to kill a small horse that should cool off just in time to stave off the beginning phase of the munchies.

RASTA PASTA A form of pasta that can take on a variety of shapes, sizes, and flavor combinations, but always contains a particular type of herb that grants the eater increased powers of perception and understanding. The general method of delivery for the pot is to sauté it in oil or butter before adding additional spices to create the base for a sauce that is then poured over boiled noodles. The layers of flavor found in most pasta dishes often mask the marijuana taste, so it can be difficult to detect the presence of weed in the dish. Just be patient, it's there.

RASTAFARIAN A religious affiliation characterized by dreadlocks, Bob Marley music, Jamaican accents, red-, white-, green-, and black-striped woven caps, and excessive consumption of marijuana. The movement started in the 1930s and was born out of the Christianity that had consumed Jamaica in the nineteenth century when British Christian abolitionists joined former slaves in the struggle to end slavery. Rastas believe that they and all members of the African diaspora are exiles in Babylon and are destined to return to Zion, led by Haile Selassie I, the former emperor of Ethiopia. Not knowing this, many white American hippies often claim to be Rasta in an effort to come across as both trendy and worldly, and to legitimize their pot habits. Everyone else, however, outside of maybe their hippie friends, is secretly embarrassed for them. **See also Jamaica; Marley, Bob**

REEFER A slang term for marijuana generally employed by people who don't smoke marijuana. Such people are also prone to calling it "dope," "wacky tobaccy," "puff the magic dragon," or "whatever you call that stuff that all the kids are smoking these days."

REEFER MADNESS A.k.a. *Tell Your Children*, a propagandizing 1936 film that used scare tactics and sensationalism to keep rebellious teenagers off the titular reefer. Supposedly funded by a church group and shot by down-on-his-luck director Louis Gasnier, whose successful silent filmmaking career combusted with the advent of talkies, *Reefer Madness* revolves around a group of youngsters whose forays into marijuana smoking lead them down a dark road of insanity, suicide, murder, and, worst of all, jazz music. Though recut and ultimately distributed as an exploitation film, *Reefer Madness* didn't find an audience until the 1970s, when Keith Stroup, founder of the National Organization for the Reform of Marijuana Laws, began screening it at pro-pot rallies. The film has since become a mainstay of the American cult-film canon. **See also NORML**

REFRIGERATION TECHNOLOGY

The development of artificial cooling for food and beverages that has been instrumental in human capacity to expand, progress, propagate the earth, and feed the hungry, using various methods such as ice storage, air compression, and gas absorption. Refrigeration is instrumental in keeping food fresh and readily available for pot smokers to binge on easily and quickly, with just a short walk from the couch to the kitchen, which is often too much work as it is. In fact, smokers nowadays don't know how good they have it. Back in the prehistoric era, before refrigeration technology existed, hunter-gatherer weedophiles had to either preplan by killing a giant deer immediately *before* getting high or go out for food *after* getting high. This usually involved climbing trees for potentially hazardous berries or haphazardly throwing a spear in the general vicinity of a cluster of animals.

REHAB A location where concerned friends and family send their pot-smoking friend after an intervention at which they express their concern and disappointment that the smoker is throwing his or her life away. **See also clean; Winehouse, Amy**

RESIN The sticky residue of burned pot that collects inside of pieces or other smoking devices. This substance is particularly harsh but can be smoked if one's connect gets burned. In dire situations, bowls and slides can be scraped and the resultant resin smoked again. Kind of the equivalent of a dog eating the same ice-cream cone twice. ▸

RIG A device used when dabbing. Traditionally, a rig consists of a water pipe with an attached metal piece, called a nail. The user heats the nail (which is sometimes fancy and battery powered, but sometimes just gets heated using an old-fashioned blow torch) and uses another metal tool to place a piece of concentrate on the nail. The smoker inhales through the pipe for a satisfying, potent high. **See also dabs**

ROACH A slang term used to describe a marijuana cigarette, more specifically the small nubbin left once a joint has been smoked as far down as is possible without burning the fingertips. Without the aid of a roach clip, a roach is actually one of the most useless things known to modern man. With the aid of a roach clip, however, it is magically transformed into a delectable afternoon treat. Over time, many roaches can be saved up and combined into a bowl or even a new joint, beautifully illustrating the process of rebirth pervasive in many religions. **See also joint**

ROACH CLIP Any nonflammable object that can be employed to hold the end of a marijuana cigarette to prevent injury to the hands and fingers of the smoker. A hemostat is the preferred instrument, although smokers without access to surgical equipment have been known to use everything from simple paper clips to artificial limbs. **See also Arrested Development**

ROGEN, SETH (BORN APRIL 15, 1982) A comedic actor whose mere presence in a movie is usually enough to signify that someone (probably Rogen) is going to be smoking some pot. A big surprise to absolutely no one, Rogen is an outspoken cannabis supporter, who launched his own company, Houseplant, in hopes of both educating users and providing quality recreational products. He is best known for his work in the films *Knocked Up, Superbad, Pineapple Express, Zack and Miri Make a Porno, This Is the End, Neighbors, Sausage Party,* and *Long Shot.* Although Rogen has received much praise for his acting ability, the off-screen version of Rogen, a happy-go-lucky pot-smoking jokester, is arguably no different than the characters he plays. He isn't acting in his films any more than Michael Jordan was when he played Michael Jordan in the film *Space Jam.* **See also Apatow, Judd; Knocked Up; Pineapple Express; Superbad**

ROLL The act of creating a joint, spliff, blunt, or other rolled marijuana-consumption device. After a lengthy debate over who is the best roller, or whose dad once rolled a joint with one hand while driving eighty miles an hour down I-90, pot smokers eventually decide who will be rolling the joint for the session. The designated roller should be one with a proven track record of well-formed joints and not just a weekend warrior who watched *Almost Famous* the night before. Technique is of the utmost importance, and experienced rollers will have a well-defined style or hallmark to their joints. The seasoned hand-roller will also consider those who use auto-rollers total wusses. ▼

ROLLER A device that takes the guesswork out of rolling a joint and produces them mechanically. The device consists of two parallel bars that spin in a circular motion. Marijuana is loaded between the rollers, which are then spun to distribute the pot in an even layer. Finally, a sheet of rolling papers is inserted between the bars, which are then spun a final time to produce a perfectly packed jay. For smokers lacking dexterity, this device allows them to smoke on their own without the need to seek out friends with more nimble fingers.

ROLLING PAPERS Thin sheets of material usually made from hemp, wood pulp, or rice that can be used to transform loose tobacco, marijuana, or other herbs into a neat, uniform tube just begging to be smoked.

ROSS, BOB (OCTOBER 29, 1942–JULY 4, 1995) The host of popular 1980s PBS TV show *The Joy of Painting*. There is arguably no single greater experience than to witness an episode of Bob Ross's show while high. His short-order painting style is simple, but the way he quickly waves his paintbrush around the canvas, throws in some "happy little clouds," and produces an amazing work of art in about thirty minutes is nothing short of magical. His voice is so calming that many viewers claim his program eliminated any need for them to smoke pot. However, they continued to do so anyway. **See also sleepiness**

RUDERALIS A species of cannabis known for its low THC content and, therefore, not commonly used for recreational purposes. Instead, its higher CBD content means that it's often used to treat medical issues like anxiety, epilepsy, and even cancer. ▶

RUNNING A recreational activity one can indulge in for health reasons, or a necessary response when one is smoking pot and encounters the flashing lights of a police car or an authoritative voice asking, "Hey, what's going on over there?" It is similar to walking, only much faster (hopefully) and carries a greater sense of urgency.

RUSH (BAND) A seminal prog-rock band from Toronto, Canada, that was active from 1968 to 2018. If one sees them in concert, smoking a joint beforehand is highly encouraged as it may be his or her only chance of surviving the thirty-eight-minute Neil Peart drum-solo that erupts in the middle of "Tom Sawyer."

RUSH (FEELING) A feeling of euphoria one experiences after engaging in activities like bungee jumping or smoking marijuana. The feeling is a result of several chemicals in one's body, such as adrenaline and dopamine, being released in the interest of self-preservation or as reward for doing something the body considers to be a good idea. Clearly the body is never wrong, so this phenomenon is considered irrefutable evidence that smoking pot is, in general, a wise decision. By this logic, similar wise decisions include jumping out of airplanes, bare-knuckle boxing, and purposely engaging and subsequently fleeing from stampeding bulls.

Ss

SAGAN, CARL (NOVEMBER 9, 1934–DECEMBER 20, 1996) An author who, in his most noted work, explains how the universe might be a cosmic calendar. For example, if the Big Bang is going to be January 1 and today is midnight on December 31, all human existence would be the last five seconds before midnight—the blink of an eye. Sagan then proceeds to enter a carpeted spaceship that zooms to Alpha Centauri while synth music blares in the background. This is his PBS series *Cosmos*. And behind the astronomy, Sagan creates beautiful metaphors that tie the ancient past to the distance future, the shores of our seas to the "great cosmic oceans" above. Sagan is like the smartest pot smoker one has ever heard—but the high never ends. **See also intellectual smoker**

SALAD BOWL A single bowl of pot that contains multiple strains of marijuana, usually resulting from a number of participants contributing a small portion from their own personal stashes. When the varieties mix, the end result can be either a glorious marriage of flavors and attributes from a mosaic of top-grade pot or a disastrous combination of dried-up schwag. If one's weed already sucks, combining it with equally poor-quality bud isn't going to make it suck any less.

SALT A table condiment consisting of sodium and chlorine (sodium chloride) that adds flavor and texture to almost any food item and is one of the primary food groups for all weed aficionados. Salt comes in a variety of strengths and flavors, such as table salt, sea salt, smoked sea salt, and kosher salt, among others. It is not only delicious but also essential in melting snow. It is also a compound that is required for the functioning of animal life, as it is a main bodily electrolyte, and it also helps in food preservation. In short, salt is a miracle. Too much salt intake may lead to high blood pressure and other health risks, though, but this is of no consequence to the recently inebriated. Pot smokers are known to pound through an entire bag of potato chips and then reach for the French fries before just emptying the saltshaker directly into their mouths and, finally, setting up an IV directly to their veins.

SAMSON A fictional drug lord played by Clarence Williams III in the 1998 film *Half Baked*. Threatened by the appearance of a rogue pot-dealing syndicate known as Mr. Smiley Face, Samson threatens the enterprising group of smokers in an attempt to eliminate the competition, and eventually unleashes his army of henchwomen to kill the group. This ends the same way all drug disputes end: The ghost of Jerry Garcia spontaneously emerges from a pouch of ashes to render Samson unconscious with his guitar. Naturally. **See also Chappelle, Dave; Garcia, Jerry; *Half Baked***

SANDWICHES The chameleon of the munchie world, capable of taking on any number of shapes and ingredient combinations. One starts with a blank slate of two pieces of bread and builds the sandwich by shoving things like lettuce, tomato, ham, turkey, bologna, pickles, and bacon between the slices. This can be a simple process or a complex one, depending on the number of ingredients as well as the amount of cannabis consumed by the person making it. ▼

SARCASM The use of excessive inflection and over-the-top word choice to illustrate the opposite of what is being stated or enacted. Typically sarcasm is used in the following manner: "Oh, yeah, I *love* the thought of going to see *Fifty Shades of Grey*. That would be *so* much fun." Sarcasm is easy to detect when sober but becomes increasingly subtle and thus difficult to pick up on when high. Pot smokers may sit still upon hearing a potentially sarcastic comment, dissect it, and wonder if it was meant to be sarcastic or not. Two hours later, when the smoker decides, no, it probably wasn't sarcasm, he'll return to reality only to find a note that says his friends left 115 minutes earlier to go to a movie, and that the smoker wasn't responding to smelling salts.

SATIVA One of the meta-categorizations of marijuana, along with indica. Sativa is slightly different from indica in that its leaves are longer and thinner (often the pot leaf represented in pop culture) as opposed to shorter and stubbier. And the high is more uplifting and, depending on circumstances, energizing. Sativa is for the daytime smoker, and many strains allow smokers to remain upbeat and productive. Sativa is also typified by its height, growing as much as twenty-five feet high, and its branches can extend up to three feet, making it largely grown as wild marijuana and not in urban areas. **See also indica**

SATURDAY NIGHT LIVE A late-evening TV comedy for which a fat joint is absolutely essential. In a lot of cases, no amount of weed can make the actors on *Saturday Night Live* funny. Except when Tina Fey was involved. And John Belushi. And Will Ferrell. And one time David Spade. But only that one time.

SAVAGES A 2012 crime thriller film starring Taylor Kitsch and Aaron Taylor-Johnson as two marijuana growers who are best known for their incredibly potent strain and for their open relationship with Ophelia Sage, played by Blake Lively. The plot involves a disagreement with a Mexican drug cartel, John Travolta as a corrupt DEA agent, and gratuitous scenes of people getting high, just in case the viewer forgot what the movie was about. Which, if they were high, they actually might have.

SCALE A device used to measure weight that can range from the complex digital variety to less complex mechanical versions. Scales are an invaluable tool for drug dealers who use them to ensure their product is evenly broken down from bulk amounts into smaller increments for resale. The credibility of a dealer can often be determined by the sophistication of the scale he or she employs. If it's digital, it's safe to assume he or she is on the up-and-up. If he or she employs the "hold something of comparable weight in each hand and see which feels heavier" approach, then it might be wise to buy elsewhere.
See also eighth; ounce ▶

SCHWAG A term used to define marijuana that is of the lowest-available quality. This grade of weed can hardly be considered pot, as it is frequently little more than a conglomeration of stems, oregano, and dried-up shake. It is not recommended that schwag be smoked unless under the direst of circumstances, such as when one flushes his higher-grade stash down the toilet during an unfortunate bout of paranoia. **See also stress**

SCORE The physical act of obtaining weed from a dealer, friend, relative, stranger, homeless person, or hyperintelligent gorilla capable of communicating through gestures. The term is so named because the feeling of transforming from a person who is in need of pot to a person possessing one's own marijuana is akin to earning a point in every game played by modern humans. ▼

SCRABBLE A game consisting of a board with 225 individual squares upon which players place lettered tiles of differing point values to form words. While it is generally not required that players get high before playing, the additional powers of concentration, focus, and creative thought garnered from smoking pot give the inebriated player a distinct advantage over those who abstain from getting high. However, there is no such word as "zoqui," even if it's attempted on a triple-word score down 100 points.

SCREEN A small, thin piece of rigid mesh material (usually metal) that is placed inside of a bowl, pipe, or other smoking device to prevent unwanted ash particles from entering the mouth and lungs of the user. Many types of paraphernalia do not come with screens. However, they can be purchased at any hardware store for several cents and cut down to the preferred size. Despite their inexpensive cost and ready availability, it usually requires no fewer than seven unintentional ingestions of hot ash before the average stoner builds up the motivation necessary to install one.

SCULPTURE The preferred deflection used to explain the existence of a large glass bong, bubbler, or pipe on the dressers of countless stoners around the world. When asked why the sculpture conspicuously smells like pot, the only acceptable response is, "How do you know what pot smells like?" This will usually result in the nosy person mumbling an apology and shuffling out of the room. ▸

SEATTLE HEMPFEST A success story of the festival circuit. Seattle Hempfest began in 1991 as a modestly scaled music and pro-legalization demonstration and has since developed into a three-day event and the world's largest demonstration of pro-marijuana advocacy. The 2008 festival attracted over three hundred thousand people. While there are tons of festivals and gatherings promoting the legalization of marijuana, Seattle's actually has some practical gains to point to. Since the first Hempfest, Washington has legalized medical and recreational marijuana. The Hempfest still continues, because why discontinue such a great party?

SECONDHAND SMOKE A by-product of the process of igniting any smokable product (tobacco, marijuana, hashish, etc.) and inhaling the resulting dark cloud. After a period of time, the smoke must be exhaled from the lungs and into the air. As a result, individuals in the surrounding area can be exposed to the THC-laden smoke and get high through no direct effort of their own. This passive form of smoking is ideal for frugal smokers who would like to get high but prefer not to actually pay for it.

SEEDS Tiny, hard, circular objects contained within the innards of a plant or fruit. Seed presence in a baggie means the weed purchase is slightly overpriced, as seeds weigh more than the plant and are also unsmokable. Smoking seeds would result in nausea, bad headache high, and painful moaning. However, seeds can be useful for the industrious smoker, as they can be planted to create new and free marijuana. Germinating and growing weed from seeds can be as simple as purchasing a pot, dirt, and plant food. However, when inebriated, smokers will typically try to bypass this process and just plant the seeds in dirt and "see if it works." Usually, they just end up with a frown and much time wasted. **See also paper towel germination** ▼

SELF-CARE In the words of *Parks and Recreation*'s Donna Meagle and Tom Haverford: "Treat Yo' Self!" Basically, self-care is anything a person does to take care of her- or himself, whether that's physically, mentally, or emotionally. It's an important way to decrease stress, reduce anxiety, and improve one's mood, but it can also prove to be a slippery slope into slackerdom. As the pot smoker knows, lighting up a joint can simultaneously be both, which may very well mean that smoking some pot is actually the number one best activity for self-care of all time.

SENSI Short for "sensimilla," a colloquial Anglicization of the Spanish term "sin semilla," meaning "no seeds," or marijuana produced from an unfertilized female cannabis plant. The upside of sensi is that, because the plant's THC-packed buds never mature into seeds, the resulting harvest is chock-full of baked-inducing goodness. The downside is that, due to the lack of seeds, it's impossible to breed sensi-producing plants. This harsh botanical reality makes sensi a pricier toke than other seedier brands, but that's all right. Seedless is always better.

SESSION A discrete instance of one or more persons inhaling marijuana with the intent of achieving a high. Sessions have been known to spontaneously instantiate in any place with a high concentration of boredom, video games, and nugs. **See also circle; nugs**

SHAGGY A key character in the popular cartoon series *Scooby-Doo, Where Are You!* Best friend (and owner of) the titular canine Scooby-Doo, it's a long-standing online theory that, while the rest of the gang is off solving mysteries, Scooby and Shaggy are hiding out with the express purpose of smoking a fatty. With his baggy clothes and unkempt hairstyle, Shaggy is the quintessential hippie of the group. He's a bit absentminded, silly, and, most convincingly, is absolutely always hungry. Sounds to us like someone has a pretty terrible case of the munchies.

SHAKE A dried-up conglomeration of marijuana particles left at the bottom of a bag of weed. Little preparation needs to be done to the actual marijuana before smoking shake, as it does not need to be removed from a stem and/or ground. Still, one must take several measures to prepare the body. It is important to have no fewer than four Marlboro Reds immediately prior, as the harsh cigarette smoke acts as a buffer for what will certainly be equally harsh shake smoke. Stretching is not necessary, although it is advisable in case one needs to run to grab a glass of water in the event of a coughing fit. Lastly, one should eliminate any expectations of enjoying this particular smoking experience and focus instead on not waiting so long before buying more pot in the future.

SHAKESPEARE, WILLIAM (EST. APRIL 23, 1564–APRIL 23, 1616) A sixteenth-century English poet and playwright whose work was popular among both aristocrats and peasants alike in his own day, but who achieved unparalleled fame and praise after his death thanks to a litany of literary masterpieces like *Hamlet*, *Macbeth*, and *Romeo and Juliet*. Shakespeare's style of writing is rife with crass humor, double entendres, and metaphors that have confounded scholars and high school English teachers for centuries. One of his works, "Sonnet 76," has sparked substantial controversy thanks to lines five through eight, which read, "Why write I still all one, ever the same/And keep invention in a noted weed,/That every word doth almost tell my name,/Showing their birth, and where they did proceed?" Some claim "noted weed" actually means "familiar clothing" in this passage, but it's quite clear what the phrase actually means: Shakespeare, the most famous person ever to put pen to paper, was a card-carrying pot smoker. ▼

SHAMPOO BOTTLES Containers of varying shapes and sizes used to house a hair-cleansing product known as "shampoo." Because shampoo has a reputation for covering up unpleasant odors, the bottles are often used for the storing and transporting of marijuana. In theory, if one were to nestle a small amount of pot in with the shampoo, unknowing humans will be fooled into believing one intends to use it to stay clean and fresh rather than as a means of getting baked. It is best not to employ this trick in the presence of drug-sniffing dogs, as they are far more intelligent than the average human and will see right through the ruse.

SHIBBY A term popularized in the stoner film *Dude, Where's My Car?* whose mystery is exceeded only by its power. The word is synonymous with any of the following words or phrases: cool, stoned, sweet, happy, mellow, drunk, awesome, message, attractive, smart, enlightened, really stoned, confused, hungry, and literally anything else the user wants it to imply. Shibby will undoubtedly be considered the most versatile word in the English language if the editors at Merriam-Webster ever get high enough to allow it to slip in. **See also** *Dude, Where's My Car?*

SHOE TOSSING The mysterious practice of tying shoes together by the laces and flinging them over power lines and telephone wires. The practice takes place in both rural and urban areas, and while not definitively known, several theories exist to explain the occurrences. Among the most popular is that shoes hanging from telephone lines mark areas where drugs are sold, and that if a buyer stands under one of them long enough, a dealer will come to hook the person up. Unfortunately, it is impossible to hang out underneath a pair of hanging shoes without everyone in the immediate vicinity knowing precisely what one is doing there. ▼

SHOES Articles of clothing used to protect the feet from injury that double as a low-tech method for hiding and transporting marijuana. Because of the undesirable odor of the human foot, some law enforcement agents are reluctant to check a suspect's shoes when searching for contraband. While this method carries with it the unfortunate side effect of making one's pot smell like feet, it's a small price to pay for avoiding bigger troubles.

SHORE, PAULY (BORN FEBRUARY 1, 1968) A stand-up comedian and actor who appeared in several low-brow comedies of the 1990s. Fans of Shore are hard to come by. However, if there are any, they remember him as the host of MTV's *Spring Break* specials or his pot-smoking persona "the Weasel" who showed up in movies like *Encino Man*, *Bio-Dome*, and *Son in Law*. Although Shore was a superstar for only a short period of time, phrases like "What's up, buudd-ddy?" or "Weezin' the juice" will forever be known in cannabis culture.

SHORT-TERM MEMORY LOSS A side effect commonly linked to marijuana use wherein the smoker has trouble remembering events that have recently taken place. This can range in anything from whose turn it is to hit the bowl to where exactly in the world the individual is at a given moment. The symptom is rarely permanent and can actually be useful, as it can shield stoners from realizing how ridiculous they act when high. **See also long-term memory loss**

SHOTGUN A complex maneuver wherein one smoker inserts a lit joint or blunt into his or her mouth, burning end first, while another positions his or her face directly in front of the other end. The first participant then blows out, unleashing a cloud of concentrated smoke into the mouth of the other. There have been no reported fatalities as a result of this practice. However, the number of burned tongues and bruised egos resulting from failed attempts is too high to calculate. **See also French inhale**

SHOWER Bathing technique whereby water is rinsed over the body from overhead, using gravity to help facilitate the cleaning, in an overall effort to cleanse the skin and hair. Hot showers especially are a favorite pastime of pot smokers. They're so satisfying that particularly high participants are at risk of staying in the shower until all people in a two-block radius lose their hot water. When the stoner is tracked down as the source of the problem, he or she will simply shrug his or her shoulders, which will in no way satisfy the neighbors.

SILVERMAN, SARAH (BORN DECEMBER 1, 1970) A comedian and actor who has done stand-up, performed in movies like *Wreck-It Ralph* and *A Million Ways to Die in the West*, and wrote a book called *The Bedwetter: Stories of Courage, Redemption, and Pee.* She starred in her own TV show, *The Sarah Silverman Program*, on Comedy Central, where she delivered the classic stoner line, "It's always 420 somewhere, right?" Silverman's act revolves around the social taboos of racism, religion, gender roles, and stereotypes, and she often plays the naive rich white girl with a mic. Silverman has been called the funniest woman alive. That's largely because of her slacker image and hilariously ballsy act, which is best appreciated while high. She's not shy about her marijuana use either, as she's been seen carrying her vape pen on the red carpet and ripping bongs with her parents.

SIMPSONS, THE An animated TV series that was one of the best shows on TV until the writing team ran out of pot in the late 1990s and stopped being funny. Despite that fact, the show, which follows the trials and tribulations of Homer, Marge, Maggie, Bart, and Lisa, is still going strong, surpassing *Gunsmoke* as the longest-running prime-time series in 2009. While the program is not as synonymous with recreational drug use as others, there is no arguing that the viewer benefits greatly from a steady dose of marijuana, especially when watching newer episodes. **See also South Park**

SKATEBOARDING A recreational activity undertaken by long-haired, rebellious youths who hate the establishment almost as much as they love attempting the same trick three hundred times without any hope for success. To participate, one merely needs a piece of wood attached to two sets of wheels and a complete disregard for one's safety. When not terrorizing shoppers outside of local malls and convenience stores, skateboarders can often be spotted smoking pot before, after, and during skateboarding sessions. This is most likely used to dull the pain resulting from repeated encounters with concrete. ▼

SKINS A slang term for rolling papers popular among time-strapped smokers who can't be bothered with multiple syllables. The term derives from the fact that if a joint were a person, the papers would be its skin.

SKUNK A slang term used to describe highly potent and odoriferous weed. The term derives from a small furry mammal of the family Mephitidae that is generally black with one or more white stripes running down the length of its back. The animal has the ability to secrete a highly offensive smell from anal scent glands located near the base of the tail. While encountering the mammal is often an undesirable experience, encountering skunky weed is almost always a cause

for celebration. Usually in the form of smoking it.

SLEEPINESS A state of being often attained shortly after consuming large quantities of cannabis. When one has reached this state, one feels an inexplicable desire to lie down in a warm bed and rest one's head on soft pillows. Sleepiness can strike without warning, and pot smokers will often be forced to settle for the closest flat or semiflat surface, sometimes including tables, floors, stairways, and ironing boards. There are several things one can do to stave off the effects of sleepiness. However, they generally involve getting up off of the couch, so it's almost always guaranteed the pot smoker will just give in instead. **See also passing out**

SLICED BREAD An essential ingredient in several marijuana-inspired delicacies including sandwiches and toast cream. It has been deemed to be such an amazing wonder of modern technology that it serves as a benchmark for all human accomplishments. That's right, in an era where one can call a friend 3,000 miles away while simultaneously streaming a video of cute animals of choice, people still look to sliced bread as the pinnacle of human achievement. Truth be told, the apple pipe is far more impressive. **See also apple pipe; toast cream**

SLIDE An element of a bong that acts similarly to a carb, allowing air to flow into the chamber and push the smoke into the user's lungs when removed from the bong. Unlike with a carb, the user does not need to actively cover a hole to work the apparatus, but instead simply leaves the slide in place when pulling the hit and removes it when it is time to inhale the delicious smoke. In most cases the slide serves double duty as the receptacle into which the marijuana is packed before being smoked. Smokers attempting to make the transition from carb to slide should observe others first because there are few things more embarrassing than waiting for one's turn to smoke, inconspicuously inspecting the bong for a hole, scratching one's head, and sheepishly asking, "So now what?"

SLINGING The act of attempting to move drugs in any type of drive-through-style ordering situation. The term derives from the way drugs were dealt in the old days, when cars would flash their lights at the dealer and

slowly pass them by on the street. The dealer would then use a slingshot to try to make the baggie fly through the car's window. If the dealer missed, the buyer got the baggie free. If he made it, the driver also got the baggie free since they were in a car and the dealer was on foot. As such, old-school slinging as a means of dealing drugs quickly grew out of favor. ▼

SLOBBER An excessive accumulation of human saliva, which is an unfortunate side effect of sharing a joint or blunt with multiple parties. When some people take a hit, they mistake the joint or blunt for an attractive member of their preferred sex and engage in deep, passionate French kissing with it. This is a common mistake and, like most things in life, can easily be remedied with incessant name-calling.

SMILEY FACE An independent, picaresque-style comedy starring Anna Faris. Taking place over the course of a single haywire day, *Smiley Face* begins when Faris's character, an aspiring actress and consummate pot-smoking roustabout, is overcome by the munchies and unknowingly devours an entire batch of pot-infused cupcakes belonging to her roommate. Her ensuing, senselessly high misadventures, which are undertaken in the name of somehow replacing the cupcakes, include botching an acting audition, fleeing the police, and accidentally stealing an original copy of *The Communist Manifesto*. Centered more on Faris's performance than the zaniness of her situation, the film derives much of its humor from rambling, faux-philosophical pot-ologues, providing a mellower viewing experience than many of the wackier, situation-based comedies. It also doesn't hurt that Faris is cuter than the sum of all buttons. **See also** *Grandma's Boy*

SMITH, KEVIN (BORN AUGUST 2, 1970) The pot-friendly film director and screenwriter responsible for such cult classics as *Clerks*, *Chasing Amy*, *Mallrats*, and *Jay and Silent Bob Strike Back*. Smith also plays Silent Bob, a stalwart drug dealer of few words who appears in nearly all of Smith's films. Shockingly enough, the creator of comic book characters like Bluntman and Chronic didn't actually smoke that much weed until after he became the king of marijuana-friendly films. After being reintroduced to the magical substance by fellow actor Seth Rogen, he now considers himself a "massive stoner" and credits the drug for lifting him out of a creative slump. To many smokers, the effect of hearing of Smith's abstinence from the holy leaf is akin to discovering that Santa Claus, the Easter Bunny, and the Tooth Fairy are figments of the imagination. **See also** *Jay and Silent Bob Strike Back*; Mewes, Jason; VIew Askewniverse

SMOKE A by-product of combustion that results when burning any form of matter. It is usually a thin gray or black wispy substance that floats in the air and dissipates over time. Smoke can be either undesirable or desirable, depending on the circumstances. When it is evidence that one's house is about to burn to the ground, it is especially unwelcome. When it is evidence that one's friends are getting high and one should join in, it is most welcome.

SMOKE-IN A large gathering of pot smokers in numbers too great for authorities to arrest everyone. A form of peaceful protest, the first of which was held in Washington, DC, on July 4, 1970, when twenty-five thousand stoners participated. It continues to this day. **See also protests**

SMOKING The preferred method for ingesting marijuana among the majority of weed aficionados. One generally inserts the marijuana into a bong, bowl, joint, blunt, or other receptacle, ignites it with a lighter or matches, inhales the resulting THC-laden by-product known as smoke into the lungs, and exhales. When done correctly, several minutes later the subject will be stoned. When done incorrectly, several minutes later the subject will be confused and embarrassed—but certainly not stoned. ▼

SMOOTHIES A beverage made by blending together fruit, yogurt, milk, and THC. The lecithin in the milk absorbs the THC, creating a sweet, healthy snack from which one can get high. **See also drinkables**

SNOOP DOGG (BORN OCTOBER 20, 1971) A West Coast rapper and Dr. Dre protégé who's got the smooth, composed delivery that makes listeners think he's permanently high. Which he might be. What Alex Trebek is to mustaches, Snoop is to marijuana. Few people can shave a mustache or stop smoking weed and have it become a national news story. Snoop is one of those people. He quit the herb after getting caught with some by a state trooper in 2002. The dry spell lasted about three months. Now he owns Leafs by Snoop, a cannabis brand that offers eight different strains of weed and one high-CBD strain; he can also be found cooking up a storm with Martha Stewart on *Martha and Snoop's Potluck Dinner Party.* Next time you're listening to his music, try playing the Get-High-As-Snoop game. The rules are as follows: While listening to any Snoop album, every time the emcee says his own name or spells his own name (S-N-Double-O-P D-O-Double-Jah-Zee), take a hit of weed. By the end of the album, the listener will be in another universe, known colloquially as the Doggy Dogg World. **See also CBD; chronic; Dr. Dre;** *Martha and Snoop's Potluck Dinner Party;* **Warren G**

SNOOTCHIE BOOTCHIES A catch-phrase uttered by Jason Mewes frequently when portraying his trademark character, Jay, in one of Kevin Smith's many pot-fueled films. Its meaning is pretty open to interpretation and serves as a deflection to draw attention away from an exceptionally crass and uncalled-for remark. For example one might say, "Last night I stole all your pot and then set your house on fire to disguise it. Snootchie bootchies!" The person hearing this news would potentially be so confused by what was meant by "snootchie bootchies" that he or she would completely ignore the far more offensive aspects of the statement. Its effectiveness is questionable. **See also** *Jay and Silent Bob Strike Back;* **Mewes, Jason; Smith, Kevin**

SNOW A variety of precipitation that falls from the sky in colder regions of the world predominately during the winter months. Most people focus on the negative attributes of snow, like how it turns into ice, blocks roads, makes walking difficult, and how it must be shoveled off of driveways and sidewalks. Pot smokers, on the other hand, look on the bright side and focus on its enjoyable aspects, like how it can be used as a replacement for bong water, a foundation for snow angels and snowballs, or as a surface for snowboarding.

SNOW BONG An ordinary bong that has been enhanced with the addition of crisp, clean, wintry snow. Preferably white and definitely not yellow. The user packs the chamber completely full of snow instead of water and then proceeds to smoke as normal. The snow will then cool the smoke as it makes its way to the user's lungs. For some pot smokers, this is literally the only good thing about winter.

SNOW WHITE A character in a fairy tale involving seven dwarfs, a magic mirror, an apple, and of course a prince that is the namesake of a white-tinted strain of marijuana known for its potent, mellow high. With big round leaves and fat buds, the pot is just as beautiful as the fairy-tale character. And if one kisses it, Snow White (the weed) also awakens and fills the user with love. Except, also like the fairy tale's postscript, that feeling lasts only about five hours before the slow descent back to reality begins.

SNOWBOARDING A winter sport that evolved from a combination of skiing, surfing, skateboarding, and smoking pot. The modern-day snowboard consists of a single piece of flat material with two foot bindings to anchor the snowboarder to the apparatus. Once secured to the board, the subject hurls him- or herself down a steep mountain while avoiding ice patches, trees, and other snowboarders stopped on the trail to pack a bowl. Unlike skiers, snowboarders do not employ the use of poles, preferring instead to grab the board in midair. This frees the hands to allow the snowboarder to smoke a joint on the way down the mountain.

SNUFFING An oft-overlooked form of pot etiquette wherein the smoker, after he or she has taken a hit and before passing to the next person, uses a lighter to extinguish the burning marijuana and prevent any of the precious leaf from being wasted. Some absentminded pot smokers will often snuff the bowl but subsequently remember an important and elaborate story that must be shared with the group immediately and forget the

necessary proceeding step of passing it along in the circle. Depending on how long the session has been in progress, this can go unnoticed by the rest of the circle for several minutes or several hours. **See also short-term memory loss**

SOCIAL SMOKER A person who smokes very infrequently and exclusively during social situations like parties and, well, pretty much just at parties. They are extremely prone to smoking gaffes like volcanoing, babysitting, and slobbering simply because they do not smoke frequently enough to have learned how to avoid these embarrassing faux pas. This is often the first stage of a pot smoker's life cycle where the subject is capable of metamorphosing into any number of other smoker personas. For this reason one should avoid getting them wet or feeding them after midnight because there's no telling what might happen. **See also active smoker; antisocial smoker; casual smoker; enhancement smoker; intellectual smoker; paranoid smoker**

SOCK DRAWER A widely utilized and obvious location for hiding private items ranging from condoms to money and jewelry to marijuana and assorted paraphernalia. The assumption of the hiding place is that no self-respecting individual would resort to rifling through smelly socks when looking for contraband. **See also shoes** ▼

SOMETIMES A GREAT NOTION A book by *One Flew Over the Cuckoo's Nest* author and noted LSD consumer Ken Kesey. While less widely read than his most popular book, *Sometimes a Great Notion* is considered by many a superior book. The novel follows the story of striking loggers in the fictional town of Wakonda, Oregon. Kesey employs a strange literary technique in the book, writing in the first person from the perspective of several different characters. While difficult to follow sober, pot-smoking readers can detect subtle clues that Kesey leaves explaining at all times who is speaking. This allows the reader to see the motives of each character and the story from their perspective while realizing they all struggle to communicate clearly with each other. As a semi-underappreciated beat/hippie book, it's required reading for Hipster Pot Smokers 101 at any college or university. **See also intellectual smokers; Project MKUltra**

SOUTH PARK An animated comedy airing on Comedy Central in which "all characters and events in this show—even those based on real people—are entirely fictional. All celebrity voices are impersonated… poorly." The show is no stranger to marijuana use, featuring the drug in several episodes and creating an anthropomorphic towel character whose sole purpose is to get high and preach the values of towel ownership. In the show's fourteenth season, the town of South Park, Colorado, is blessed with a string of medical marijuana dispensers, prompting several male townspeople to give themselves testicular cancer in order to receive prescriptions for the drug. **See also Streisand, Barbra**

SPACED OUT A common state among absentminded pot smokers resulting in an unusually slow reaction time to external stimuli. The term gets its name from the fact that subjects will usually just sit and stare off into space for extended periods of time. They might be looking at something interesting, like a pretty picture or a funny movie. However, they are often just gazing off into the distance. There is no surefire cure for spacing out, although lighting up another joint has an uncanny ability to snap them back to attention, albeit temporarily.

SPARK A small glowing ember of matter that has the ability to ignite certain gases to create fire, and an essential element for smoking pot. It also serves as a form of pot slang used as a call to action when followed by the words "it" and "up." ▼

SPICOLI, JEFF The comic relief in the classic 1982 coming-of-age movie *Fast Times at Ridgemont High*, played with subtlety and authenticity by Sean Penn in what was no doubt the highlight of his acting career. As the token and tokin' surfer/stoner at Ridgemont High, Spicoli carries on a low-key feud with his history teacher, Mr. Hand, orders a pizza during class, crashes his friend's car, and utters the famous line, "All I need are some tasty waves, a cool buzz, and I'm fine." In the film, classmates reveal that Spicoli, the archetypal California pothead who utters words like "gnarly" with no irony, has been stoned "since the third grade."

SPLIFF A slang term that generally refers to a long conical marijuana cigarette containing both tobacco and cannabis. One might choose to roll such a joint in order to extend the life of a dwindling stash of weed, as a clever misdirection in an elaborate bogarting scheme, or to mask the smell and taste of particularly low-grade schwag in order to avoid public humiliation. Some self-loathing smokers will roll them instead of a full joint because they are embarrassed by their smoking habit and are trying to cut back. One should never roll a spliff for this reason because one has nothing to be ashamed of.

SPOOF An ingenious contraption that is used to mute the smell of marijuana. The device consists of a paper towel or toilet paper roll stuffed with dryer sheets, which are occasionally sprayed with cologne, Febreze, or any other fragrance. With spoof in hand, the smoker will take a hit as normal, but when it comes time to exhale he or she will do so into one end of the tube. Unfortunately for stoners, the spoof's scent-masking abilities share one important characteristic with the fairies in J.M. Barrie's *Peter Pan*—they only exist if the user believes in them.

SPORTS Activities of physical exertion that pit the athletic talents of one individual or group of individuals against others in a scored matchup. Sports are widely variant in their approaches and play; however, many resemble war in style and strategy, none more so than football. One common thread linking sports together is their reliance on hand-eye coordination and good instincts in order to be successful. As such, sporting smokers may think to themselves that they can get high and achieve a sort of Zenlike state in which the mind, body, and ball (or puck) become one. Instead, pot smokers often find their drive to win, lung capacity, and overall athletic grace decreases. This often results in coaches benching the smokers, where,

fortunately, they can still indulge in a feast of unlimited Gatorade and have a first-row seat to a fascinating game of physical achievement that they once partook in. **See also gym** ▼

SQUARE A geometric shape that makes for a poor configuration for smoking pot in groups as it requires an even number of people to create. It is also a term used to refer to anyone who does not indulge in smoking, eating, smelling, touching, looking at, or even thinking about marijuana. Oftentimes squares look down on cannabis smokers and will say mean things about them. Sometimes, however, their prejudice is not truly their fault. They have merely been misinformed, and there is still hope that they can be shown the light. But one should not hold his or her breath. **See also circle**

STASH A stockpile of marijuana that is almost always hidden in a location believed by the owner to be completely obscure and undetectable, but is actually wildly obvious and cliché (e.g., inside a cigar box, velvet pouch, mattress, or hollowed-out dictionary). If one's stash is located by anyone other than a fellow, friendly pot smoker, there is only one appropriate response: "So that's where that went. Now I can finally hand it over to the proper authorities."

STASH CAN A clever apparatus used for hiding illicit items like marijuana. To create, one simply takes an ordinary soda can and removes the top with a can opener. After discarding the contents, one inserts a smaller glass jar with a twist-off lid and attaches said lid to the underside of the removed can top. Now, one simply places any contraband inside of the jar and seals the device with the lid/top combo. The result is a completely foolproof hiding place. Unless, of course, somebody tries to drink it. **See also pop**

STEAMROLLER A type of pipe used to smoke marijuana. A steamroller consists of a cylinder that's open on both ends with a bowl attached to the top. One opening acts as the carb, while the other acts as the mouthpiece. All one needs to do to use is cover one of the openings with his or her hand while lighting the bowl, suck on the pipe until it's sufficiently filled with smoke, and then remove the hand to inhale. Almost certain coughing attacks to follow. **See also carb; coughing**

STEMS The structural support system for the cannabis plant that allows for the blooming of buds and flowers. While this function is admirable, once the buds have been harvested the stems are more or less useless and should be discarded before selling. If one discovers a stem in one's stash, one should alert the dealer from whom it was purchased immediately. If the dealer is unwilling to rectify the situation, there is absolutely nothing one can do about it, as there is currently no customer service center in existence that one can call to report poor drug-dealing service. ▶

STEVE-O (BORN JUNE 13, 1974) Arguably the single dumbest human being ever to have walked the face of the earth. This even includes several hominid species that preceded modern Homo sapiens like Australopithecus and Ardipithicus ramidus. He is best known for his "work" on the MTV show *Jackass,* where he performed various acts of self-destruction ranging from hurtling himself off poorly constructed ramps to stapling his scrotum to his leg. Due to the inherently painful nature of his vocation, Steve-O routinely engaged in recreational drug use, dabbling in everything from whip-its and marijuana to cocaine and ecstasy. His love of marijuana was so deep-seated that he was arrested in May 2003 in Sweden because he claimed to have swallowed a condom filled with cannabis to smuggle it into the country for later use. This may seem like a low point for the D-list celebrity, but his low point actually came several years later, in October of 2006, when he appeared on the Internet talk show *Tom Green Live!* hosted by Tom Green. In a single episode, Steve-O ignored calls from viewers while eating hash brownies, smoking cigarettes, doing whip-its, and drinking to excess. The show ended with

him chugging an entire bottle of salad dressing, vomiting profusely, and collapsing on the floor. Despite his transgressions, the pot-smoking community remains appreciative of his willingness to sacrifice his body in the interest of mindless entertainment. Fortunately, Steve-O has been sober for over ten years, so perhaps there's hope for him yet.

STEWART, KRISTEN (BORN APRIL 9, 1990) An American actress best known for playing Bella Swan in the incredibly successful movie adaptations of the young-adult book series Twilight. Her peculiar and aloof public behavior led many to believe she may dabble in the green stuff. In 2008, a picture of the starlet sitting on the steps of a building and smoking what appeared to be a pot pipe fueled these suspicions. Later that year, a photograph surfaced in which she was wearing a bikini decorated with the universal symbol for marijuana leaves. General consensus is that she must be smoking something to be so conspicuous about her pot use. **See also vampires**

STICKY ICKY A slang term used to describe bud that is especially potent, dank, skunky, etc. High-grade marijuana that has been properly cured is slightly sticky to the touch, as opposed to schwag, which is generally dry as a bone. Industrious DIY dealers often attempt to resuscitate their dried-up low-grade pot by adding sticky substances such as honey, molasses, or sugar and passing it off as sticky weed. There is a special place in hell for these people, right alongside telemarketers and meter maids.

See also schwag; stress ▼

STOKE The physical act of cleaning a bong, pipe, bubbler, bowl, or any apparatus used for the purpose of smoking marijuana. Over time, tar, resin, and bong water can cause a piece to become discolored and even obstruct the chamber, making it nearly impossible to get high efficiently. This is unacceptable and should be remedied at the earliest

convenience. Depending on how thorough the owner of the dirty piece is, this can range in anything from filling the paraphernalia with water, closing both ends, and shaking it around to painstakingly rubbing the inside with pipe cleaners and lovingly applying dedicated cleaning solutions like Formula 420. Some smokers claim that, similar to the way a well-seasoned grill imparts flavor to meat, an unclean bong makes for more potent bud. See also Formula 420

STONED The state of being intoxicated via marijuana consumption. "Getting stoned" is one of the most common phrases to refer to smoking weed, yet its origin remains an unsettled question to most stoners. Some claim the term derives from an old alcoholic drink called Stone Fence. Another theory claims "being stoned" refers to the act of a stone: doing nothing. But most etymologists agree the term derives from 1930s slang for being intoxicated, as people would wobble around as if they had just been stoned by an angry mob. That tradition carries on today, just with less blood and death.

STONER A person or animal that frequently gets high by smoking or ingesting buds from the *Cannabis sativa* plant. Nonsmoking members of society often use the term as a derogatory insult. However, many individuals who enjoy marijuana use it as a term of endearment. So, depending on the circumstance, the remark "You are such a stoner" is very likely to receive a response of "Thanks, you too."

STONER FILM A subgenere of movies, usually comedies, whose theme or storyline includes overt reference to marijuana use or drug culture. Some examples include: *Super Troopers, Dazed and Confused, Half Baked, How High, Pineapple Express, Harold and Kumar Go to White Castle,* and *Dude, Where's My Car?* Stoner films can also include any movie so filled with bad acting and stunted line delivery that it becomes comedy gold. The genre can also be interpreted to include crazy, mind-blowing movies, which would include titles such as: *Being John Malkovich, 2001: A Space Odyssey, Pi, Mulholland Drive, Donnie Darko,* and *Waking Life.* Ultimately, a stoner film is any movie about which someone who smokes weed asks a fellow smoker, "Yeah, but have you ever seen it *high?*" **See also movies**

STRAIGHTEDGE Lifestyle choice of individuals who refrain from alcohol, drugs, and, in some extreme cases, premarital sex. Straightedge individuals occasionally mark themselves on their hands with a big black X, signaling to the rest of the world they are no fun at all. Coming out as straightedge can be a shocking revelation to friends and family, and many will reject the straightedger out of fear, confusion, general negative feelings of "those types," or just because they find it "icky." As such, straightedgers often find themselves ashamed, alone, and depressed, at which point they find the only friends who never judge them: drugs and alcohol. They are soon reacclimated into society. **See also clean; square**

STREISAND, BARBRA (BORN APRIL 24, 1942) A Grammy, Tony, Oscar, and Emmy-winning entertainer, the bestselling female singer ever with over 150 million albums and singles sold worldwide, and former giant robot Godzilla figure who destroyed the town of South Park, Colorado. Though Strcisand performs in the adult contemporary genre, a musical style known for its sophistication and seeming maturity, she is a known pot smoker who admitted to *Rolling Stone* in a 1972 interview that she used to get high during gigs to try to relieve the tension. She also claimed to get weed from other celebrity stoners who would hear about her habit. "[They] started sending me the best dope in the world," she said. "I never ran out." She then quickly added, "Hmm, I wonder if I should tell that story." The revelation caused elderly Jewish women everywhere to start crying, wail their arms in the air, and proclaim, "My poor Barbra! Where did I go wrong?!" She would not, however, smoke pot with Seth Rogen for reasons unknown. **See also Rogen, Seth; South Park**

STRESS A classification of marijuana that is considered to be of exceptionally low quality and is often used interchangeably with schwag. Weed that falls into this category often contains an excess of stems and seeds and is quite unpleasant to smoke. It is not uncommon for a group of underprivileged pot smokers to purchase a bag of stress and spend an entire evening complaining how awful it is and how they should never buy it again, only to go out the following evening and do the exact same thing. This could be a result of short-term memory loss or it could just be that pot smokers love to complain. Especially about pot. **See also schwag**

STRIKEOUT A game of sorts wherein participants must take a hit of marijuana, down a shot of spirits, and chug a beer before exhaling. Once the act is successfully completed, it is recommended that contestants raise their fists in the air in triumph, although it is not necessary. It is not uncommon for creative players to add any number of additional acts to the game, ranging from doing push-ups to beating the first level of the original *Mario Bros.* game before exhaling. Regardless of the variation, the game is very similar to tic-tac-toe in that the only winning move is not to play. **See also highdea**

SUBLIME A California ska punk band known as one of the few bands that enjoys a consensus among music lovers and pot smokers as great music. Sublime is therefore a common band to put on in the background during smoking sessions of mixed company. Their music is bass-heavy, reggae-styled, fun-branded punk, and they still remain a fixture of alternative radio airplay years after their last proper album. Sublime released two albums before lead singer Bradley Nowell died of a heroin overdose in 1996, two months before the release of the band's major-label debut. **See also Dave Matthews Band**

SUGAR A nickname given to a lovely person and a primary edible table condiment that adds sweetness and flavor to most any food. Sugar comes in many forms, but the most widely used is the high fructose corn syrup that appears in soda, cookies, and so many other American food products. There is some debate about the health effects of high fructose corn syrup, with some calling it the primary force behind the American obesity epidemic. Pot smokers call it the most flavorful joyride their tongue has ever experienced. Sugar is such a flavor enhancer that the only thing stopping pot smokers from eating an entire box of sugary cereal is the size of their stomachs and the terrible knowledge in the back of their heads that sugar may lead them to lose all their teeth, and thus never be able to eat their favorite snacks again. **See also cereal ▼**

SUNGLASSES Protective headgear with lenses worn by pot smokers to disguise the unfortunate aftereffect of smoking marijuana known as blood-shot eyes. Some nonsmokers also wear them as a means to shield their pupils from the harmful ultraviolet rays given off by the Earth's sun. It is important to avoid wearing them at night, as their inherent darkening properties will make seeing difficult. Also, wearing them at night makes the wearer look like a complete and utter idiot to everyone in their immediate vicinity, regardless of how high they may be. **See also bloodshot eyes ▼**

SUPER HIGH ME A 2008 documentary film starring comic Doug Benson in which the protagonist, a regular pot smoker, abstains from smoking weed for thirty days before spending the ensuing thirty days high ²⁴/₇. The film parodies the Morgan Spurlock documentary *Super Size Me*, which attempted to measure the effects of eating McDonald's for thirty straight days on a person's health. Benson's film makes the same attempt with consuming weed. Stunningly, the comic's verbal SAT score, psychic ability, and sperm count all improved while he was high. To marijuanaphiles, the film serves as indisputable scientific proof to pot's mental and physical health benefits. **See also Benson, Doug**

SUPER SMASH BROS. A series of video games published by Nintendo that takes popular characters from various games and pits them against one another in a battle royale–style fighting system. While many fighting games require an encyclopedic knowledge of complicated button combinations to employ various supermoves, the Smash Bros. games keep things simple with dedicated buttons performing each attack. The simple game play makes it an ideal party game for groups of smokers seeking to relive their childhoods with an epic battle between Mario, Link, Fox, and Donkey Kong. While pot-smoking players are at a distinct disadvantage when playing more complicated games, Super Smash Bros. titles offer them an opportunity to button mash their way to victory, even providing them with enough downtime between lives to take a fairly decent hit from a joint or bowl.

SUPER TROOPERS A 2001 American film starring the Broken Lizard comedy troupe. The movie follows a group of Vermont state troopers as they attempt to keep their stretch of highway safe from excessive speeders, pot-smoking teenagers driving to Canada to score poutine, and an elusive drug-smuggling syndicate bringing truckloads of marijuana into their mild-mannered state. Rather than portray the squad as stereotypical cops on power trips, the film shows them in a more relatable light as a lazy group of pranksters who don't take their jobs seriously and abuse their positions only if the result is going to be really, really funny. After two of the officers inadvertently thwart a large marijuana delivery, squad members do everything in their power to act like actual police officers and track down the culprits, even going so far as to smoke the confiscated ganja themselves in order to better understand the enemy. Shockingly, their research does not get them much closer to catching the actual criminals. **See also cops; police station**

SUPERBAD A 2007 bromantic comedy starring Michael Cera and Jonah Hill as high school seniors in search of alcohol as a means to increase their chances of getting laid. Their odyssey to procure booze takes them from one questionable situation to the next and inevitably ends in tears when neither protagonist manages to score with his respective love interest. Scholars maintain that, had the main characters chosen marijuana as their preferred aphrodisiac, they could have scored pot from a fellow student, gotten the girls high at lunch, and gotten laid before fifth period. The resulting film would have been approximately twenty minutes long and increased the use of marijuana among high school students by 3,000 percent overnight.

SURFING An aquatic sport in which participants stand atop oblong boards and navigate cresting waves. Though the activity of surfing was a pivotal aspect of Polynesian society, and was observed by Europeans as early as the 1700s, surfing didn't exist as an American cultural institution until the 1950s. Weed is often cited as the choice drug among surfers as it quiets the mind and allows one to picture oneself as part of the primal, elemental waters that spawned all life from the womb spring of the earth heart. Or something. Though surf culture, including slang, music, and clothing, continues to evolve, the ideological root of the surfing mindset—a calm, focused hunger for that next gnarly wave—remains strong within the contemporary boarding community. ▼

Tt

TAKING WOODSTOCK A 2009 Ang Lee film documenting Woodstock from the perspective of Elliot Teichberg (Demetri Martin), the man responsible for bringing the music festival to Bethel, New York. The film portrays the power of pot to reunite estranged families, as Elliot's strict and miserly parents become loving and affectionate after ingesting four hash brownies apiece. Director Lee exercises his artistic license here, as four hash brownies would surely render the old folks catatonic or worse. **See also Woodstock**

TALKATIVE SMOKER A person who is incapable of shutting up once he or she has ingested cannabis. They are usually under the false impression that they are the first person to have ever gotten high and will regale innocent bystanders with every aspect of their experience. Especially if nobody is listening. If their constant babble becomes irritating (and it will), simply encourage them to continue smoking until they are so baked they can barely stand up, let alone fill everybody in on how much they love *Family Guy*. **See also active smoker; artistic smoker; casual smoker; enhancement smoker; intellectual smoker; lazy smoker; paranoid smoker; social smoker**

TARANTINO, QUENTIN (BORN MARCH 27, 1963) Writer, director, auteur, and one of the best moviemakers of his generation. Tarantino is known for injecting his scripts with excessive and unforgiving violence, including scenes of cutting off someone's ear (and pouring gasoline in the wound), shooting a man in the crotch and waiting for him to bleed to death, beating characters to death with a baseball bat, and vehicular homicide. Tarantino is also known for injecting his films with occasional drug references, such as the scene in *Pulp Fiction* where Mia Wallace (Uma Thurman) inadvertently snorts a line of heroin, and the scene in *Jackie Brown* where Melanie Ralston (Bridget Fonda) rips a bowl. The director does not shy away from his own experiences with marijuana, but insists he does not smoke pot while in the director's chair. Thankfully, this self-imposed ban does not appear to extend to when he is writing his films. **See also** *Pulp Fiction*

TATTOO A body modification technique using ink and a needle to dye the skin a different pigment for artistic reasons, to be rebellious, or, in far too many instances, because the person is too inebriated to know better. The thought process goes as follows: A tattoo would be a great way to achieve self-expression. I should get a tattoo. I should get a tattoo now. If I don't get a tattoo now, I'll never do it. #YOLO! The thinking leads to some bad decision-making, regret, and tears. It also may lead to scar-replacement laser surgery, as nobody can continue living a dignified life with a giant anime dragon displayed on one's chest.

TEXT MESSAGING The number one choice for wasting time at work and an easy way to avoid actually talking to people in real life. Texting is overall a great way to quickly send short communications without having to go through the trouble of formally saying hello to someone. This makes it both an ideal format for close friends to talk as well as a dangerous technology for the pot smoker to possess. Text messaging puts smokers at risk for contacting old flames, communicating unintelligible personal insights, and sending out their pent-up anger at whoever finished off the last of the munchies.

THAI STICK A somewhat dated but still kickin' strain of marijuana that originated in Thailand. This is definitely more like one's parents' weed, or even grandparents'. It was most popular during the 1960s and 1970s. Thai stick is high-quality bud wrapped around a stem and bound with rope-like strands of hemp plant. The end result looks like a little cigar—and it knocks the smoker out of commission longer than an organ solo from The Doors. Thai sticks are rumored to have been dipped in opium, cannabis oil, and even embalming fluid. But those rumors were probably started by embarrassed smokers who didn't want to admit that Thai stick turned them into one-toke jokes. **See also one-toke joke**

THAT '70S SHOW A long-lived TV series that aired on the Fox network in the summer of 1998 and ran for eight consecutive seasons until the spring of 2006. The title leaves little to the imagination, as the show is simply a sitcom following a group of six teenagers growing up in the 1970s. Coincidentally, the size of the group is roughly the maximum capacity for a smoking circle, an activity the gang frequently engages in as their primary means of entertainment in the imaginary Podunk town of Point Place, Wisconsin. Because of the inherent evils associated with marijuana use, the characters never say outright that they are getting high. Instead the show employed not-so-subtle effects such as adjusting the camera angle, billowing artificial smoke in the background, and having the characters magically appear in better spirits whenever they "do that thing where they all sit around in a circle."

THC Short for tetrahydrocannabinol, a chemical found inside the trichomes of the cannabis plant and known to cause marijuana's enjoyably intoxicating psychotropic effects. Though the biological mechanism by which THC induces euphoria and alters autonomic physical processes such as pain response and appetite are not fully understood, the chemical is one of the safest recreational drugs. One lab study estimates that to self-administer a lethal dose of THC, one would have to smoke 1,500 pounds of cannabis in fourteen minutes. Negative side effects of THC include the inability to differentiate between a sitcom and a drama, eating all of the munchies, and the staunching of one's motivation to go out and purchase additional munchies to replenish the supply. **See also trichomes ▼**

THINKING The process by which the brain manages all feelings, impulses, desires, and any humanlike activity not directly involving the five senses, and the way in which people or animals perceive and understand the world around them. Thinking is an unavoidable part of life, but people really dig in to the exercise after smoking a joint. So deep can thought become that smokers disappear into themselves as their eyes roll to the back of their heads. This means the smoker is either experiencing the greatest high of his or her life, or he or she just keeled over and requires immediate medical assistance. **See also spaced out**

THOMPSON, HUNTER S. (JULY 18, 1937–FEBRUARY 20, 2005) Creator

of gonzo journalism, the practice of writing subjectively and in the first person, and author of landmark American books such as *Fear and Loathing in Las Vegas*, *Hell's Angels: A Strange and Terrible Saga*, and *Fear and Loathing on the Campaign Trail '72*. Thompson is a favorite of pot smokers, mostly because of his erratic and seemingly irrational behavior. This was most aptly seen during Thompson's actual run for sheriff of Pitkin County, Colorado, in 1970, when he ran on a platform of decriminalizing drugs for personal use only, building pedestrian malls, banning any building so tall as to obscure the view of the mountains, firing a majority of the conservative county officials, renaming Aspen as "Fat City," and shaving his head so he could call his crew-cut-wearing Republican opponent "my long-haired opponent." Thompson narrowly lost the election, but the campaign did accomplish one thing for weedophiles: It finally gave them a reason to vote. **See also Fear and Loathing in Las Vegas**

TIE-DYE A resist-dying technique that results in a pattern of cloth typically worn by hippies and Grateful Dead fans. Tie-dye is related to dreadlocks, ripped blue jeans, ratty sandals, and, by extension, drug use, largely because the multicolored, interconnected, geometrical patterns are the sorts of things drug users see when they close their eyes while heavily intoxicated. However, for some smokers, closing one's eyes is too much work, so they must rubber-band a cotton shirt together before dipping it in colorful dye, waiting twenty-four hours, washing it, and then wearing or displaying it. **See also Grateful Dead, The**

TIME A measuring system through which the sequence of events and things can be determined. Time is one of the seven fundamental physical quantities, along with distance, velocity, mass, momentum, energy, and weight. Time is also one of the easiest fundamental quantities to measure. While high, however, time loses all objective reality. Sitting on a couch and thinking for sixty seconds can feel like twenty minutes. Playing video games for two hours can feel like fifteen minutes. Twenty-five years spent getting high can feel like five months, as smokers ask themselves, "What did I do that whole time?"

TIME TRAVEL The act of moving from one point in time to another by traveling close to the speed of light, entering a wormhole, or other methods unknown to the general layperson. On a small scale, anyone who has ever smoked pot has likely experienced some form of time travel. This generally comes in the form of resting one's eyes "just for a minute" only to open them several hours later.

TINCTURE An alcohol-based solution that extracts the THC and cannabinoids from the cannabis plant. Tinctures are more effective at isolating those desirable compounds and can often take effect more quickly than other methods of ingesting marijuana. There are also lots of options for use, including ingesting the tincture directly in small amounts or incorporating it into favorite meals or drinks. Some people choose to make their own if they have the proper ingredients, but they're also available for purchase if

users would rather go the easy route. **See also drinkables; edibles ▼**

TOAST CREAM A culinary experience best enjoyed under the influence of weed. One part toasted wheat bread, one part ice cream spread over aforementioned toasted bread, it yields a delicious snack. Invented in 1923 in Troy, New York, by the son of a vacuum salesman, toast cream has been applauded by pot smokers and gourmands the world over. Its simple ingredients and ease of assembly are perfectly suited to the childlike state immediately after two large bong hits.

TOKE A popular term in weed aficionado parlance for the act of smoking marijuana. While the word sounds slightly similar to the tokay gecko, a lizard common to rainforests throughout the world, it is unclear if there is any association between the two. **See also midnight toker**

TOLKIEN, J.R.R. (JANUARY 3, 1892–SEPTEMBER 2, 1973) A twentieth-century English author who is best known for his epic fantasy novels, *The Hobbit*, *The Silmarillion*, and The Lord of the Rings trilogy. Tolkien's writings take place in an imaginary realm called Middle Earth populated with fantastical creatures like wizards, elves, dragons, dwarves, orcs, and trolls. But the most prominent creatures featured in his novels are squat, good-natured beings called hobbits, who want nothing more in life than a fine meal, a cold mug of beer, and a nice relaxing toke of pipe weed. While Tolkien makes no direct reference to what exactly pipe weed might be, one can draw some conclusions based on the fact that hobbits spend the majority of their time eating, talking about eating, or complaining that they aren't eating enough. **See also pipe weed**

TORONTO FREEDOM FESTIVAL A now canceled annual rally aimed at decriminalizing marijuana and celebrating pot culture. Part of the Global Marijuana March, this May soiree traditionally found more than thirty thousand weed aficionados gathering in Queen's Park to stage a political protest, enjoy like-minded conversations, and, of course, score bountiful spliff-fuls of chronic. Started in 1999, the festival was an officially recognized city event, boasting sponsorships and a variety of live music and comedy performances. Unfortunately, it was canceled when it was unable to acquire the appropriate permits. Fortunately, the "Save the Toronto Freedom Festival" *Facebook* page lives on and is busy being just about as effective as you might have guessed. **See also *Facebook*; Global Marijuana March**

TRAILER PARK BOYS A Canadian mockumentary series about a bunch of people who live and cause trouble in a trailer park. One character, Ricky, is known for being dumb, spouting phrases that are just slightly off, and growing marijuana; his story continues in the related movie *Trailer Park Boys 3: Don't Legalize It*, which centers around his concerns that legalization could put him out of business.

TRAMPOLINES Round, elevated surfaces containing a tight, bouncy material pulled over coiled springs. Trampolines are apparently death traps for children, as children get too much height and land on the lawn, often resulting in broken bones. Trampolines now come equipped with walls for child safety, causing grand-parents everywhere to talk about how "they didn't care about safety in my day" and "spoiled kids these days!" The walls are welcome news for pot smokers, as they allow unfettered safety while engaging in one of the most underrated post-joint activities: jumping on a trampoline. **See also pogo sticks** ▼

TREES A slang term used to refer to marijuana. The euphemism is especially useful when one wishes to disguise one's intention to get high, as the term can also apply to any number of large plant life that provide breathable oxygen and are not considered illegal to possess, such as weeping willow, birch, and oak. Asking someone, "Can I buy some marijuana?" can be very risky. However, asking, "Can I buy some trees?" is much less likely to raise any suspicions.

TRICHOMES Tiny bulb-topped filaments that cover the outer surface of cannabis plants and contain the THC that turns boring smoke into a heavenly toke. Often theorized to be a biological defense mechanism designed to make the plant both resilient to harsh weather and unpalatable to herbivores, these narcotic hairs also serve as natural indicators of a marijuana plant's maturity and, ergo, its smokability. Trichomes are naturally occurring evidence that coating one's self with drugs is an exceptionally good self-preservation strategy since no one will ever let weed go extinct. **See also THC** ▼

TV A visual entertainment and information medium using moving images accompanied by sound. Commercially available since the 1930s, TVs are a fixture of American culture and society. TVs are also a staple of the pot smoker's experience. Hours and hours of TV viewing can take place without a smoker even blinking an eye. When it starts to seem like there is nothing to watch, all the smoker needs to do is light another joint and anything on TV becomes instantly entertaining.

TWAIN, MARK (NOVEMBER 30, 1835–APRIL 21, 1910) The pen name of Samuel Langhorne Clemens, a famous American author known for such works as *Adventures of Huckleberry Finn* and *The Prince and the Pauper*. Called "the father of American literature" by William Faulkner, the Missouri-born author is equally well-known for having been a prolific fount of insightful, humorous quotes of the type that thoughtful smokers enjoy repeating, such as "Giving up smoking is the easiest thing in the world. I know because I've done it thousands of times." Though little is known about Twain's own dalliances with psychotropics, some scholars believe that the author did, on occasion, indulge in hashish, a drug that was quite popular among American artists and bohemians during the mid-nineteenth century. Regardless, given his laid-back demeanor and liberal stance on issues like women's suffrage and abolition, Twain is an obvious pick for any respectable pot smoker's answer to the "if you could go back in time and smoke a jay with anyone…" question.

TWEAKING OUT The act of freaking out while under heavy marijuana, mushrooms, or LSD intoxication. Tweaking out may involve spasming of the eyes and neck, cradling in a corner, shaking, covering one's ears, possibly moaning. Other smokers will attempt to calm the tweaker, first by casually asking, "You OK?" before moving on to the only known cure for tweaking out: a slap across the face and some ice cream. **See also OK**

TWITTER A social networking site whose function is to compile as many of its members' brain farts as possible. All tweets must be conducted in 280 characters or less, making it nearly impossible to use for pot smokers, whose most profound thoughts include at least a half dozen "man"s, "dude"s, or "whoa"s. This means the most insightful thing a weedophile could say on *Twitter* is simply, "If animals could speak, would they talk in their native country's tongue, or would they create a subset animal language?" The only proper response from friends is to unfollow said smoker until he learns his lesson.

Uu

UFC (ULTIMATE FIGHTING CHAMPI-ONSHIPS) Backyard wrestling turned professional sport employing mixed martial arts and anything-goes cage-match fighting to determine the best animal-man on the planet. UFC does establish some rules: no eye goug-ing, head butting, hair pulling, fish hooking, ankle biting, or groin attack-ing, as well as some others. But the matches still sometimes end in violent puddles of blood, skin, and lost teeth. The sheer madness that an ultimate fighter must present is enough to hook a pot-smoking viewer into at least two or three rounds of action, which will be viewed with shock and awe in the comfort of his or her home.

UFO (UNIDENTIFIED FLYING OBJECT) Anything in the sky that cannot immediately be identified as something that belongs there. Until proven otherwise, most people who view UFOs assume them to be space-crafts piloted by alien beings hell-bent on abducting them for their own nefarious purposes. In almost all cases, it winds up being a plane, satellite, or a piece of ash that floated off of the joint while someone wasn't paying attention. The chances of witnessing a UFO rise exponentially when smok-ing marijuana. ▼

UNCOOL A person, place, thing, or action that is the opposite of cool. This term may seem like a fairly minor insult to those who aren't indoctri-nated. However, for pot smokers this piece of slang is reserved for only the most undesirable of situations, like running out of pot or noticing an instance of bogarting. If one has been called "uncool" by a pot smoker, the only way to get back in his or her good graces is to offer to pack the next bowl. All will instantly be forgiven. **See also cool**

UNDERWEAR Refers to any garment worn underneath traditional clothing that is used to create an extra layer of protection and warmth for the most sensitive areas of the human body. It also makes for a discreet location to conceal marijuana and other illicit drugs. When employing this method of concealment, please, for the love of God, store the pot in an airtight plastic bag.

UNICORNS Mythical beasts that are 95 percent horse and 5 percent narwhal. They are rarely seen in the wild; however, smoking large quantities of marijuana can greatly increase the likelihood of a sighting. Since they are imaginary, little is known about their behavior. Scholars speculate that their blood has magical healing powers and that if you catch one you will be granted seventeen wishes. Unfortunately, one cannot use any of those wishes to wish for more wishes, as unicorns are far too clever to fall for that sort of thing.

UNRESPONSIVE A state of being usually achieved somewhere around joint number four of a smoking session,

wherein participants are unable to react to external stimuli. This is not necessarily an undesirable state, as one can only assume the subjects would have very little to offer in the way of intelligent discourse anyway. Fortunately this state is only semipermanent and should dissipate after several hours as long as no additional marijuana is ingested. ▼

UP IN SMOKE A classic marijuana-themed buddy comedy, and the first feature film starring reefer-lovin' comedy duo Cheech and Chong. As the name suggests, the entirety of *Up in Smoke*—starting from the moment that Tommy Chong's character,

Anthony Stoner, and Cheech Marin's character, Pedro de Pacas, share an enormous joint filled with Maui Wowie and dog turds—revolves around the weed-smoking antics of two clueless, but lovable, pot smokers. In one of the film's most famous scenes, the duo escapes from Mexico in a van made entirely of cannabis, ultimately resulting in the gnarliest-ever hotboxing of a motor vehicle. *Up in Smoke* was the twelfth-highest-grossing film released in 1978 and has proudly retained its reputation as "that Cheech and Chong movie, man...with the van and all the pot and it's on fire, right? And, like, everyone gets so baked...oh, man. Pass those chips over here, dude." **See also Cheech and Chong**

URANUS The farthest planet in the solar system if one eliminates demoted dwarf planet Pluto (RIP: July 1, 1,000,000 B.C.–August 24, 2006). The planet itself is icy, barren, and relatively useless, but its name can be used as a reliable method for determining how high a particular individual is at any given time. Simply mention the planet's name and count how long it takes the individual to stop laughing. If any longer than 2.3 seconds, the subject is either twelve years old or undeniably high. ▼

Vv

VALUE MENU A list of inexpensive items ranging from hamburgers to French fries and chicken nuggets usually priced around $1 that can be found at various fast-food restaurants throughout the United States. Wendy's claims to have invented the concept in 1989 when it released the Super Value Menu, with Burger King and McDonald's refusing to officially enter the game until 1998 and 2002, respectively. Items from the value menu are an essential part of the pot smoker's diet due to their widespread availability and because their low cost allows the smoker to put money toward more important things. Like buying more pot.

VAMPIRES Folkloric undead monsters known for drinking human blood, turning into bats, and falling in love with teenage girls. Once dreaded the world over for their mind-control powers, bloodlust, and alleged ability to change others into marauding night stalkers, classic vampires were often portrayed as immortal, once-human creatures that were vulnerable to sunlight, garlic, crosses, silver, holy water, and wooden stakes. Modern pop culture, including the writings of Anne Rice (*Interview with the Vampire*), Joss Whedon (*Buffy the Vampire Slayer*), and Stephenie Meyer (*Twilight*), has portrayed them as fetchingly handsome, occasionally heroic, guilt-stricken heartthrobs who, despite their age and unconventional diet, manage to meet, seduce, and bed an endless number of hotties. This is great news for pot smokers, as it has left legions of attractive women desperate for men with pale complexions, spacey demeanors, and chronic munchies. **See also Stewart, Kristen**

VAPORIZER A method for smoking pot that defies the laws of physics and eliminates a key element in the equation: Marijuana plus fire equals high. Also known as "vapes," there's a wide range of products from which a smoker can choose. Vapes typically include a battery, some type of heating element, and a place to attach a concentrate cartridge, but there are also dry herb vaporizers, which use flower instead of oil-based concentrate. Some vapes are relatively simple and inexpensive, while others, like the coveted Volcano Vaporizer, can be pretty pricey. Vapes continue to be highly controversial and have even been associated with severe illnesses and deaths. As a result, vapes are banned in some locations for safety concerns. **See also concentrate; Volcano Vaporizer** ▼

VCR An archaic device used for viewing ancient historical documents called movies on equally archaic cartridges called videocassettes. While they have been replaced by DVD players, Blu-Ray players, and every streaming site imaginable, they have found a second life in the pot-smoking community as discreet hiding places for ganja. Each VCR contains a crevice large enough to house a videocassette, in which one can store minimal quantities of marijuana. One then covers the hole with a small flap. The only risk is that someone will decide to finally dispose of the VCR—and the hidden stash along with it.

VEGETARIAN JOINT A term popularized by the movie *Igby Goes Down* to describe the common practice of vegetarians rolling very thin joints. This is apparently in contrast to meat eaters, who roll big fat blunts. The practice of asking smokers who roll thin joints if they are vegetarians has skyrocketed as a result of the film. Just be careful when asking this question, as, in some circles, being called a vegetarian is the equivalent of being called a narc. **See also pinner**

VERMONT A state that was welcomed into the Union in 1791 and no one's regretted it since. The Green Mountain State is named for its green mountains—in French so no one can understand it—but it could also be called the Green Bud State, as it is the only New England state that produces high-quality sticky icky. Vermont has everything a stoner could ask for: natural beauty, medical and recreational marijuana laws, Ben & Jerry's world headquarters, and the jam band Phish, who come from the mean streets of Burlington.

VIDEO GAMES Pieces of software that allow common everyday people to live out obscure fantasies like fighting in the Battle of the Bulge, racing in the Indy 500, or running around searching for a princess who is never where she says she'll be while avoiding goombas, turtles, and flying fish. Because of pot's inherent ability to increase focus, marijuana use and video games go hand in hand like peanut butter and fluff. One might not believe they are a good combination right away, but once one tries it, he or she is hooked for life. ▾

VIEW ASKEWNIVERSE A fictional universe created by infamous film director Kevin Smith. Instead of creating a utopian universe, Smith chose to create one that is identical to the one inhabited by himself and the rest of humanity, with a few distinct differences: All of the McDonald's restaurants have been replaced with Mooby's. The traditional serious God with white beard and sandals has been replaced with a carefree Alanis Morissette. And two pot-smoking drug dealers are the most intelligent, business-savvy individuals in the entire universe. **See also Smith, Kevin**

VIOLENT SMOKER An oxymoronic term used to describe a breed of smoker that, in theory, becomes uncongenial and violent after smoking cannabis. Not much is known about this variety, as none have ever been observed in the wild. In all likelihood, they do not exist. **See also antisocial smoker**

VOLCANO An unfortunate gaffe commonly performed by inexperienced smokers whereby, after taking a large hit from a bowl or bong and with their mouth still firmly attached, a smoker begins to cough uncontrollably, sending the burning contents of the bowl erupting toward the sky. This is generally met with nostalgic laughter from experienced smokers, immediately followed by feelings of remorse for the wasted pot and regret that they neglected to take their hit first.

VOLCANO VAPORIZER A popular brand of vaporizer that has become synonymous with that particular form of drug paraphernalia. The crème de la crème of vaporizers, the Volcano works by heating the herb in a conical base to a preselected temperature that then releases the vapor into a heatproof bag. The user can then detach the bag and inhale the THC-laden vapor sans potentially harmful by-products commonly found in marijuana smoke. The Volcano is one of the more expensive models on the market, so it is recommended that only quality marijuana be used with the device. Although there is no supporting evidence, it is rumored that the machine will actually sprout legs and skip town at the first sign of schwag, shake, or any pot that has been "stepped on." **See also** **vaporizer**

Ww

WACKY TOBACCY A derogatory term often used by old people and anyone who has never smoked pot to refer to marijuana. The term is derived from the fact that marijuana shares several similarities with tobacco (they are both dry, smokable, and often rolled into cigarettes), combined with the fact that it makes the user act strange, disoriented, or "wacky." Also, the two words almost kind of rhyme. Whenever anyone suggests that the group smoke some "wacky tobaccy," it is best to run away as quickly as possible as the person is most certainly a narc.

WAFFLES A breakfast food consisting of batter cooked to a golden crisp that is served at every waffle house in America. Waffles are best when combined with syrup. However, waffles are known to absorb the syrup when placed directly together. That's why experienced pot smokers who eat waffles know to put the syrup on the side and dip the waffle, maximizing the syrup's flavor. Waffles are also frequently combined with fruit, either by direct infusion (blueberry waffles, for example) or by cutting up the fruit and garnishing the waffles. The combination is perfect, as not only does it taste great but it also gives smokers the false sense that since they're eating fruit, waffles constitute a healthy meal. Thirty pounds later, they'll learn their lesson. ▼

WAKE AND BAKE The process by which a person wakes up in the morning and, rather than leaping out of bed to greet the day, opts instead to stay in bed and get high. This activity will often take precedence over going to the bathroom, walking the dog, eating breakfast, job hunting, or any number of other common morning rituals. While sporadic participation in this practice is harmless, there is the potential risk that, if done consistently, one can forget what it's like *not* to be stoned.

WAKING LIFE The experience of being alive, awaking in the morning (or early afternoon, for some smokers), eating breakfast, maybe showering, brushing teeth, dressing, going out into the world, interacting with other humans, learning, teaching, thinking, living—the polar opposite of being asleep. When sober, waking life can seem boring, normal, unspectacular, completely ordinary, etc. When stoned, waking life can appear scary, fun, silly, unserious, satirical, surreal, absurd, and totally sweet. It requires a high level of functionality, a skill set most smokers lack, and is not recommended for anyone who does any job that requires the use of safety glasses.

WAR ON DRUGS A battle that has raged ever since Richard Nixon first used the phrase in 1971 and whose intention is to work with military personnel, police, and foreign countries to find and stamp out the illegal drug trade. More than forty years in, drugs have proven to be a formidable opponent. The tactics of drugs have changed, starting as a proper army but gradually breaking up into a loose network of tribal leaders and networks all over the globe. Since the enemy is not a nation-state, the war is not being fought in a traditional manner. Adding to the problems is that drugs don't subscribe to the Geneva Conventions and thus are unpredictable and untrustworthy. Progress is about as slow as an absolutely wasted pot smoker, particularly since the ideal outcome of the war consistently changes depending on which political leaders are in power.

WARREN G (BORN NOVEMBER 10, 1970) Rapper, producer, and stepbrother of Dr. Dre, whose massive 1994 hit "Regulate" has kept him financially well off and set him up for the rest of his life. Warren has used his riches to give back to his community of Long Beach, California, and in 2005, the week of August 1 to August 6 was dubbed "Warren G Week." That week, Warren spoke to the youth of the community about the importance of working hard to get ahead and the dangers of destructive decision-making. To underscore his point, in 2008, the rapper ran a red light, and when police pulled him over they found enough marijuana to arrest Warren on drug possession with intent to sell. Warren probably insisted he was just trying to show kids what *not* to do. All charges were dropped. **See also Dr. Dre**

WASHINGTON, GEORGE (FEBRUARY 22, 1732–DECEMBER 14, 1799) A

Founding Father, military general, and the first president of the United States. All around a pretty cool dude…but he gets even cooler when you learn that he was actually growing hemp on his land at Mount Vernon. Unfortunately, it's not exactly the same as the marijuana we know today and was instead used for industrial purposes like making rope and cloth. More like distant plant cousins. There's no real evidence Washington ever tried to smoke it…and if he did, it would have been a huge waste of time. **See also hemp ▼**

WASTED A state of being achieved through overindulgence in marijuana, sometimes in combination with other substances, that is beyond high, stoned, baked, or even ripped. This state is usually achieved when the rational portion of a smoker's brain loses a battle to the portion that really wants to keep taking gravity bong hits. The latter portion has little concern for the well-being of its host. Scientists believe this area of the brain is also responsible for drunk-dialing ex-partners, lighting the wrong end of the cigarette, walking home at 4 a.m. in the rain without a coat, and watching countless hours of mindless TV.

WATER A chemical compound necessary for human life that is created by combining two parts hydrogen with one part oxygen. The average human requires around six glasses of the life-sustaining liquid when not smoking pot. However, that number skyrockets while under the influence and can approach infinity depending on the harshness of the bud being smoked. When used properly, water can also serve as a medium for cooling marijuana smoke before it is inhaled into the lungs, although this process creates a foul-smelling by-product known as bong water. In instances where there is enough available water only to fill a bong or use as a means of hydration but not both, one may be tempted to use it for smoking purposes and then drink the bong water. This is always a terrible idea. **See also bong water**

WATER BOTTLE A hollow plastic container used for transporting the life-sustaining substance known as water. While relatively inexpensive and unassuming, it is arguably the single most important piece of equipment any pot smoker can have in his or her arsenal, as dehydration is a common side effect of smoking weed and other methods for transporting water, like cups or one's hands, are far less efficient and prone to spillage.

WEED Arguably the most popular euphemism used to refer to marijuana by modern men and women. While the word carries a negative connotation in horticultural circles (e.g., "these damn weeds are killing my azaleas!"), it could not be used more lovingly in the pot-smoking world (e.g., "If it weren't for weed, I don't think I'd bother getting up in the morning"). **See also every entry in this book**

WEED TEA A drink created by steeping marijuana in boiling water for an extended period of time. Because THC is not especially water soluble, the psychedelic properties of the resulting brew are fairly mild. To increase the potency of the tea, one can add ingredients with high fat contents like milk, butter, or vegetable oil. On its own, weed tea is not very appetizing, so one can add flavor enhancers like honey, sugar, or tea leaves. Of course, one could also abandon the notion of weed tea altogether and simply smoke the stuff. **See also drinkables ▼**

WEED THE PEOPLE A documentary from filmmakers Ricki Lake and Abby Epstein that's available through the popular streaming service Netflix. This film dives into the medical marijuana industry, particularly the effects of cannabis on children with cancer, and challenges governmental limitations on what may very well be a life-changing treatment. **See also Netflix**

WEEDS A Showtime dramedy created by Jenji Kohan. The show stars Mary-Louise Parker as lovable sociopath Nancy Botwin, who sells marijuana in her conformist California suburb to maintain her family's posh lifestyle after her husband dies suddenly. Over the seasons, the original foundation of the show shifts rapidly and frequently, often before the viewer can say "unexpected plot twist." For example, at various points in the show, Armenian mobsters and Mexican drug lords hold the entire ensemble cast at gunpoint for one reason or another. Tuned-in pot smokers are rewarded for following along by long shots of hot cast members smoking what looks like luscious herb at least once per show.

WHITE WIDOW A notoriously potent, high-yield strain of cannabis named for the abundant number of THC-rich trichomes that cover its exterior,

giving the plant its trademark frosted appearance. Originally developed in Amsterdam, and winner of the 1995 Cannabis Cup, White Widow is actually a crossbreed of the Indian indica strain and the Brazilian sativa strain that's infamous for its pure, intoxicating strength.

WILFRED A comedy series that ran from 2011 to 2014 and starred Elijah Wood (of hobbit fame) as Ryan, a suicidal young man whose life is turned upside down by his neighbor's dog, Wilfred. Although everyone else sees Wilfred as a regular dog, Ryan sees him as a crude, pot-smoking man wearing a grubby dog suit. It's initially unclear whether Wilfred is real…but all pot smokers know the truth.

WILLIAMS, KATT (BORN SEPTEMBER 2, 1971) A stand-up comedian, actor, and rapper who some have claimed is the heir to Dave Chappelle. While both are admitted pot smokers and use the drug extensively in their bit, in many ways Williams is the complete opposite—animated, quick, long-haired, goateed, and slickly dressed. (He wore a green blazer, shirt, and tie during his stand-up special *The Pimp Chronicles Part 1*.) Among other marijuana-inspired bits, Williams advises people to smoke more weed, especially if they are unemployed, because what else are they gonna do? Upon the release of the stand-up special, Williams became a hero to out-of-work stoners everywhere. **See also Chappelle, Dave**

WILLIAMS, MONTEL (BORN JULY 3, 1956) Soft-spoken but tough-talkin' host of *The Montel Williams Show* who became an outspoken supporter of medical marijuana ever since police blew up his spot in 2003 when security found a pipe in his bag at Detroit Metro Airport. Williams was diagnosed with multiple sclerosis in 1999 and found that nothing worked as well as marijuana to ease his pain. Now, Williams continues to support legalization and has founded his own company to produce a line of cannabis products, most recently featuring various medicinal-quality CBD products. **See also CBD**

WILLIAMS, RICKY (BORN MAY 21, 1977) A former NFL running back and the antithesis to every cliché professional sports athletes are supposed to live up to, automatically making him every stoner's favorite athlete whether they've ever seen him play or not. Despite a promising start to his NFL career, Williams retired from the NFL for the first time at age twenty-seven after failing three drug tests in violation of the NFL's drug policy. Eventually, Williams returned to the NFL and went off pot in order to play…but failed yet another drug test, was suspended for all of 2006, and instead joined the CFL for a season before returning to the NFL until 2011. It should come as no surprise that Williams is an unabashed and outspoken medical marijuana supporter, making him a pariah in NFL circles and a fascinating figure outside of it. **See also Moss, Randy**

WINEHOUSE, AMY (SEPTEMBER 14, 1983–JULY 23, 2011) An extremely talented English soul and jazz singer who was best known for winning five Grammys (tying the record for most in one night by a female artist) and her iconic 1960s-style *Dreamgirls* image and musical stylings. Winehouse struggled with addiction and was known to use heroin, ecstasy, cocaine, and heavy amounts of alcohol, sometimes in combination. Along with her husband at the time, Blake Fielder-Civil, she was arrested in Norway for marijuana possession in 2007. Unfortunately, despite several trips to rehab, Winehouse died of alcohol poisoning in 2011. **See also rehab**

WOLFE, TOM (MARCH 2, 1930–MAY 14, 2018) Author, journalist, and one of the trailblazing figures in the New Journalism era. Wolfe was freelancing for *Esquire* when he was assigned a story about the hot rod and custom car culture in Southern California. Wolfe struggled with the story and waited until the night before it was due before he wrote his editor a letter with his notes about what he wanted to say on the subject. *Esquire* printed the letter intact, and the article served as a new form of journalism. This was continued with Wolfe's 1968 book *The Electric Kool-Aid Acid Test*, which followed Ken Kesey and his friends (called the "Merry Pranksters") as they traveled the country using LSD and other psychedelics and describing what they considered their revelations about life. Though surrounded by drug culture, Wolfe has claimed he never took LSD and tried marijuana only once, a claim that belies his knack for describing in enormously vivid detail everything about his subjects' house, clothes, facial expressions, and tone of voice, as well as Wolfe's penchant for wearing the

all-white suit. **See also Thompson, Hunter S.** ▼

WOO BLUNT A normal cigar-shaped marijuana receptacle that has been enhanced with cocaine. One should only roll a woo blunt with the express knowledge of everyone in the group. Even when done openly, this practice is frowned upon by many smokers who feel that pot is good enough on its own and doesn't need the help of cocaine, its distant cousin twice removed.

WOODSTOCK A massive, three-day-long American music festival held near Woodstock, New York, in August of 1969. What started as a fledgling business venture for two open-minded investors (John Roberts and Joel Rosenman) and two young concert promoters (Michael Lang and Artie Kornfeld) turned into a landmark cultural occurrence that found four hundred thousand Americans coming together for a long weekend of free love, cheap drugs (including weed), and undeniable rock and roll. Woodstock was host to thirty-two bands, including the Grateful Dead, Jimi Hendrix, The Who, Creedence Clearwater Revival, Janis Joplin, Santana, and Jefferson Airplane. Originally scheduled to be held at an industrial park in nearby Wallkill, New York, the festival was moved (after Wallkill's local government backed out due to hippiephobia) to the land comprising cooperative local Max Yasgur's dairy farm and Filippini Pond. Despite massive crowds, impassable traffic jams, and rampant drug use, peace and love prevailed. **See also *Taking Woodstock***

WURTZEL, ELIZABETH (BORN JULY 31, 1967) An American writer and journalist, famous for publishing her memoir, the bestselling *Prozac Nation,* at age twenty-six. The book details her struggle with drugs, including marijuana, and depression, and her subsequent use of Prozac, which she credits with saving her life after multiple hospitalizations and a suicide attempt. Since the publication of *Prozac Nation,* Wurtzel has gone on to write several other books, including *Bitch: In Praise of Difficult Women* and *More, Now, Again: A Memoir of Addiction.* She also attended Yale Law School and passed the New York state bar exam in 2010. Her writing is credited with disproving the long-held belief that smoking enough marijuana can make anything funny and enjoyable because one will find that even after ten-plus joints her books are neither.

Xx, Yy, Zz

XERIC A term used by overeducated potheads to describe marijuana that is exceptionally dry. Premium bud is usually a little sticky to the touch and should never turn to dust in one's hands. The term has yet to catch on among the larger pot-smoking community, primarily because it is impossible to use it in a sentence without sounding like a pretentious jerk.

XI A letter in the Greek alphabet that has little practical application in the modern world aside from its usefulness as one of several potentially high-scoring two-letter words in the popular board game Scrabble. The word's small size makes it ideal for people attempting to play the game while high, as it is easy to remember and very difficult to misspell. **See also Scrabble ▼**

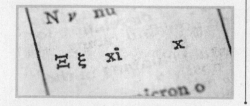

YEATS, WILLIAM BUTLER (JUNE 13, 1865–JANUARY 28, 1939) One of several authors whose likeness appears only in black and white who dabbled in the use of hashish and used the drug as inspiration and in various writings. Yeats was introduced to the drug in 1890, and he wrote about it in his essay "Concerning Saints and Artists" as only an Irish lyrical poet could: "I had never taken it before, and was instructed by a boisterous young poet, whose English was no better than my French. He gave me a little pellet, if I am not forgetting, an hour before dinner, and another after we had dined together at some restaurant. As we were going through the streets to the meeting-place of the Martinists, I felt suddenly that a cloud I was looking at floated in an immense space, and for an instant my being rushed out, as it seemed, into that space with ecstasy." Yeats's dramatic retelling of such an unremarkable drug trip is possibly the most absurd pot description of all time. **See also Alcott, Louisa May; Dickinson, Emily** ▼

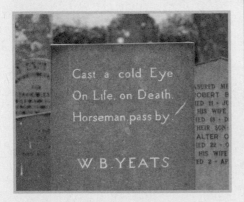

Cast a cold Eye
On Life, on Death.
Horseman pass by.

W. B. YEATS

YOUTUBE A popular video-sharing website that has morphed into a dumping ground for videos of men being hit in the groin, animals doing any range of cute things, and clips of wildly untalented singers and dancers flailing around for the amusement of the anonymous Internet community. Smoking marijuana can enhance the contents of the site, and several clips cannot attain their full humor quotient without its help.

ZEN A state of being achieved through excessive marijuana use that is generally described as an extreme feeling of contentedness. The term derives from a sect of Buddhism whose followers practice meditation as a means of achieving enlightenment. While the average pot smoker is not necessarily seeking spiritual oneness, the similarities between smokers and Buddhist monks is startling. Replace the orange robes with an orange hoodie and the word "om" with the word "um" and nobody would ever know the difference. **See also philosophy**

ZOINKS! An exclamation of surprise, confusion, annoyance, or relief made by the animated character Shaggy on the "popular" Hanna-Barbera cartoon *Scooby-Doo, Where Are You!* Despite Shaggy's iconic status within the pot-smoking community, the slang term has yet to catch on in the real world. This could be due to the real world's lack of ghosts, mummies, and other monsters hiding inside suits of armor ready to jump out and scare hapless victims, thus eliminating the need for the use of the term. **See also Shaggy**

ZOMBIELAND A zombie-themed horror comedy in which a group of three strangers and one kid sister make their way across a newly decimated, ghoul-infested America. To cut right to the chase, this movie features a sequence in which Bill Murray, playing himself, gets baked off his ass with Emma Stone and Woody Harrelson, and the three of them re-enact scenes from *Ghostbusters*. The end? Hardly. Also of interest to movie-loving pot smokers are the various scenes of gratuitous but hilarious zombie violence and an opening-credit sequence that promises to be either the most captivating or blood-chillingly terrifying thing a person has ever seen, depending on what and how much that person has recently smoked. **See also *Adventureland***

ZONG A bong with a Z-shaped tube that doubles its capacity for smoke and allows a four-foot bong to fit in a two-foot space. It is rumored to have been invented by Thomas Edison.

However, the only evidence to substantiate this are sixteen primitive recordings filled with nothing but giggling and extended periods of contemplative silence.

ZONKED A term used to describe being really tired, stoned, and generally spent. Once one has achieved this state, there's no coming back without the proper application of time and sleep. One could try smoking more pot in a misguided attempt to get so high that one actually comes back around full circle and sobers up. However, if this does succeed, the ensuing down leaves the smoker so zonked he or she is likely to sleep for eighteen hours straight. **See also passing out**

IMAGE CREDITS

Images © 123RF/Eldad Carin, lightwise, belchonock, NejroN, Leonard Zhukovsky, Shawn Hempel, victor kuznetsov, wtnpss, Pablo Hidalgo, Michael Nosek, Jiri Vaclavek, Dmitry Tishchenko, Alexander Zuluaga, amarosy, Nikolay Antonov, Laschon Maximilian, nasaimages, kirillvasilevcom, realcontent, Roman Budnyi, Roman Budnyi, lightfieldstudios, imogi; Getty Images/digitalimagination, ggprophoto, KarenMower, KenTannenbaum, atiatiati, Cabezonication, surabky, zigifoto, RichLegg, LauriPatterson, Sezeryadigar, carlofranco, razyph, sborisov, myshkovsky, eskymaks, GibsonPictures, rimglow, golddiamondphotography, MarioGuti, hsyncoban, eyegelb, HighGradeRoots, francisblack, brazzo, guruXOOX, Morrison1977, rgbspace, FilippoBacci, VasilevKirill, Gleti, ilbusca, channarongsds, Kuzmik_A, Oleksandra Troian, TRADOL LIMYINGCHAROEN, Marco Bagnoli, Daemon Barzai, Eivaisla, Michaela Dusikova, Roman Didkivskyi, leonardo monteverde, Jose S, nito100, Hailshadow, Mirjana Ristic, José Antonio Luque Olmedo, CasarsaGuru, powerofforever, AYEHAB, Magone, Thomas Pajot, Alexander_Volkov, Moha El-Jaw, Nastco, Charles Wollertz, Roman Budnyi, Indigoai, HighGradeRoots, Antwon McMullen, Talaj, Rancic Aleksandar, elena marchew, maridav, jpbcpa, South_agency; pixabay.com; unsplash.com.

Get down to growing your own ganja—
NO GREEN THUMB REQUIRED!

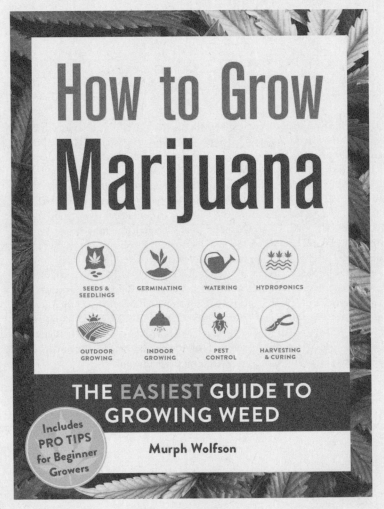

How to Grow
Marijuana

SEEDS & SEEDLINGS **GERMINATING** **WATERING** **HYDROPONICS**

OUTDOOR GROWING **INDOOR GROWING** **PEST CONTROL** **HARVESTING & CURING**

THE EASIEST GUIDE TO GROWING WEED

Includes
PRO TIPS
for Beginner
Growers

Murph Wolfson

Pick Up or Download Your Copy Today!

adamsmedia
An Imprint of Simon & Schuster
A CBS COMPANY